On Earth as in Heaven

On Earth as in Heaven

The Lord's Prayer from Jewish Prayer to Christian Ritual

David Clark

Fortress Press
Minneapolis

ON EARTH AS IN HEAVEN

The Lord's Prayer from Jewish Prayer to Christian Ritual

Cover image: Figure of a young woman with a veiled head praying with her arms outstretched, Via Salaria (fresco), Roman, (3rd century AD) / Catacombs of Priscilla, Rome, Italy / Bridgeman Images.

Rock wall background brown ©iStock/Thinkstock

Cover design: Tory Herman

Print ISBN: 978-1-5064-1438-6

eBook ISBN: 978-1-5064-1439-3

The paper used in this publication meets the minimum requirements of American National Standard for Information Sciences — Permanence of Paper for Printed Library Materials, ANSI Z329.48-1984.

Manufactured in the U.S.A.

This book was produced using Pressbooks.com, and PDF rendering was done by PrinceXML.

This book is dedicated to all of the people around the world who have been part of my YWAM family over the past twenty years. In our friendship, prayer, worship, proclamation, and labor, I can say that I've truly tasted the communion of the Trinity (John 17:21). Thank You! I will always remember and treasure that which we have shared.

Contents

Introduction ix

1. A Prayer Revival 1

2. Prayer and Covenant Renewal 25

3. Matthew's Vision of Heaven and Earth 59

4. Order and Chaos in the *Didache* 87

5. Luke on Prayer 117

6. Tertullian: "Prayer Alone Conquers God" 163

7. Conclusion 193

Appendix: Praying the Lord's Prayer 207
Index of Ancient Sources 211
Index of Modern Authors 223

Introduction

The Quest for the Origin

It was on a hot, humid day in the summer of 1832 that the discovery was made. For several weeks Henry Schoolcraft and his men had been traversing lakes, portaging through thick forests, and winding along streams in pursuit of their goal. For 290 years, the object of their pursuit had been a mystery. Others had tried, only to be thwarted by Minnesota's impenetrable terrain and unforgiving climate. But this expedition was destined to succeed. Plunging down a thorny trail discernible only to the eye of their Ojibwa guide, crossing a shallow pond, and ascending one last hill, Schoolcraft at last caught sight of it: "At length, the glittering of water appeared, at a distance below, as viewed from the summit of one of these eminences. It was declared by our Indian guide to be Itasca Lake," the source of the Mississippi.[1] With this discovery, one of the last geographical mysteries of North America had been solved. The birthplace of the continent's greatest river had been found.

Schoolcraft stands in a long line of adventurers, historians, philosophers, scientists, and theologians who have been driven to discover. The quest for *origins* is a common theme in the narrative of Western civilization. A river is a mystery until its headwaters are found. A historical event cannot be comprehended apart from its

---

1. Henry Rowe Schoolcraft, *Personal Memoirs of a Residence of Thirty Years with the Indian Tribes on the American Frontiers* (Kindle Edition, 2012), 388.

antecedents. And a natural phenomenon is indecipherable until the physical laws driving it are understood.

Often times, great discoveries are significant beyond their practical value. For those of us living in the twenty-first century, the identification of the "true source" of the Mississippi might seem like a minor issue. But in the days when the Western part of the United States was veiled in mystery, such a find had enormous symbolic value. Knowing the geography of North America opened the door for new territories to be settled, new farms to be planted, new forests to be harvested, and new trade routes to be established. Our understanding of the continent was the precursor of its colonization.

The principle at work here applies to much more than geographical discovery. In Western civilization, we have come to equate *knowledge of the source* with the ideas of *freedom* and *opportunity*. We are persuaded that the discovery of truth—the unveiling of false assumptions and interpretations—is the path to liberation. When we arrive at the ideas behind the rules or the doctrines or the laws that govern us, we are free to decide whether we agree or disagree. We're no longer dependent on others to interpret reality for us. We escape deception, control, and manipulation.

As for religious thought in the West, our watershed moment came with the Protestant Reformation. In its wake ordinary Christians, for the first time in history, were able to individually engage with the source of their faith: the Scriptures. The promise of the Reformation was that this "discovery" of the source would lead to liberation. Luther and others had argued that by restricting translation and discouraging personal access to the Bible, the Roman Catholic church had maintained a tight control over its teachings. The common people were at the mercy of the priests, who were no longer to be trusted. The church had adulterated the truth of God's word. The Reformers argued that if the people could read the Scriptures for themselves, they would find no mention of Purgatory or prayer to the saints, or any other of the many encumbrances of tradition. If given access to the source, the pure word of God, they would find spiritual freedom.

Five hundred years later, it comes as no surprise that we who are the heirs of the Reformation are obsessed with the idea of encountering the Bible at its place of origin. To decipher the original language, to find the historical author, to unravel the mysteries of ancient cultures, to engage the communities that produced the texts, to determine the historical circumstance behind every parable and teaching—this is our endeavor. We walk in the conviction that armed with a proper understanding of the Bible, we as individuals will need no teacher. We will not be at risk of deception or control. When we as individuals have discovered the original sense of Scripture, we will *know the truth and the truth will make us free.*

Or so we have been told.

Isolated and Bored

Many of us who were raised in this mindset are now questioning whether this *individualized* approach to Scripture has really resulted in the emancipation that the Reformation promised us. The unintended consequence of the Reformation has been that our *individual* control over the Scriptures has led to our isolation from one another. Rather than coming to Christ through the mediation of the church, we are now free *as individuals* to come to Christ directly. We have idealized a spirituality in which every man is a priest unto himself. The idea of *Sola Scriptura*—"just give me the Bible!"—has been a foundation of our faith. But when the church is no longer needed to mediate our relationship with God, participation in the life of the church ultimately becomes optional. Equipped with all the "tools" necessary to unlock the original meaning of Scripture, we've become less dependent on any teacher—either past or present—to teach us what the Bible says. Tragically, we've been driven away from one another and from the historical community of faith.

And if the angst of our loneliness were not enough, this disconnectedness has also resulted in a general boredom with the biblical text. Our lack of deep engagement with one another and with history has led to our acceptance of a small set of "right answers" and "right interpretations." We read the Bible very narrowly. Our understanding of the texts is all-too-often devoid of complexity, nuance, or even the possibility of reinterpretation. Once we've found *the source*, the *original meaning*, we tend to think that there's little else to discover. Sadly, many people who grew up in the church no longer find reading the Bible all that interesting.

And yet there remains the hope of reigniting our fascination with the message of Scripture. There's much more to be discovered, but we have to know where to look. We have to be willing to go beyond the source.

Let us consider once again the metaphor of the Mississippi. When Schoolcraft discovered Lake Itasca, he discovered the river's origin. As we have noted above, such a discovery was essential to our understanding of the river. But Lake Itasca and the Mississippi River are not one-and-the-same. As the river flows over 2,300 miles to its mouth in the Gulf of Mexico, its character is shaped along the way. I can stand in New Orleans knowing that the water before me came from Lake Itasca. But I must also recognize that over that journey from the source to where I now stand, the water has changed. Other rivers have flowed in, leaves and branches have fallen into the water, fish and living organisms have shaped its makeup, different types of soil have been swirled into the mix, and human factors such as garbage and chemicals have also had an impact. To fully know and understand the story of the Mississippi River, I must take into account all that has happened along the path that it has traveled.

This same idea holds true for the Scriptures. Whereas the quest for the original sense of bblical texts must remain a priority, we must not be deluded into thinking that the fullness of their meaning is to be found exclusively in the *original sense*. We must absolutely maintain our commitment to finding the authorial intent of every word in the Bible. But we must bear in mind that this is only the beginning of the journey. The meaning of a biblical text emerges from the history of its meaning. It is only when we have engaged a text in the long story of its interpretation that we can begin to understand the height and depth and breadth of God's word. Markus Bockmuehl notes that a text's footprint "comprises not just an original setting but a history of lived responses to the historical and eternal realities to which it testifies. The meaning of a text is in practice deeply intertwined with its own tradition of hearing and heeding, interpretation and performance."[2] Students of the Bible, therefore, must become students of history. The story of Scripture is not just what it *once said* at a fixed time in the past, but rather what it *has said* in the past, what it is *saying now*, and what it *will say* in the future.[3]

Reception History

The study of how the Bible has been interpreted in diverse historical settings is commonly known as *reception history*.[4] There is a growing movement among scholars to bring this approach to the forefront of biblical studies. Several factors are contributing to this development. First among these is a growing recognition that the historical-critical method (which has dominated biblical research) is unable to paint the full picture. Ulrich Luz characterizes the current state of scholarship as "ever more obsessed with detail" and taking "such exaggerated interest in the original sense of letters and strokes of the text that there is little room for any unified understanding of the whole." He argues that, "the historical-critical understanding of a text isolates its original sense from the present-day exegete as well as from all exegetes of the past by attempting as far as possible to exclude from the process of interpretation the present situation of the exegete and all that has since occurred in history."[5]

What Luz here questions is the notion that the original sense of

---

2. Markus Bockmuehl, *Seeing the Word: Refocusing New Testament Study* (Grand Rapids: Baker Academic, 2006), 65.

3. Luz notes: "One way or the other, understanding biblical texts means dealing with history. In contrast to the widespread current idea that the historical is, in the end, relative and therefore secondary, we must say that for biblical texts the history to which they refer and which they reflect is primary" (Ulrich Luz, *Studies in Matthew* [Grand Rapids: Eerdmans, 2005], 274–75).

4. *History of interpretation* or *effective history* are other terms often used to describe this same field of study. For a fuller description of the nuances pertaining to these various terms, see Luz, *Studies*, 352.

5. Ibid., 268.

a biblical text can be isolated and "cleanly" retrieved from the past. Many scholars no longer accept the proposition that we can simply put ourselves "in the shoes" of the biblical authors and discuss their ideas as if the two or three thousand years that stand between us are of no consequence. More and more we are accepting the idea that the Scriptures have come to us in a mediated fashion, shaped and influenced by centuries of interpretation and application. And while in the case of the Mississippi there still remains opportunity to explore the actual source, we cannot travel through time to engage Matthew or Paul as they write.

It is in this understanding that the philosopher Hans-Georg Gadamer has argued that we deceive ourselves if we think that this kind of time travel is possible: "We think we understand when we see the past from a historical standpoint—i.e., transpose ourselves into the historical situation and try to reconstruct the historical horizon. In fact, however, we have given up the claim to find in the past any truth that is valid and intelligible for ourselves."[6]

Gadamer's words should not be taken as a call to abandon our quest for the original sense of biblical texts. But we must validate his insistence that we can never really find the meaning of a historical text as something that stands alone and untouched in the distant past. Too much stands between us and the point of origin. He therefore challenges us to read Scripture with a historical consciousness. That is to say, with a simultaneous awareness of what happened two thousand years ago, what has happened since, and what is happening now. Consequently, we must stop trying to drive a wedge between history and the knowledge of it. The original voice of a biblical text comes to us only through the historical voices of its interpreters. It is only when we listen to this polyphonic message of a text that we are able to approach the fullness of its meaning.[7]

Another reason that reception history is gaining traction lies in its openness to a more pluralistic understanding of the biblical message.

---

6. Hans-Georg Gadamer, *Truth and Method* (London: Continuum, 1989), 302–3.
7. Ibid., 285.

When we acknowledge that the meaning of a text is a story that continues to be written, we validate our personal interpretation even as we accept understandings that differ from our own. We accept that our own interpretation tells us a lot about ourselves, and we seek to learn what the perspective of others tells us about them. Luz asserts that

> Biblical texts claim repeatedly that they offer basic orientation for living. They want readers to enter them with their whole lives, bringing the cargo of their own situation and responding to what the texts offer. These texts need to be experienced and lived afresh. Their deconstruction and re-interpretation take place in history. It is the human search for identity, human life and practice and suffering. It is not mere intellectual patchwork but life as it is lived.[8]

As we move beyond author to engage the reader, we find that biblical texts open up new meaning through encounter. In every unique situation wherein a reader discovers what a passage *means to her*, the meaning of that passage has been more fully revealed to her and to others. Rather than insisting that the meaning of a text is locked in the past, we see it as an ongoing narrative that continues to unfold.

This is not to say, however, that any and all interpretations of biblical passages should be considered valid. Trash does get thrown into the river. Many times in history people get it wrong. Studying the original context of a text is important because that's where we find the directionality and the parameters established by the author. A text cannot mean what it never intended to say. Many interpretations are possible, but not *any* interpretation is possible. So we must always tether our understanding of Scripture to the author's intent.

One final benefit of reception history lies in its potential to break the impasse that now ensnarls modern biblical studies. As long as the *original sense* of a text is the sole object of our pursuit, the debate will endlessly continue as to what that original sense actually is. The study of a text's original meaning (exegesis) is not an exact science. Scholars will take various approaches to build structures of plausibility around

---

8. Luz, *Studies*, 325.

what they believe a biblical passage means. They may point to the historical setting of the author and audience, the literary context, the range of meaning for the words employed, etc. But every construct of meaning can be deconstructed. In other words, no matter how plausible one person's argument may seem, another will find a way to undo everything she has said, and present a totally new interpretation.

Let us consider, for example, the Greek word πάτερ (*pater*). Because this word denotes the Father who is addressed in the Lord's Prayer, how one constructs its meaning will have a significant impact on the interpretation of the entire prayer. Given that this word is written in the language of the first century Mediterranean region, one scholar might define it in light of the Greco-Roman family, and interpret the Lord's Prayer accordingly. Another scholar might then come along and deconstruct this interpretation, arguing that even though the Lord's Prayer is written in Greek, Jesus would have taught this prayer in Hebrew. Thus, the key to understanding this term lies in the understanding of אָב (*av*). This second scholar might then go on to cite various ancient Hebrew prayers that address God in this same way, and construct an interpretation of the Lord's Prayer that stands in the light of Jewish prayer. But a third scholar might argue against these previous constructions, and insist that Jesus actually spoke this prayer in Aramaic, and thus the proper term is אַבָּא (*abba*). This third scholar might then argue that Jesus' prayer has nothing to do with first century Jewish prayer, and she may then go on to construct an interpretation of the Lord's Prayer that is completely unique from the others.

Sadly, much of contemporary biblical scholarship involves these endless cycles of construction and deconstruction. Scholarly support can be found for a wide variety of interpretations, and often times we end up no closer to finding the *original sense* of the text than when the debate first began. We are left with the conclusion that the diversity of interpretations owes itself more to subjective than to objective rationales.

As a method of biblical study, reception history is not unwilling to reach for the original sense of a text. What sets this approach apart, however, is its awareness that the original sense comes to us in a mediated fashion. The reception historian bears in mind, particularly in regard to the teachings of Jesus, that *all we have is interpretation*. We have no books written by Jesus himself. We have no audio recordings or video footage of his teachings. What we have is Mark's interpretation of Jesus, Matthew's interpretation of Jesus, Luke's interpretation of Jesus, and John's interpretation of Jesus. This is not to say that the words of the historical Jesus are impenetrably hidden behind the veil of the Gospels. But *it is* to recognize that the study of the Gospels is in fact an exercise in reception history. We are not engaging with the exact words (*ipsissima verba*) of Jesus in a raw, untouched form. Even as we validate the fidelity of the Gospel author's witness, we also recognize the value of his interpretation—and the long line of interpretations that follow.

The Lord's Prayer

Many years ago, when I was first exposed to the idea of reception history, I asked myself what it might look like to trace the interpretation of a biblical text from its inception to the modern day. I thought about what passages might be suitable for such an endeavor. What texts have a discernible history of interpretation? What texts have consistently, since the first century, been used in sermons, songs, commentaries, and theological treatises? And what verses afford us the opportunity to see not only how they were taught, but how they were put into practice? As I contemplated these questions, I landed on the Lord's Prayer. Not only is there a steady stream of writing on this text, but its consistent use as a *prayer* provides us the opportunity to see how it was lived out by Christians across the centuries.

My initial thought was to research the complete, two-thousand-year reception history of the Lord's Prayer. In consultation with others, however, I came to the realization that such a task was beyond the scope of my time or capabilities. Thus, I chose to focus my studies on the first two hundred years of this prayer's story, from its origin in the proclamation of Jesus to its implementation in the liturgical practice of the early Catholic Church. This research became the basis of my PhD dissertation entitled *The Lord's Prayer: Origins and Early Interpretations*.[9]

I discovered a remarkable narrative about how the meaning of the Lord's Prayer progressed in the earliest stages of its reception history. Whereas a continuity of interpretation was easily discernible, my findings illuminated the wonderful freedom that various authors and communities enjoyed as they articulated the significance of this prayer within their own faith and practice. Insomuch as the prayer remained tethered to the life and teaching of Jesus there were, to be sure, boundaries within which it was interpreted. But the clear message from the early Christian communities is that this prayer was intended to open up new meaning for new people in new situations. Its truth was not limited by a singular historical context, but rather was to be found in a continuum of lived responses.

This current book is a retelling of that story, in what (I hope) will be a more accessible and engaging format. We will here follow the trail of the Lord's Prayer from first-century Israel all the way to third-century North Africa, exploring what it meant to Jesus and various early Christian communities that came after him. As we have noted above, our aim will not be to determine the *univocal* (singular) meaning of this prayer at a fixed point in the past. Rather, listening to the voices of many interpreters and communities, we hope to discover its *equivocal* (open to more than one) meanings in history.

Along the way in this journey we will have two corollary objectives. One is the task of application. As we discover the diverse interpretations of this prayer in its early reception history, we must consider the implications for our present time. When we see the possibilities of meaning that were open to previous generations, we realize that we too have the freedom to make this prayer our own. Each early interpreter of the Lord's Prayer had an agenda, and a certain methodology by which they deciphered its meaning. We too, can bring our agenda to the Lord's Prayer, and pursue a path of interpretation

---

9. David A. Clark, *The Lord's Prayer: Origins and Early Interpretations* (Turnhout, Belgium: Brepols, 2016). For those seeking further explanation or documentation of the material in this present book, I encourage you to consult that work as a "companion."

that aligns with our vision. The Lord's Prayer as a text does not resist this type of personal appropriation. The record from history is, in fact, that it welcomes it.

The second corollary objective goes beyond the text of this book. That aim is simply that we would say this prayer in the unity of the Church. In this day when we as Christians tend to focus more on our differences than our similarities, we desperately need to identify the "common denominators" of our faith. The Lord's Prayer is the one prayer that every Christian knows, and that every Christian can pray together. Even as we bring our own "cargo" to this prayer, the words we say together remain the same. We need not have a uniform understanding of this prayer in order to pray it in unity. We are a diverse family of faith that approaches the Father as one body. This prayer reminds us of all that we share in the midst of our differences: a common Father, a common vision, a common need for forgiveness, a common need for bread, a common weakness, and a common enemy. The "our" of the Lord's Prayer denotes not just *our little group*. It speaks of all Christians, everywhere. When we pray with this understanding in mind, we give room to the Spirit to make us one, thus fulfilling a desire that Jesus himself expressed in prayer.

It is my hope that as we reflect on the Lord's Prayer in history, our eyes will be opened to see the communities of faith that have come before us. May we understand their hopes and aspirations, their worldview, their ministries, their struggles in community life, and the deep convictions that fueled their passion for Jesus. This book is much more than a survey of a doctrine or liturgical practice. The reception history of the Lord's Prayer tells us about real people and their vision to know and proclaim Jesus in the real world. In their story, we see our own story, as we perceive where we ourselves have come from. There is a legacy that we have inherited. But the narrative is not complete. In our generation we are giving shape to what the Lord's Prayer will mean for our children, and for many generations to come. It is in this awareness—the knowledge that we participate in the *living history* of this prayer—that we make it our goal to be faithful to our predecessors, even as to our own selves we are true.

1

A Prayer Revival

Jerusalem was surrounded, and the food was running out. Thousands of pilgrims had recently arrived to celebrate Passover in that fateful spring of 70 CE, perhaps unaware that the Roman siege was about to begin. Now they were trapped. As days passed into weeks, and weeks into months, the desperation intensified. Bandits ransacked family homes demanding that any food be turned over on pain of death. Families resorted to eating hay, leather, cloth—anything they could chew. Rumors of cannibalism circulated throughout the city. In the evenings some dared to venture outside the walls under the cover of darkness to scavenge along the perimeter for leaves and herbs. When caught, they were tortured and crucified near the walls so that all of the inhabitants could see their fate. Each night, more starving scavengers were captured, and soon the Romans had no more space to plant their crosses.

The Roman general Titus pleaded with the Jewish leaders to surrender. He insisted that he had no intention of destroying their city. But they refused, and the siege wore on. As the battering rams finally breached the first wall, the Roman soldiers poured in. They plunged through one line of defense after another, pushing the Jews deeper into the city. A valiant stand was made at the seemingly impenetrable Antonia Fortress, but once again, the Judean defenses succumbed. The battle now raged within the outer courts. Titus had warned his soldiers not to harm the temple itself. But the six-month siege had left its mark on his men. When they finally broke down the inner gates, their fury was insatiable. The temple was soon in flames. Man-to-man combat spread throughout the inner court. Jewish soldiers mounted the altar itself to fend off the onslaught, but to no avail. Soon, the monument upon which the sacrifices of Israel had been offered for centuries was shrouded in corpses. An eyewitness would report, "Now round about the altar lay the dead bodies heaped one upon the another, as at the steps going up to it ran a great quantity of their blood, where also the dead bodies that were slain above (on the altar) fell down."[1]

As the temple was finally taken, the last Jewish fighters scattered throughout the city. Romans soldiers scoured the streets, breaking through household doors only to find piles of emaciated corpses—men, women, and children long dead from starvation. The last fighters had retreated to the tunnels and caverns underground. There remained no option for the Romans but to torch the city. As the smoke of Jerusalem ascended, the soldiers lifted their standards upon its remaining towers. Among the ashes of the Holy Place, Titus made an offering to his gods. Jerusalem was now desecrated and destroyed.

Forty years earlier, a young prophet had envisioned this destruction and wept.

> Oh Jerusalem, Jerusalem. . . . Behold your house is forsaken. . . . For the days will come upon you, when your enemies will set up a barricade around you and surround you and hem you in on every side and tear you down to the ground, you and your children within you. And they will not leave one stone upon another in you. (Luke 13:34–35; 19:43–44)

And so it came to pass.

For those of us living almost two thousand years later, it can be difficult to grasp the full weight of these events. For the people of first-

---

1. *Bellum judaicum* 6.29 (Flavius Josephus, "*Bellum judaicum*," in *The Works of Josephus: Complete and Unabridged,* trans. William Whiston [Peabody: Hendrickson, 1987]).

century Israel, the temple that fell to the ground on that day was more than just an important religious building. It was the one place, and the only place, where they could fulfill their commitment to offer worship to YHWH.[2] According to the Torah, ancient Judaism was not a religion that could be practiced by anyone, anywhere. It was intrinsically tied to a *place*. According to Deuteronomy, Moses had been careful to tell their ancestors that there would be a *single altar* that would serve as the focal point of their worship. Other nations—the nations they were driving out—sacrificed on multiple altars. Israel would offer sacrifice in one place only: "But you shall seek the place that the Lord your God will choose out of all your tribes to put his name and make his habitation there. There you shall go, and there you shall bring your burnt offerings and your sacrifices, your tithes and the contribution that you present, your vow offerings, your freewill offerings, and the firstborn of your herd and of your flock" (Deut 12:5-6).

There was *one place* where the presence of God would dwell on earth. In the era of the Judges, the presence of YHWH had moved from town to town within the tents of the tabernacle. But when David secured Mount Zion as the location to build the temple, a final place had been established. YHWH himself would declare, "This is my resting place forever; here I will dwell, for I have desired it" (Ps 132:14).

The Jewish people would come to view Jerusalem and its temple as having cosmological significance. On this view, the universe was a series of concentric circles, and the temple formed the center.[3] The temple was "the place where heaven and earth converge and thus from where God's control over the universe is effected."[4] Without a

---

2. Throughout this book I will use "YHWH" as another reference for God. Known as the tetragrammaton, these four letters represent the name of God that could not be spoken. Many scholars will read this name as "Yahweh," even though there is no certainty that this is the actual pronunciation.

3. In the Mishnah (*m. Kelim* 1:6-9), this idea was described as follows: "There are ten [degrees of] holiness(es): The land of Israel is holier than all lands. . . . The cities surrounded by a wall are more holy than it [the land]. . . . Within the wall [of Jerusalem] is more holy than they. . . . The Temple mount is more holy than it. The rampart is more holy than it. The court of women is more holy than it. . . . The court of Israel is more holy than it. The court of the priests is more holy than it. . . . [The area] between the porch and the altar is more holy than it. The sanctuary is more holy than it. The Holy of Holies is more holy than they" (*The Mishnah: A New Translation*, ed. Jacob Neusner [New Haven and London: Yale University Press, 1988]). See also *Jub.* 8.19; *Sib. Or.* 5.248-50.

4. Carol Meyers, cited by N. T. Wright, *Jesus and the Victory of God* (Minneapolis: Fortress, 1996), 407.

temple, the God of Israel would have no place on earth from which to exercise his authority among people. Without a temple, there could be no sacrifice for sins. Without the temple sacrifices, so this view held, the people of Israel could not maintain relationship with YHWH.

As we thus consider all that the temple stood for in the eyes of the Jewish people, it would be natural to think that when Titus and his soldiers entered the precinct, tore down the altar, and desecrated the Holy Place, the end should have come. Judaism should have collapsed, or at least entered into significant decline. And yet, in spite of all that this building represented, its demise did not result in the end of Judaism. In fact, after its fall the Jewish people continued to worship YHWH, and their community continued grow and thrive.

What is seen in this story is that history does not always follow predictable patterns. Sometimes what we would expect to happen *doesn't* happen, and in such cases, we must find an explanation. The fact that Judaism didn't fall along with the temple seems to indicate that in spite of all that the temple was *supposed* to mean and *supposed* to do, perhaps the Jewish people were not so dependent upon this structure after all. Upon closer historical analysis, we find that long before the Roman attack in 70 CE, a monumental shift had been taking place in Jewish faith and practice. For hundreds of years, Jews had been discovering how to worship and encounter the presence of YHWH independently of the temple and its sacrifices. The central feature of this personalized approach to worship was the practice of prayer.

Throughout Israel and the Diaspora, the people had been meeting in synagogues or "houses of prayer" for the purpose of reading the Torah and praying together. As they gathered, they were experiencing the presence of God in a new way. A revival was taking place. Even though the Scriptures said nothing about synagogues or prayer meetings, they were appearing everywhere. It was this renewal movement that ultimately ensured the continuance of Judaism after the temple's fall. And it was this same renewal movement that gave birth to Christianity.

Our present task is to explore how this prayer movement started, what it looked like, and how Jesus was a part of it. Jesus was in many ways a product of his Jewish culture. He and his followers rode the wave of this revival. If we are to understand what prayer meant to Jesus—and more specifically what the Lord's Prayer meant to him—we must first look at this fascinating prayer movement and the cultural forces that gave it birth.

The Historical Background

Movements need not be characterized by a single leader or organizational structure. It often occurs that different groups of people in different places—who may or may not even be aware of one another—share the same frustrations and longings. As these sentiments find expression, societies often reach "tipping points" wherein forces that may have previously been undetected suddenly result in massive change.[5] With the sack of Jerusalem in 70 CE, Judaism came to a tipping point that brought enormous changes to the way the people expressed their faith. This was not a change that the Jewish people sought, but it *was* one for which they were well prepared.

As we look at the landscape of Judaism in the first century, there are three discernible "pockets" where we may observe the development of a prayer movement: the synagogue communities, the Pharisees and their followers, and the community that identified itself as the "*Yahad*," known to the world by the Dead Sea Scrolls.[6] Whereas our tendency may be to view these Jewish groups (particularly the Pharisees) with suspicion because of the way they are presented in some Gospel passages, we must remember that Jesus was Jewish, and these were his people. He interacted with them and their ideas, and his own movement stood in continuity with them in many regards —particularly as it relates to prayer.

---

5. Contemporary sociological theory, as popularized by Malcolm Gladwell, *The Tipping Point: How Little Things Can Make a Big Difference* (New York: Little, Brown and Company, 2002), characterizes this phenomenon as a moment when ideas, trends, or behaviors cross a threshold to become widely embraced in society.
6. *Yahad* is an umbrella term for the Essene communities represented by the Dead Sea Scrolls (DSS). Meaning "unity," *Yahad* was the preferred self-designation of the movement. The term appears fifty times in 1QS, seven times in 1QSa, and additionally in 4Q174, 4Q177, 4Q252, 4Q265, and CD.

The Birth of the Synagogue

Luke begins his Gospel by telling the story of a priest from a small town in Judah who had been chosen by lot to offer incense in the Jerusalem temple. To be selected for such a task was an honor not only for Zechariah but for his entire village as well. A group of men accompanied him to Jerusalem so that at the very moment he was inside the sanctuary, they could stand outside and pray. Simultaneously, those men of the village who were not able to make the journey paused from their workday at the hour of incense so that they could pray as well. Zechariah's presence in the Holy Place was a significant event for everyone. This was their opportunity, even if vicariously, to stand in the presence of YHWH.[7]

The tradition that Luke recounts had a long history among the villages of Israel. Whereas there was no mandate in the Torah for this type of prayer gathering, these meetings became very meaningful. Over time, the people of many villages decided to keep coming together for prayer and Torah reading, even if a local priest wasn't being sent to Jerusalem. In the early years, they would meet at the city gates, which frequently had large chambers. While the original purpose of these rooms may have been storage, trade, or town meetings, they became the ideal place for Torah study and communal prayer. It was here that the synagogue was born.

By the time Jesus came on the scene, these local gatherings were now operating in dedicated buildings. Because they were used for prayer and Torah study, they were increasingly seen as holy places. Baths were constructed by the doors so that those coming in could ritually wash before entering. The architecture began to resemble the temple of Jerusalem, and some synagogues were even built facing toward the holy city. While they were never intended to replace the temple, the local synagogue soon became the focal point of Jewish worship. Those Jews who lived far from Jerusalem might only visit the

---

7. This gathering known as the *maamad* is described in *m. Taanit* 4:2–3. See Jakob J. Petuchowski, "The Liturgy of the Synagogue," in *The Lord's Prayer and Jewish Liturgy*, ed. Jakob J. Petuchowski and Michael Brocke (New York: Seabury, 1978), 46.

temple three times a year, if that often. The synagogue, however, was a place where they could go to pray every day. And while their role in the temple sacrifices was relegated to that of a mere spectator, in the synagogue any Jewish man could lead prayer and read the Torah.[8]

While the temple was standing, the prayers of the synagogue did not necessarily stand in rivalry to the animal sacrifices. Throughout the era of the Second Temple, the two operated (for the most part) in tandem. When the temple fell, however, the synagogue was prepared to "carry the load" of Jewish worship. For many years it had already been assuming the primary role.[9] The significance of the temple sacrifices had long been waning in the hearts and minds of the people. It was in the synagogue that they found life. This was where they could they could read the Torah, experience the presence of YHWH for themselves, and offer the sacrifice of prayer.

The Pharisees

The Gospels certainly do not paint the Pharisees in a very positive light. There's a reason, however, behind Jesus's ongoing conflict with this group. Jesus said very little against the Romans who worshiped pagan deities, or the rich, Hellenized Sadducees who denied the resurrection of the dead. He reserved his ire for the Pharisees, and this was for the simple reason that they were so much like him in their beliefs and practices. Jesus instructed the people to follow the teaching of the scribes and Pharisees because they sat on the "seat of Moses" (Matt

8. For an excellent overview on the history and development of the synagogue, see Donald Binder, *Into the Temple Courts: The Place of the Synagogues in the Second Temple Period* (Atlanta: Society of Biblical Literature, 1999).

9. Schiffman notes, "In the aftermath of the Great Revolt of 66–74 there was no longer any cult. The priest no longer sacrificed; the Levite no longer sang; Israel no longer made pilgrimages to the holy Temple. Henceforth, only prayer and the life of rabbinic piety could ensure Israel's continued link to its Father in Heaven. It is naïve to assume that this eventuality came upon Pharisaic-rabbinic Judaism with no warning" (Lawrence Schiffman, "The Dead Sea Scrolls and the Early History of Jewish Liturgy," in *The Synagogue in Late Antiquity*, ed. Lee Levine [Philadelphia: The American Schools of Oriental Research, 1987], 53). Haran also comments, "In the period of the Second Temple . . . prayer as an act of worship was also implanted in a distinct institutional framework in the form of a synagogue, which was an entirely new innovation. In the course of time this institution enabled Judaism to do without the Temple altogether" (Menahem Haran, "Temple and Community in Ancient Israel," in *Temple in Society*, ed. Michael V. Fox [Winona Lake, IN: Eisenbrauns, 1988], 21–22).

23:2).[10] To be sure, there were drastic changes that Jesus wanted to see happen in their attitudes and practices, but he certainly wanted them as allies.

The New Testament and the Jewish historian Josephus both depict the Pharisees as highly influential men. Josephus notes that the Pharisees are "able greatly to persuade the body of the people; and whatsoever they do about divine worship, prayers, and sacrifices, they perform them according to their direction."[11] If we consolidate what the Gospels say about the Pharisees, we see that they were influential in the synagogues (Mark 3:1–6; Matt 23:6); they upheld the traditions of the elders (Mark 7:1–13; Matt 15:1–9); they insisted that God alone can forgive sins (Mark 2:6–7; Matt 9:2–3; Luke 5:20–21); they emphasized fasting (Mark 2:18; Matt 9:14; Luke 5:33); they did not eat with unwashed hands (Mark 7:1–8; Matt 15:1–2); they made determinations regarding the binding nature of oaths (Mark 7:9–13) and dietary laws (Mark 7:14–23); they believed in the resurrection of the dead (Mark 12:18–27; Matt 22:23–34; Luke 20:27–40); they considered the two greatest commands to be loving God and loving one's neighbor (Mark 12:28–33; Matt 22:34–40); they believed that the Messiah would come from the line of David (Mark 12:35–37; Matt 22:41–46; Luke 20:41–44); and they did not believe that a rabbi should teach on the basis of personal authority (Mark 1:22; Matt 7:28–29).[12] In sum, there was much upon which Jesus and the Pharisees could agree.

For centuries, the Pharisees had played an enormously important role in the life of Israel. They helped the people work through several monumental changes taking place in Israelite society. When Joshua had first led the tribes into the land of Canaan, Israel was an agricultural society. The people lived off the land that they farmed and the animals that they raised. Accordingly, the law that Moses gave presupposed an agriculturally based lifestyle. The lamb that was to be

10. Archeological excavations from a third-century synagogue in Chorazin, Galilee uncovered a large stone chair with the Aramaic inscription "the seat of Moses." See Zeev Yeivin, "Chorazin," in *The New Encyclopedia of Archaeological Excavations in the Holy Land*, ed. Ephraim Stern (New York: Simon & Schuster, 1993), 1:301–4.
11. *Bellum judaicum* 6.259.
12. This list is taken from Ellis Rivkin, *A Hidden Revolution* (Nashville: Abingdon, 1978), 271.

set aside for the Passover was to be taken from each family's own flock (Exodus 12). At the Feast of Harvest, the people would offer grain from their own crops (Leviticus 2). Three times each year the people had to present themselves at the temple, and these feasts corresponded with the agricultural calendar (Exod 34:22–24). As long as the people lived off of their crops and herds, following the Torah was fairly straightforward.

But over time Israelite society became more complex. We know from the Gospels, for example, that Joseph was a carpenter, not a farmer. For many centuries new types of vocations had been developing throughout the land. There were merchants and tradespeople of many sorts. Consequently, keeping a set of rules that had been written for farmers and herdsmen became increasingly difficult. The Jewish people wanted to remain faithful to the law, but in many cases that law required new interpretations that would accommodate the changing structure of society.[13] It was the Pharisees who helped the people of Israel navigate this transition by means of the "unwritten laws" (or "oral Torah") that addressed many issues not clearly outlined in the Scriptures.[14] These were the "traditions of the fathers" (Mark 7:1–3)

---

13. The Jewish scholar Ellis Rivkin believed that the Pharisees were responsible for a "hidden revolution" that had taken place in Israel, rooted in what the people had perceived as a flaw in the written law. He describes the general dissatisfaction that led to this revolution as follows:

> The Pentateuchal system was bogged down in a commitment to immutable laws administered by a priestly class whose power, authority, and privileges were tightly tied to preserving a system built on the joint interests of priests and peasants. It was a system that was not at all geared to fast-paced urbanization and its destructive impact on the individual, loosened from the soil, and dislodged from his rural moorings. The Pentateuch focuses almost exclusively on the agricultural blessings that will follow on obedience to God's Law and the agricultural disaster which the sinful people will reap should they prove disloyal to Yahweh. The ultimate punishment is to be driven from the land; the ultimate reward, to gather in overabundant harvests in peace and tranquility. And though the individual is promised a long and fruitful life, and though he is to benefit from the blessings which God will shower on an obedient Israel, there is no provision made for that individual who, though law-abiding himself, is swept into exile along with the majority who have sinned. Thus, salvation was ultimately dependent not on what the individual did but what the community of Israel as a whole did. . . . And though this flaw may have been most grievously felt by artisan, craftsman, and shopkeeper whose activities are nowhere taken into account in the Pentateuch, it was not excluded from the day-to-day experience of the peasant, especially when the coming and going of foreign armies disrupted the tranquil cycle of sowing and reaping. (Ibid., 244)

14. Rivkin notes:

> Their unwritten laws, the halakhah, were operative in all realms: cultus, property, judicial procedures, festivals, etc. The Pharisees were active leaders who carried out their laws with vigor and determination. They set the date for the cutting of the omer. They set up the procedures

to which Jesus referred. In his eyes, the Pharisees often missed the "weightier matters of the Law" (Matt 23:23), but even he conceded that their instruction was necessary for maintaining Torah-faithfulness in changing times.

At the heart of Pharisaic teaching was a very noble idea. They believed that the presence of God was not limited to the temple. They viewed the home and the village as holy places, where people ought to imagine themselves as priests constantly ministering before the Lord. In the Jewish mindset, standing in the presence of YHWH required ritual purity. It was for this reason that the Pharisees placed so much emphasis on the rules surrounding all things that were "clean" or "unclean." They believed that people in their homes should uphold the same standard as the priests in the temple.[15] Thus, at the core of Pharisaic instruction is a personalization of worship. Every person had access to the presence of God, every person was like a priest, and every person was called to holiness.

The entire Pharisaic system was designed "to bring into alignment the moment of sanctification of the village and the life of the home with the moment of sanctification of the Temple on those same occasions of appointed times."[16] Nowhere was this alignment seen more clearly than in their practice of prayer.[17] Just as the sacrifices of

for the burning of the red heifer and compelled priestly conformance. They insisted that the High Priest carry through his most sacred act of the year in accordance with their regulations. They determined judicial procedures, the rightful heirs to property, the responsibility of slaves for damages, the purity status of Holy Scriptures. (Ibid., 176)

15. This understanding of the Pharisees emerges from the work of Jacob Neusner, which Meier summarizes in the following way: "the ideal of holiness pursued by the Pharisees was the priestly holiness proper to the temple . . . the Pharisees achieved their program by the careful handling of food in all its aspects: proper harvesting and paying of tithes on the harvest, proper purity of vessels used for food, proper purity of those taking part in ordinary daily meals" (John P. Meier, *A Marginal Jew: Companions and Competitors*, vol. 3 [New Haven and London: Yale University Press, 2001], 312). See Jacob Neusner, *The Rabbinic Traditions about the Pharisees before 70* (Leiden: Brill, 1971), and Jacob Neusner, *From Politics to Piety: The Emergence of Pharisaic Judaism* (New York: Ktav, 1979).

16. Jacob Neusner and Bruce Chilton, *Judaism in the New Testament* (London: Routledge, 1995), 32.

17. As seen in *Antiquitates Judaicae* 18:15, Matt 6:5, and Luke 18:9–14, the Pharisees were deeply committed to prayer, and their instructions on how it should be practiced were very influential. The prayer *par excellence* was the Amidah (also known as the *Tefillah* or *Shemoneh Esreh* (eighteen benedictions). Although the actual text was not codified until the late second century, there is clear evidence that this prayer was shaped by the Pharisees, most notably in its declaration regarding the resurrection of the dead: "You are mighty, bringing low the proud; powerful,

the temple were offered three times a day—in the morning, afternoon, and evening—so the Pharisees instructed their followers to pray at these times.[18] In their daily communal prayers they didn't see themselves as mere bystanders, which is what they were in the temple. In their homes and synagogues, the people imagined themselves to be priests, bringing their own offerings before God. Joseph Heinemann has argued that these daily prayers provided a spiritual connection for the people that went beyond anything they could experience as mere observers in the temple:

> communal prayer, which constituted a radical innovation of the Second Temple period . . . made an indelible impress on the entire religious life of the people by providing them with a completely novel form of religious expression. Communal fixed prayer . . . is a self-sufficient and independent form of worship, and is not a subordinate of, nor a "accompaniment" to, a more primary ritual or ceremony. It requires neither a holy shrine, nor a priestly "officiant" cast, which alone is empowered to perform it.[19]

This "novel form of religious expression" was being driven forward by the Pharisees. They were the champions of the idea that the temple's sanctity extended far beyond the confines of the Jerusalem structure. Because the home, the village, and the synagogue were holy, every man and woman could lift up an offering to YHWH: the offering of prayer.

The *Yahad*

Whereas the Pharisees and the people of the local synagogues were in the "mainstream" of first-century Jewish society, the people of the

judging the arrogant; ever-living, raising up the dead; causing the wind to blow and the dew to descend; sustaining the living, quickening the dead. O cause our salvation to sprout as in the twinkling of an eye. You are praised, O Lord, who quickens the dead" (Jakob Petuchowski, "Jewish Prayer Texts of the Rabbinic Period," in *The Lord's Prayer and Jewish Liturgy*, ed. Jakob J. Petuchowski and Michael Brocke [New York: Seabury, 1978], 27).

18. The custom of thrice-daily prayer dates back at least as far as Daniel (see Dan 6:10). Luke refers to the people praying at the hour of incense (Luke 1:10) and the disciples going to the temple at the ninth hour, "the hour of prayer" (Acts 3:1). By the time the Mishnah was recorded in the late second century, the debate among the Rabbis was not about *whether* the pious would pray three times a day but rather according to what structure. *M. Ber.* 4:1 states, "The morning prayer [may be recited] until midday . . . the afternoon prayer [may be recited] until the evening. . . . And [the prayers] of the additional service [may be recited] at any time during the day" (Neusner, *Mishnah*).

19. Joseph Heinemann, *Prayer in the Talmud: Forms and Patterns* (Berlin: de Gruyter, 1977), 14.

Yahad chose to cut themselves off completely. While the Gospels don't speak of any direct interaction between Jesus and the Qumran community, they shared some important ideas. The *Yahad* viewed the priesthood and the sacrificial system of their day as completely illegitimate. Consequently, they found alternative ways to express the ideas behind *temple* and *sacrifice*. It would be some of these very same innovations that Jesus and his followers would later adopt as they envisioned a form of worship with no physical temple.

The story of the *Yahad* begins in the second century BCE, during the time of the Hasmonean rule. Various disputes had arisen among the priesthood regarding the rules of succession, the calendar, and regulations governing ritual purity. Under the leadership of a man known as the "Teacher of Righteousness," a group of priests and their followers withdrew in protest from Jerusalem to establish a community along the shores of the Dead Sea, in a place now known as Khirbet Qumran.[20]

One of the distinguishing features of this community was their total rejection of the temple sacrifices. Their community rule, known as the Damascus Document, clearly prohibited any of their members from participating in the activities of the Jerusalem temple:

> None who have been brought into the covenant shall enter into the sanctuary to light up His altar in vain; they shall "lock the door," for God said, "Would that one of you would lock My door so that you should not light up my altar in vain." They must be careful to act according to the specifications of the Law for the era of wickedness, separating from corrupt people, avoiding filthy wicked lucre taken from what is vowed or consecrated to God or found in the Temple funds.[21]

As a result of this conscientious rejection of the temple, the obvious

---

20. I hold to what is commonly called the "Standard Model" for interpreting the Dead Sea Scrolls, which has three basic tenets: (1) The Qumran Community formed part of the Essene sect; (2) the origin of the Qumran community came in reaction to the Hasmonean takeover of the high-priesthood; and (3) the scrolls themselves belonged to the community that inhabited the Khirbet Qumran ruins. For a summary, see Peter W. Flint and James C. VanderKam, *The Dead Sea Scrolls after 50 Years: A Comprehensive Assessment* (Leiden: Brill, 1998–1999).

21. CD 6:11b–16a. See Michael O. Wise, "The Damascus Document (CD) (Geniza A B, 4Q266–272)," in *The Dead Sea Scrolls: A New Translation*, ed. Michael O. Wise, Martin G. Abegg Jr., and Edward M. Cook (San Francisco: HarperSanFrancisco, 2005), 49–78.

challenge that the *Yahad* faced was how to offer sacrifices. The Torah had expressly forbidden that animals be offered anywhere other than the *one* altar. It would be unconscionable for this community to sacrifice animals on their own, outside of the designated place. Someday they hoped to get back to Jerusalem. Their prophets had predicted that they would eventually gain victory over their enemies, and that the true priesthood would be restored.[22] But until that day, they would have to find a substitute for sacrifice. The solution that they found was to offer the sacrifices of prayer. Atonement for their own sins and for the land of Israel would now be effected through the righteousness of the community and through the offerings of their lips. A passage from scroll 1QS states, "They shall atone for the guilt of transgression and the rebellion of sin, becoming an acceptable sacrifice for the land through the flesh of burnt offerings, the fat of sacrificial portions, and prayer, becoming—as it were—justice itself, a sweet savor of righteousness and blameless behavior, a pleasing free-will offering."[23]

Whereas it might seem striking that a Jewish community would attempt such a radical innovation, the *Yahad* actually stood in the line of an old tradition. It had long been held that there was more to maintaining relationship with YHWH than just offering animal sacrifices. The prophet Samuel had said to Israel's first king, Saul, "Has the Lord as great delight in burnt offerings and sacrifices, as in obeying the voice of the Lord? Behold, to obey is better than sacrifice, and to listen than the fat of rams" (1 Sam 15:22). Saul's successor David would pray, "For you will not delight in sacrifice, or I would give it; you will not be pleased with a burnt offering. The sacrifices of God are a broken spirit; a broken and contrite heart, O God, you will not despise" (Ps 51:16). The prophet Hosea had declared, "For I desire steadfast love and not sacrifice, the knowledge of God rather than burnt offerings" (Hos

---

22. See 1QM 1:14–16; 2:5–6.
23. 1QS 9:3–5. See Michael O. Wise, "The Charter of a Jewish Sectarian Association (1QS, 4Q255–264a, 5Q11)," in Abegg et al., *Dead Sea Scrolls*, 112–35. Bertil Gartner describes this replacement as a "transfer of meaning, from the carrying out of blood sacrifice to the living of a life according to the precepts of the Law, thus making a sacrifice of deeds and of lips" (Bertil Gartner, *Temple and Community in Qumran* [Cambridge: Cambridge University Press, 1965], 21).

6:6). And Isaiah denounced the people and the priests, saying, "'What to me is the multitude of your sacrifices?' says the Lord; 'I have had enough of burnt offerings of rams and the fat of well-fed beasts; I do not delight in the blood of bulls, or of lambs, or of goats. When you come to appear before me, who has required of you this trampling of my courts? Bring no more vain offerings'" (Isa 1:11–13a).

Thus it was ingrained in the Jewish mindset that there did exist such a thing as a "spiritual sacrifice." The animal sacrifices of the temple were symbolic offerings that communicated the worshiper's repentance, need for forgiveness, and the desire to maintain covenant relationship. Whereas these animals had to be offered as a simple act of obedience, the people believed that there were other ways to communicate these same desires and needs. It was upon this alternative approach that the *Yahad* staked its legitimacy.

In correlation with the notion of "prayer as sacrifice" was the *Yahad*'s concept of *community as temple*. In the absence of a physical building, they developed the idea that the community of believers itself was the dwelling place of YHWH.[24] 1QS states:

> When such men as these come to be in Israel, then shall the party of the Yahad truly be established, an "eternal planting," a temple for Israel, and—mystery!—a Holy of Holies for Aaron; true witnesses to justice, chosen by God's will to atone for the land and to recompense the wicked their due . . . they shall be an acceptable sacrifice, atoning for the land and ringing in the verdict against evil, so that perversity ceases to exist.[25]

Just as the *Yahad* had replaced the notion of animal sacrifices with prayer, so they replaced the concept of a physical temple with one that was now spiritual. Gartner notes that "they transferred the whole complex of ideas from the Jerusalem temple to the community. This undoubtedly meant that some measure of 'spiritualization' had taken place, since the idea of the temple was now linked with the community, and since the temple worship was now performed through the

---

24. Modern visitors to the archeological site at Qumran can see an "all purpose" room that was most likely used for prayer and other functions. It seems that there was no structure dedicated exclusively to prayer and worship.
25. 1QS 8:4–7, 9–10 (Wise, "Charter," 129).

community's observance of the Law and through its own liturgy and cultus."[26]

What we see is a continuation in the symbolic imagery of the temple even if they did not have access to the actual structure. In this they anticipated what would occur within both Christianity and Rabbinic Judaism. For them, the material substance of the temple and its sacrifices was of secondary importance. The building itself was only a symbol of the community of Israel. And the material sacrifices were metaphors for prayer. Prayer had become "justice itself," and a "pleasing free-will offering." Prayer was their lifeline to the presence of God.

Putting the Pieces Together

As we have looked at the various "pockets" of this prayer movement in the first century, we can now discern two primary threads that held it together. First, we have seen that the temple was taking on an increasingly metaphorical meaning among various Jewish groups. For the *Yahad*, the idea of the temple was now expressed through the fellowship of the community. The Pharisees were teaching that the sanctity of the temple extended to the home and the village and that everyone was called to live in the same ritual purity as the priests. The synagogues were seen as "mini versions" of the temple, holy places for prayer and Torah study. In sum, the *idea* of the temple was now transcending the Jerusalem structure. The temple now symbolized the presence of YHWH, and it could be manifested in a diversity of settings.

Second, we have noted that prayer was coming to be seen as a form of spiritual sacrifice. There was a long-standing tradition in Judaism that animal sacrifice was ultimately a symbol for that which YHWH really wanted: a contrite heart and intimate relationship. For the *Yahad*, atonement would be entirely dependent on the offering of prayer. The rest of the Jewish people would continue to present sacrifices and offerings in the temple, even as prayer was gradually

---

26. Gartner, *Temple*, 18.

taking center stage. The people were tired of just being observers in the temple as the priests made offerings on their behalf. They wanted to present their own offerings; they wanted a role. And this is what was they were finding in prayer.

These threads were integral to the discipleship program of Jesus. He was fully engaged in this prayer movement. But there was one factor in particular that set the teaching of Jesus apart from the rest, and this was his declaration concerning the temple. In the teaching of the Pharisees and in the functions of the synagogue, we have seen that the people sought to *extend*—but not replace—the temple's purpose. They didn't want to see the eradication of the Jerusalem structure, they simply wanted to amplify its significance into new realms of their lives. As to the *Yahad*, their separation from the sacrifices of the temple was viewed as temporary affair. They hoped to see a restoration of true priesthood so that their participation in the sacrifices could resume. Jesus was radically different from them in the sense that in his movement, the Jerusalem temple would not play a central role. In his mind, it had become obsolete and he predicted its demise. In its place he would raise up a new house of prayer where people of all nations could present their offerings directly to YHWH. This new temple, enigmatically, would be the body of Jesus himself.[27]

Jesus and the Temple

When we look at the historical origins of the temple in Jerusalem, the biblical text is clear that God never commanded such a building to be constructed, nor was it necessary for offering sacrifices. For centuries before the temple was built, sacrifices and offerings were made inside the tabernacle, a mere configuration of tents. When David first presented the idea of building "a house" for YHWH, God's first response was this: "For I have not lived in a house since the day I brought up Israel to this day, but I have gone from tent to tent and from dwelling to dwelling. In all places where I have moved with all Israel,

27. This argument will be built upon the assumption that John 2:19–21 gives an accurate account of Jesus's words. See notes 32 and 33 below.

did I speak a word with any of the judges of Israel, whom I commanded to shepherd my people, saying, 'Why have you not built me a house of cedar?'" (1 Chron 17:5–6)

It was not God's idea. Yet it seems that YHWH did eventually acquiesce to David's vision of building a temple. God's purpose was that it would serve as a focal point for prayer. Solomon appealed to this purpose when he later dedicated the temple:

> Yet have regard to the prayer of your servant and to his plea, O Lord my God, listening to the cry and to the prayer that your servant prays before you, that your eyes may be open day and night toward this house, the place where you have promised to set your name, that you may listen to the prayer that your servant offers toward this place. And listen to the pleas of your servant and of your people Israel, when they pray toward this place. (2 Chron 6:19–21)

The temple was to serve the dual purposes of being a place of sacrifice and a focal point for prayer.

Somewhere along the way, however, the institution began to drift from its original purposes. The literature of the Second Temple period reveals that many Jews were unhappy with the "system" that had developed around the building and its rituals. As we have observed, the *Yahad* asserted that the whole operation was illegitimate. They were not alone in their discontent. Various texts from the pseudepigrapha contain scathing critiques of the priests and the temple functions.[28] Complaints ranged from illegitimate priestly succession, to following the wrong calendar, to sexual impurity among the priests. Alongside these ritual concerns, there was a social element as well. The Sadducean priests were aristocratic and wealthy. Something along the lines of banking system had been established through which many of the common people became indebted to the priests. At the outset of the first revolt (66–70 CE), the rebels burned down the house of Ananias the High Priest and the archives where the records of debts were kept. In their eyes, the temple and the priests had become symbols of economic oppression.[29] All this is not to say that the people as a

---

28. E.g., *1 En.* 89:73–74; *Pss. Sol.* 1, 2, 4, and 8; *T. Levi* 14:5–8; *T. Mos.* 4–7.

whole stood in opposition to the temple. The vast majority continued to participate in the feasts and the prescribed rituals. But the historical record does indicate that there were many Jews dissatisfied with the priestly hierarchy and the temple system. Jesus was among them.

An Illegitimate Institution

When we look at what the Gospels say about Jesus and the temple, there are some positive elements to this relationship: he participated in its festivals; he taught there frequently; he was willing to pay the tax; and his teachings seemed to presuppose the legitimacy of its rituals. In the book of Acts, we see that the early Christian community in Jerusalem did not see any contradiction between their faith in the risen Christ and their continued presence in the temple.[30] Yet despite these signs of a seemingly favorable attitude, the facts "on the ground" were that Jesus and the temple system were on course for a dramatic collision. He no longer believed that the temple was operating in the best interests of the people. In his mind, the time had come for something better. In the kingdom of God as Jesus proclaimed it, the Jerusalem temple would simply be obsolete, for he himself would take its place.[31]

In the eyes of Jesus, there were three "legs" upon which the temple's claim to legitimacy had once stood: its inviolable sanctity; its absolute necessity for the forgiveness of sin; and its favor with God. In the course of his ministry and his proclamation, he dismantled each of these three claims. First, with regard to the notion of sanctity, in Matthew 12:1–8 he demonstrated that the holiness of the temple and

---

29. Regarding the destruction of Ananias' house and the archives, see Josephus, *Bellum* 2.427. With regard to the general attitudes toward the temple as seen in the aforementioned pseudepigraphal writings, Nickelsburg notes, "This evidence need not indicate a continuous anti-temple movement over time, or a single anti-temple party at any given time. Nor do the polemics necessarily stem from a single concern or kind of criticism. Nonetheless, taken together they falsify the notion that all Jews in the postexilic period held the temple in high regard" (George Nickelsburg, *Ancient Judaism and Christian Origins* [Minneapolis: Fortress, 2003], 155).

30. See Matt 5:23–24; 17:24–27; Mark 14:49; Luke 2:41–51; 24:3; John 5:1; 7:10; Acts 2:46; 3:1; 5:42. We note in particular that the disciples' ongoing participation in the life of the temple, even after the resurrection of Jesus, indicates that they found no need to actively oppose its operation.

31. Cf. Wright, *Jesus*, 432–33.

the Sabbath were no longer paramount. "Something greater than the temple" had come, and that was Jesus himself. Second, in dealing with the issue of forgiveness, Jesus proclaimed to a paralytic that his sins were forgiven without the need of the temple priests or sacrifices (Mark 2:1–12). If Jesus on his own authority could proclaim the forgiveness of sins, then in his view the sacrifices of the temple were no longer necessary.[32] And finally, Jesus declared that the favor of God was no longer upon the temple. Its destruction was imminent. We will look at this dismantling of the "third leg" in greater detail.

Predicting the Temple's Fall

All three Synoptic authors recount Jesus's prediction that the temple would fall. In Mark 13:2 he declares, "Do you see these great buildings? There will not be left here one stone upon another that will not be thrown down."[33] Shortly after giving this prophecy, Jesus "cleansed" the temple, a symbolic act foreshadowing the divine judgment that was to come. As he turned over the tables and drove out the money changers, he cried, "It is written, 'My house shall be called a house of prayer,' but you make it a den of robbers" (Matt 21:13). Looking at his words more closely, we find that there are two important OT passages to which Jesus was making reference.

The notion of the temple a "house of prayer for all nations" comes from Isaiah 56:6–7, which declares:

> And the foreigners who join themselves to the Lord, to minister to him, to love the name of the Lord, and to be his servants, everyone who keeps the

---

32. Dunn notes:

> He pronounced the man's sins forgiven outside the cult and without any reference (even by implication) to the cult. It was not so much that he usurped the role of God in announcing sins forgiven. It was rather that he usurped the role of God which God had assigned to priest and cult. . . . He who took upon himself the priestly task of pronouncing absolution, without the authorization of the Temple authorities and without reference to the cult, might well be seen as putting a question mark against the importance and even the necessity of the cult, and, more threateningly, as undermining the authority of those whose power rested upon that system. (James Dunn, *The Partings of the Ways* [London: SCM, 2006], 61–62).

33. Wright argues that this prediction was the one upon which his validation as a prophet most depended: "As a prophet, Jesus staked his reputation on his prediction of the Temple's fall within a generation; if and when it fell, he would thereby be vindicated" (*Jesus*, 362).

Sabbath and does not profane it, and holds fast my covenant—these I will bring to my holy mountain, and make them joyful in my house of prayer; their burnt offerings and their sacrifices will be accepted on my altar; for my house shall be called a house of prayer for all peoples.

The idea of the "den of robbers" is from Jeremiah 7:9–15:

Will you steal, murder, commit adultery, swear falsely, make offerings to Baal, and go after other gods that you have not known, and then come and stand before me in this house, which is called by my name, and say, 'We are delivered!'—only to go on doing all these abominations? Has this house, which is called by my name, become a den of robbers in your eyes? Behold, I myself have seen it, declares the Lord. Go now to my place that was in Shiloh, where I made my name dwell at first, and see what I did to it because of the evil of my people Israel. And now, because you have done all these things, declares the Lord, and when I spoke to you persistently you did not listen, and when I called you, you did not answer, therefore I will do to the house that is called by my name, and in which you trust, and to the place that I gave to you and to your fathers, as I did to Shiloh. And I will cast you out of my sight, as I cast out all your kinsmen, all the offspring of Ephraim.

The Jewish leaders who heard Jesus's brief references to these passages were fully aware of what they said in their entirety. And they knew that through these words, Jesus was accusing them. Those who offered the sacrifices (i.e., the priests) were thieves, murderers, and idolaters. YHWH would judge the temple as he judged Shiloh, leaving it barren and desolate. In its place he would establish the eschatological temple of which Isaiah spoke, the "house of prayer for all peoples."[34]

When Jesus was subsequently arrested, tried, and crucified, his prediction of the temple's destruction would be used against him. A false witnesses at his trial declared, "We heard him say, 'I will destroy this temple that is made with hands, and in three days I will build another, not made with hands'" (Mark 14:58). And one of the thieves hanging with him taunted him saying, "Aha! You who would destroy the temple and rebuild it in three days, save yourself, and come down

34. Throughout the course of this book I will refer to God in the masculine gender (he, him, his). The rationale for this decision is my desire to maintain consistency with the ancient sources upon which this work is based, and is not intended as a "statement" on this matter.

from the cross!" (Mark 15:29). None of the Gospel authors actually depict Jesus saying that *he himself* would destroy the temple. But what is clear across the Gospel accounts is that Jesus predicted two things: the temple would be destroyed (by someone), and he would rebuild it in three days.[35]

With regard to the second prediction, it seems somewhat surprising that Jesus would say this when, in a literal sense, it would never come true. Why would he deliberately give them the impression that after the temple's destruction he himself would rebuild it in three days? The answer is that in this cryptic prophecy, Jesus was asking his hearers to make a mental shift. After his resurrection, they would understand, as John would write many years later, that "he was speaking about the temple of his body" (John 2:21). Stated simply, he wanted his followers to conflate the ideas of the temple and his body. Both the physical building and his physical body would be brought down. But only one would be rebuilt.

To sum it all up: Jesus said that he was going to replace the temple. Once the old structure and the corrupt system that went along with it was out of the way, his body would become what the temple was always intended to be, a house of prayer for all nations. The full weight of Jesus's prediction and prophetic acts concerning the temple were directed toward one aim: the restoration of prayer. His vision was to restore to Israel the intimate experience of God's presence that they had been missing for so many years. For too long they had settled for a counterfeit temple, and now he was going to give them the real thing.

---

35. There are five passages in the Gospels that speak an association between the death and resurrection of Jesus and the destruction of the temple. In four instances, it comes in the form of an accusation against Jesus, as seen in Mark 14:58: "We heard him say, 'I will destroy this temple that is made with hands, and in three days I will build another, not made with hands.'" See also Matt 26:61, 27:40; Mark 15:29. Only John puts this claim in the mouth of Jesus himself: "Jesus answered them, 'Destroy this temple, and in three days I will raise it up.' The Jews then said, 'It has taken forty-six years to build this temple, and will you raise it up in three days?' But he was speaking about the temple of his body." There is debate as to whether John's account is historical. I am obviously making the case that it is. It should also be noted that in John, what Jesus actually says differs slightly from the account of the false witnesses and the thief on the cross. They had accused Jesus of saying that *he himself* would destroy the temple. John's account presents Jesus saying that it is the Jews who would do the destroying: "*You* (2nd person plural) *destroy this temple and in three days I will raise it up.*" For more on this topic, see Nicholas Perrin, *Jesus the Temple* (London: SPCK, 2010), 99–113.

This idea would eventually become incorporated into Christian thought. The "body" of Jesus would come to be understood as a metaphor for the true temple: the community of believers. And prayer was seen as the sacrifice that they, as priests, would offer. The *Yahad* had once described their community as "a temple for Israel" and "a "Holy of Holies for Aaron," offering "an acceptable sacrifice, atoning for the land." In the same way, Peter would say to his readers, "You yourselves like living stones are being built up as a spiritual house, to be a holy priesthood, to offer spiritual sacrifices acceptable to God through Jesus Christ" (1 Pet 2:5). Here, Christians are priests. The spiritual sacrifice they lift up is prayer, and the spiritual house is the fellowship of believers, the church.

Conclusion

We close by looking back to the siege of Jerusalem once again. History has it that shortly before Titus arrived, the members of Jerusalem's Christian community managed to escape.[36] They had heeded Jesus's warning: "But when you see Jerusalem surrounded by armies, then know that its desolation has come near. Then let those who are in Judea flee to the mountains, and let those who are inside the city depart, and let not those who are out in the country enter it" (Luke 21:20–21). Not everyone, however, heard or heeded these words, and they suffered the horrible consequences.

After the city was decimated and the Romans regained control, the Jews would no longer be allowed to offer sacrifices. No legitimate sacrifice has been offered there since that day. But Judaism survived. Under the direction of the Pharisees, the Jewish people reorganized, and the heart of the new "Rabbinic" Judaism now moved to the town of Yavneh. It was from there that the Rabbis forged a new path for the

---

36. The church historian Eusebius claimed that before Titus arrived, "the people of the church in Jerusalem had been commanded by a revelation, vouchsafed to approved men there before the war, to leave the city and to dwell in a certain town of Perea called Pella" (*Hist. Eccl.* 3.5.3, in Eusebius of Caesaria, "*Historia ecclesiastica*," in *A Select Library of the Nicene and Post-Nicene Fathers of the Christian Church*, ed. P. Schaff and H. Wace, trans. Arthur McGiffert [New York: Christian Literature Company, 1890]).

Jewish people. Rabbi Isaac would declare, "At this time we have neither prophet nor priest, neither sacrifice, nor Temple, nor altar—what is it that can make atonement for us, even though the Temple is destroyed? The only thing that we have left is prayer."[37]

Prayer had been gradually taking the place of animal sacrifice long before Isaac made his proclamation. Many people had grown tired of merely observing the priests as they offered the sacrifices in the temple. They were looking for a more personalized expression of worship. While the temple stood, few Jews would challenge its necessity. But once it was gone, they discovered that they been in a long process of preparation to live without it.

The Pharisees had taught that the presence of YHWH was not limited to the Jerusalem sanctuary, that it could be experienced in the home and the village. In the synagogues, the people were gathering regularly, taking ownership of their worship and experiencing YHWH's presence through prayer. The *Yahad* had learned how to maintain relationship with YHWH even without the Jerusalem structure. Prayer was becoming a true spiritual sacrifice that was acceptable and pleasing to God.

It is in the context of these developments that we understand why and how prayer was such a central element of Jesus's teaching. He launched his ministry during a prayer revival in which he himself was deeply engaged. He took this revival in a radical new direction. Whereas most of his contemporary Jews were willing to offer up both spiritual *and* animal sacrifices, Jesus saw the temple and its functions as obsolete and in need of replacement. The house of prayer that he would build could only be established once the Jerusalem structure was gone. Jesus himself—his body—would be that new temple, the house of prayer for all nations. This pivotal "transfer of meaning" crystallized at the very end of Jesus's ministry. Even though the Jerusalem temple would continue to operate for another four decades after his death, his disciples could now move forward without it. They now understood that the call to follow Jesus was a call to prayer.

37. *Tanhuma, Way-yislah* 9 (Heinneman, *Prayer*, 20).

2

Prayer and Covenant Renewal

Sara's life was the story of one tragedy after another. For many years her family had been living as refugees in Assyria, having been forcibly deported from their homeland in northern Israel. Now settled in this foreign land, her father Raguel had been trying desperately to find her a suitable match. There was no lack of candidates. In fact, several young men had agreed to take her as a bride. The only problem was that every time they would get to the honeymoon suite, the groom would die. It so happened that a nasty demon named Asmodeus was in love with Sara, and in his jealously he would slay each young man before the marriage could be consummated. Falsely accused of having murdered the seven grooms herself, Sara in her despair cried out to God, "Either take my life, or deliver me from this shame!" (Tob 3:11–16).

At the same time that Sara prayed, another Jewish refugee, in another part of the land, was also praying. Tobit was also a victim of tragedy. Despite his many righteous deeds, things always seemed to go wrong for him. Like Daniel, he had once risen to a prominent position in the royal court, only to be driven away when the king he served died. He was then caught illegally burying the bodies of dead Jews that he found in the streets, and all of his possessions were taken away. Finally, to add insult to injury, a sparrow defecated into his eyes while he was standing near a wall, leaving him totally blind. Nothing could go right for poor Tobit! In his shame and embarrassment he saw that the tragic comedy of his own life was a crude reflection of Israel's story. It was becoming too much to bear. So he cried out to God, "Either take my life or deliver Israel from her shame" (Tob 3:1–6).

As the prayers of these two righteous people rose to heaven, an angel was dispatched to come to their aide. His name was Raphael, and his four-fold mission was to find a spouse for Sara, outsmart Asmodeus, heal Tobit's eyes, and show both Sara and Tobit that there was still reason for hope in Israel. To accomplish this task, Raphael engaged the services of two characters: Tobit's son Tobias, and a salubrious fish. The story is a bit complex, but the crucial details are that Tobias marries Sara, burns the fish's heart and liver to drive away the demon, and then uses the gall to heal his father's eyes. In the end, both Sarah and Tobit acknowledge that God has heard their prayers, and they can be confident that he will restore their nation.

Despite what we may consider its humorous elements, the book of Tobit actually contains a serious and theologically rich message. At the end of the story, Tobit makes prayers and prophecies regarding the future of his people and all the nations of the earth. In his prayer he declares that all peoples will come to Jerusalem to worship the God of Israel: "A bright light will shine to all parts of the earth; many nations shall come to you from afar, and the inhabitants of all the limits of the earth, drawn to you by the name of the Lord God, bearing in their hands their gifts for the King of heaven. Every generation shall give joyful praise in you, and shall call you the chosen one, through all ages forever" (Tob 13:11–12). And then he later prophesies again:

> But God will again have mercy on them and bring them back to the land of Israel. They shall rebuild the temple, but it will not be like the first one, until the era when the appointed times shall be completed. Afterward all of them shall return from their exile, and they shall rebuild Jerusalem with splendor. In her the temple of God shall also be rebuilt; yes it will be rebuilt for all generations to come, just as the prophets of Israel said

of her. All the nations of the world shall be converted and shall offer God true worship; all shall abandon their idols which have deceitfully led them into error, and shall bless the God of the ages in righteousness. (Tob 14:5–7)

By the way that it combines fantasy and reality, the story of Tobit is what we today would call "historical fiction." Similar in nature to a parable, the purpose of Tobit was not to recount actual events, but rather to illustrate a truth. The text appears to have been written to address insecurity about the future of the Jewish people.[1] What the author is seeking to communicate is that through prayer, Israel can be restored to greatness. Tobit and Sara represented all those who were feeling discouraged and ready to give up. When they prayed, God acted mightily on their behalf. Just as God had restored the lives of these unfortunate individuals, so he would lift up the entire nation. Tobit prayed and prophesied that the scattered tribes would return to the land, and the temple would be gloriously rebuilt. The exaltation of Israel would be so amazing that the surrounding nations would recognize the God of Israel as the one and only true God. They would forsake their idols and come to Jerusalem to worship him alongside the Jewish people whom they had once held in scorn.

Tobit is significant as an indicator of the way many Jews of the Second Temple period thought about prayer. Their approach to prayer was very different than our own. Our prayers typically combine elements of worship, thanksgiving, confession, and petition for present needs. Unless they are marking some solemn occasion, rarely do our prayers contain historical reflections on the experiences of our family, community, or nation.[2] And this is where the typical American prayer

---

1. It is generally accepted that the book of Tobit was written in the late third or early second century BCE. The intended audience was the Jewish community of the Diaspora, who awaited their restoration to the land of Israel while living among the gentiles. See Jill Hicks-Keeton, "Already/Not Yet: Eschatological Tension in the Book of Tobit," *Journal of Biblical Literature* 1 (2013): 97–117.

2. Gibson provides a helpful overview of how many American Christians interpret the Lord's Prayer. His survey suggests that most people are praying the Lord's Prayer with a vague, if any, sense of the community to which it refers and make no connection between it and any particular historical narrative. See Jeffrey Gibson, *The Disciple's Prayer: The Prayer Jesus Taught in Its Historical Setting* (Minneapolis: Fortress, 2015).

in the twenty-first century differs so much from ancient Jewish prayers.

When the Jewish people of old prayed, they thought about history. Whatever was happening in the present could only make sense in light of how God dealt with their people in the past and what he had promised to them for the future. Individuals saw their own fate as being deeply intertwined with that of their nation. Yes, they prayed for their personal needs, but these needs only mattered because they formed part of a bigger picture. Tobit and Sara saw their own lives as reflections of the Jewish experience in history. They believed that their personal restoration was somehow tied to the healing of the entire nation. In traditional Jewish prayer there is a deep consciousness of how individuals are connected to their community, how God has dealt with the community in the past, and how he will deal with it in the future.

In the previous chapter, we talked about the prayer revival that was taking place in various Jewish settings during the first century. Our task in this present chapter will be to look specifically at the Lord's Prayer as a traditional Jewish prayer. Just like other prayers of the period, it is rich in historical awareness. It makes reference to what God had done for Israel in the past, and it articulates the hopes that all Jewish people held for their future. The people that were first called to pray in this way—who would address God as "Our Father"—were the Jewish followers of Jesus. Thus, long before we can talk about the Lord's Prayer within Christianity, we must consider what it meant within first-century Judaism.

Our approach to this task will take place in two stages. First, we will look at other Jewish prayers that were in use during Jesus's time. We will explore the historical events to which they referred, the hopes they articulated, and the community identity that they reinforced. Then, in the second part of our study, we will look at the actual text of the Lord's Prayer. It will be seen that this prayer bore numerous similarities to other Jewish prayers of the period. But there was one overarching characteristic of the Lord's Prayer that made it unique.

Whereas other prayers expressed the notion that Israel's hopes were yet to be made reality, the Lord's Prayer expressed the idea that the time of fulfillment had come. Other prayers metaphorically presented Israel as still awaiting their restoration. The proclamation of Jesus, however, was that through him, Israel could fulfill the covenant that they had made with YHWH in the Sinai desert. They could now move forward with their vision to bring all nations to salvation. The Lord's Prayer is the prayer of a people who are closing a dark chapter in their history and now beginning to see the realization of their hopes. It is the prayer of a renewed Israel.

How the Jewish People Prayed in the Time of the Second Temple

The story that forms the backdrop for all Jewish prayer is the historical narrative of Abraham and his family. Abraham, the father of Israel, was given a promise that through his seed all the families of the earth would be blessed.[3] After spending four hundred years as captives in Egypt, Israel passed through the Sinai wilderness on their way to land that had been promised to Abraham. While they were in the desert, YHWH deepened the covenant that he had originally made with Abraham. He promised them that if they would honor the commandments given to them, then they would be his "own possession among all the peoples" and "a kingdom of priests and a holy nation" (Exod 19:5–6). It was on this same journey in the desert, however, that the people of Israel first demonstrated stubborn refusal to honor this pact. Despite the miracles that they had seen and the provision of the manna, they put YHWH to the test with their grumbling and doubting. Consequently, that first generation coming out of Israel was forbidden from entering the Promised Land.

As the second generation after the exodus prepared to enter Canaan under the leadership of Joshua, Moses delivered a series of teachings, according to the book of Deuteronomy. The purpose of these teachings was to remind the people about all they had been through and to

---

3. See Gen 12:2–3; 22:17–18.

clarify the terms of their agreement with YHWH. Moses declared, "Hear, O Israel: The Lord our God, the Lord is one . . . you are a people holy to the Lord your God. The Lord your God has chosen you to be a people for his treasured possession, out of all the peoples who are on the face of the earth" (Deut 6:4, 7). If the people of Israel would honor the statutes and commands given to them by Moses, then they would see the fulfillment of all that YHWH had promised to Abraham. They would be a model people. All the nations of the earth would know that YHWH was the one true God and that Israel was his chosen people: "And if you faithfully obey the voice of the Lord your God, being careful to do all his commandments that I command you today, the Lord your God will set you high above all the nations of the earth. . . . And all the peoples of the earth shall see that you are called by the name of the Lord, and they shall be afraid of you" (Deut 28:1, 10). This renewed contract between God and Israel is commonly referred to as the "Deuteronomic covenant."

The biblical history that follows the making of the covenant tells the story of Israel's struggle to honor their end of the bargain. Time and time again, the people drifted away from God. There would be seasons of revival and renewal under the leadership of righteous kings such as David, Josiah, and Hezekiah. But these were only periodic interruptions in a general pattern of unfaithfulness.[4] God's judgment eventually came upon the northern ten tribes, who in 722 BCE were overthrown by the Assyrians and driven from their homeland. Then, in the late sixth century BCE, YHWH's anger was displayed against the people of Judah. Jerusalem was sacked, the temple was destroyed, and the people were taken into captivity.

After a period of seventy years, a small portion of the exiles returned from Babylon and began to rebuild the temple. During this time in Israel's history, the nation experienced a mixture of blessings and challenges. One positive aspect of the exile was that it seemed to have purified the people from their tendency to worship both YHWH *and* other gods. Under the leadership of men such as Ezra, Nehemiah, and

---

4. This metanarrative can be seen, for example, in the prayer of Daniel (Dan 9:3–19).

Zerubbabel, the people of Israel rebuilt the ruined temple. In this time, commonly known as the "Second Temple" period, Israel became a truly monotheistic people for this first time since the patriarchs. The political fortunes of the nation, however, were not encouraging. The majority of the twelve tribes never returned from their exile. The Jewish Diaspora would remain scattered throughout the Mediterranean world and Mesopotamia. In Palestine itself, there would be seasons of political independence, such as the reign of the Hasmoneans. But for the greater part of this Second Temple era, Israel would be under the dominion of foreign powers.

The Hope of Israel

During this season of spiritual purification and political oppression, a clear hope for the future began to emerge. Israel had long been waiting for the coming of the "promised one," the Messiah, who would restore the nation to greatness. Throughout the Second Temple period, the Jewish people were united around a group of specific expectations that they believed would characterize this restoration. These expectations were as follows: (1) Israel's oppressors would be crushed; (2) YHWH would regather the tribes from the nations; (3) the presence of YHWH would return to Zion to inhabit a glorious temple; (4) the Jewish people would experience a revival of worship and righteousness; and (5) upon seeing the exaltation of Israel, all the nations would come to worship YHWH, the one and only true God.[5] All of these hopes are encapsulated in the various "servant" passages of Isaiah. These passages describe YHWH's promises to the people, promises that came to be understood as the work of the Messiah to come. This is how God's promised actions are described:

1. He will crush the oppressor: "I will make your oppressors eat their own flesh, and they shall be drunk with their own blood as with

---

5. See E. P. Sanders, *Judaism: Practice and Belief 63 BCE–66 CE* (Philadelphia: Trinity Press International, 1992), 288–90; and N. T. Wright, *The New Testament and the People of God* (Minneapolis: Fortress, 1992), 280–338.

wine. Then all flesh shall know that I am the Lord your Savior, and your Redeemer, the Mighty One of Jacob" (Isa 49:26).

2. He will regather the tribes: "I will bring your offspring from the east, and from the west I will gather you. I will say to the north, Give up, and to the south, Do not withhold; bring my sons from afar and my daughters from the end of the earth" (Isa 43:5–6).

3. He will proclaim the return of YHWH to Zion: "The voice of your watchmen—they lift up their voice; together they sing for joy; for eye to eye they see the return of the Lord to Zion. Break forth together into singing, you waste places of Jerusalem, for the Lord has comforted his people; he has redeemed Jerusalem" (Isa 52:8–9).

4. He will bring revival: "By myself I have sworn; from my mouth has gone out in righteousness a word that shall not return: 'To me every knee shall bow, every tongue shall swear allegiance.' Only in the Lord, it shall be said of me, are righteousness and strength; to him shall come and be ashamed all who were incensed against him. In the Lord all the offspring of Israel shall be justified and shall glory" (Isa 45:23–25).

5. He will save the nations: "'It is too light a thing that you should be my servant to raise up the tribes of Jacob and to bring back the preserved of Israel; I will make you as a light for the nations, that my salvation may reach to the end of the earth. . . . Kings shall see and arise; princes, and they shall prostrate themselves; because of the Lord, who is faithful, the Holy One of Israel, who has chosen you'" (Isa 49:6–7).

As Jesus initiated his ministry, these were the hopes and expectations that his fellow Jews had.

These hopes constituted the "final chapter" of the Deuteronomistic narrative. When Israel's enemies were defeated, when the tribes were brought back together, when YHWH's presence returned to Zion, when Israel was made spiritually pure, and when the nations came to salvation—then the people could say that the purpose of the covenant had been achieved.

For the people of Israel living in the Second Temple era, prayer was a means expressing these hopes and affirming their identity. The Jews saw themselves as a particular people. They believed that they were the one and only nation chosen by the one and only true God. Yet at the same time they had a universal mission: they must draw all the nations of the earth to worship the one true God. Their strategy for reaching the nations did not entail sending out "missionaries." Rather, the people of the Second Temple era prayed for themselves so that when Jerusalem was exalted, the nations of the earth would simply come to worship their God. They prayed for their own purification and restoration, even as they declared their confidence that God would draw the people of the earth to himself.

Identity and Hope as Expressed through Prayer

The people of the *Yahad* at the Dead Sea saw themselves as the chosen remnant of YHWH. How they viewed their uniqueness among the nations is seen in this prayer from a text known as the War Scroll:

> Thou art the God of our fathers; we bless Thy Name for ever. We are the people of Thine inheritance; Thou didst make a Covenant with our fathers, and wilt establish it with their children throughout eternal ages. And in all Thy glorious testimonies there has been a reminder of Thy mercies among us to succour the remnant, the survivors of Thy Covenant, that they might recount Thy works of truth and the judgements of Thy marvellous mighty deeds. Thou hast created us for Thyself, O God, that we may be an everlasting people.[6]

Yet even as the Yahad believed that judgment would come upon the sinful people of Israel and all nations, there are many texts found at Qumran that also speak of the salvation of the gentiles. This would

---

6. 1QM 13 (Geza Vermes, *The Complete Dead Sea Scrolls in English: Complete Edition* [London: Penguin, 2004], 179). Translations of DSS often contain brackets indicating where there were gaps in the original text whose content has been extrapolated by the translator. For the sake of legibility I have removed the brackets from this citation and all others from the scrolls.

occur as the nations witness the blessing and restoration of Israel. The following prayers are examples:

> Your residence . . . a place of rest in Jerusalem the city which you chose from the whole earth for your Name to be there forever. For you loved Israel more than all the peoples. . . . And all the countries have seen your glory, for you have made yourself holy in the midst of your people, Israel. And to your great Name they will carry their offerings: silver, gold, precious stones, with all the treasures of their country, to honour your people and Zion, your holy city and your wonderful house.[7]

. . .

> Thou wilt raise up survivors among Thy people and a remnant within Thine inheritance. Thou wilt purify and cleanse them of their sin for all their deeds are in Thy truth. Thou wilt judge them in Thy great loving-kindness and in the multitude of Thy mercies and in the abundance of Thy pardon, teaching them according to Thy word; and Thou wilt establish them in Thy Council according to the uprightness of Thy truth. . . . All the nations shall acknowledge Thy truth, and all the people Thy glory. For Thou wilt bring Thy glorious salvation to all the men of Thy Council, to those who share a common lot with the Angels of the Face.[8]

. . .

> And they will refine by them the chosen of justice and he will wipe out all iniquity on account of his pious ones; for the age of wickedness is fulfilled and all injustice will pass away. For the time of justice has arrived, and the earth is filled with knowledge and the praise of God. In the days of . . . the age of peace has arrived, and the laws of truth, and the testimony of justice, to instruct all in God's paths and in the mighty acts of his deeds . . . for eternal centuries. Every tongue will bless him, and every man will bow down before him, and they will be of one mind.[9]

Prayers of the Synagogue

The prayers known as the *Shema* and the *Amidah* form the core of the rabbinic prayer liturgy. The tradition held that the *Shema* was said by the temple priests as they offered sacrifices in the temple. Dating

---

7. 4Q504 f1-2 4:2–12 (Florentino Garcìa Martìnez and Eibert J.C. Tigchelaar, *The Dead Sea Scrolls Study Edition (translations)* [Leiden: Brill, 1997–1998], 2:1015).
8. 1QHa 14:8–13 (Vermes, *Complete*, 277).
9. 1QHa 14:8–13 (ibid.).

back perhaps to the second or third century BCE, the custom came into practice for the people to recite the *Shema* and the *Amidah* at the hours corresponding to the temple's sacrifices and offerings.[10] Among the declarations of the *Shema* and its accompanying "blessings" are the following:

> For You are a God who works salvation, and You have chosen us from all peoples and language groups.

> And You have brought us close to Your great Name in truth—that we may give thanks to You and proclaim Your unity in love. You are praised, O Lord, who has chosen His people Israel in love.

> Hear O Israel: the Lord our God, the Lord is One. Praised be His Name, whose glorious kingdom is forever and ever. Love the Lord your God with all your heart, with all your soul, and with all your might.

> It is true that You are the Lord our God and the God of our fathers, our King and the King of our fathers, our Redeemer and the Redeemer of our fathers, our Maker, the Rock of our salvation, our Deliverer and Rescuer. Eternal is Your Name; there is no God beside You.[11]

The *Amidah* declares, "Have compassion, O Lord, in Your abundant mercies. Upon Israel, Your people, upon Jerusalem, Your city, upon Zion, Your glorious dwelling-place, upon Your temple and upon Your abode, and upon the kingdom of the house of David, Your righteous anointed, You are praised, O Lord, God of David, Builder of Jerusalem."[12] Other prayers of the synagogue express these same themes. Although the origin of the following texts cannot definitively be dated in the Second Temple era, they stand in continuity with the prayers of that

---

10. *M. Tamid* 5.1 describes the priests reciting the *Shema* as they offered sacrifices, and *M. Berakhot* 1–4 discusses the parameters for the daily recitation of these prayers. By the time the Rabbis of Yavneh codified these prayers at the end of the first century, the tradition of their recitation was firmly established. Hoffman notes that the provenance of the *Shema* can definitively be dated before 70 CE. He also notes that many scholars believe some form of the *Amidah* existed in the second or third century BCE. The most natural assumption is that the development of these prayers accompanied the emergence of the synagogue, as discussed in the previous chapter. See Lawrence Hoffman, "Reconstructing Ritual as Identity and Culture," in *The Making of Jewish and Christian Worship*, ed. Paul Bradshaw and Lawrence Hoffman (Notre Dame: University of Notre Dame Press, 1991), 24.
11. Petuchowski, "Jewish," 22–24.
12. Ibid., 29.

period. One example is the *Kaddish*, which affirms the universal rule of YHWH in language very similar to that of the Lord's Prayer: "Exalted and hallowed be His great Name in the world which He created according to His will. May He establish His kingdom in your lifetime and in your days, and in the lifetime of the whole household of Israel, speedily and at a near time."[13] Another ancient prayer that affirms the unique identity of Israel and the future salvation of the nations is the *Alenu*. Among its declarations and petitions are found the following:

> It is for us to praise the Lord of all, to ascribe greatness to the God of creation. Who has not made us like the nations of other countries, nor placed us like the other families of the earth. He did not appoint our portion like theirs. Nor our destiny like that of their multitudes . . . the Lord is God in the heavens above and on the earth below; there is none else. . . . We therefore hope in You, O Lord our God, That we may soon behold the glory of Your might, when idols will be removed from the earth, and non-gods will be utterly destroyed. When the world will be perfected under the rule of the Almighty, when all mankind will invoke Your Name. . . . Before You, O Lord our God, Let them bow down and worship. Giving honour unto Your glorious Name. May they all accept the yoke of Your kingdom, So that You will reign over them soon and forevermore. For Yours is the kingdom. And unto all eternity You will reign in glory.[14]

The clear message emerging from all of these prayers is that the people of Israel viewed themselves as a particular nation, chosen and blessed by YHWH. They believed that eventually this blessing would spread to all of the families of the earth. But the establishment of YHWH's universal blessings would not occur until he had first exalted them.

The Lord's Prayer and Covenant Fulfillment

We have seen in these ancient prayers that the Jewish people prayed with a deep awareness of all that had happened before them and how those events shaped both their present and future. The Lord's Prayer is no different in this regard. It is steeped in historical consciousness.

---

13. Ibid., 37.
14. Ibid., 43.

And if there is one particular moment in Israel's history that shapes the mindset of this prayer, it is the sojourn in the Sinai wilderness. This was the season, we might say, when YHWH offered his hand in marriage to the people of Israel. God expressed his unique love for the Jewish people and gave the terms of their covenant relationship.

Over the course of the centuries, this marriage relationship between YHWH and the people of Israel passed through difficult periods. When the people strayed, prophets such as Ezekiel and Hosea would characterize Israel as an unfaithful wife who rejected her husband in favor of foreign lovers.[15] They spoke of God's judgment on the people for their sins, and yet these prophets also spoke of restoration. YHWH and Israel would return to the "days of their youth" and their marriage vows would be renewed. Ezekiel wrote, "I will remember my covenant with you in the days of your youth, and I will establish for you an everlasting covenant.... I will establish my covenant with you, and you shall know that I am the Lord" (Ezek 16:60–62). And Hosea said, "I will allure her, and bring her into the wilderness, and speak tenderly to her. ... And there she shall answer as in the days of her youth, as at the time when she came out of the land of Egypt. "And in that day," declares the Lord, "you will call me 'My Husband,' and no longer will you call me 'My Baal'" (Hos 2:14–16). Passages such as these reminded the people of Israel that in seasons of spiritual darkness, God would always take initiative to bring the hearts of the nation back to himself.

It was in this vein that Jesus understood his own ministry. He saw himself as the one sent by the Father to restore the relationship between Israel and their God. One way to interpret his mission is to think of him as the one who came to restore the marriage.[16] In this light, Jesus's forty-day fast in the wilderness can be seen as a ceremony

---

15. See Hos 1:2–2:13 and Ezek 16:1–52.
16. So Wright:

> The age to come, the end of Israel's exile, was therefore seen as the inauguration of a new covenant between Israel and her god. Building on the earlier promises of restoration articulated by Isaiah, Jeremiah, and Ezekiel, the post-exilic and then the post-biblical writings gave varied expression to the belief that their god would soon renew his covenant. ... When Israel finally 'returned from exile,' and the Temple was (properly) rebuilt, and reinhabited by its proper occupant—this would be seen as comparable with the making of the covenant on Sinai. It would be the rebetrothal of YHWH and Israel, after their apparent divorces it would be the real forgiveness of sins; Israel's god

for renewing the vows.[17] Reenacting "the days of Israel's youth," he metaphorically returned to the wilderness. Once there, he faced all of the same trials and temptations that Israel had faced. But where the people of the exodus had failed, he succeeded and reaffirmed the commitments of the Deuteronomic Covenant. This accomplished, he then showed the Jewish people the secret of his success and taught them how to be a renewed Israel. The Lord's Prayer became the new set of vows that Israel could make with YHWH. Through this prayer, the marriage relationship could be restored.

Jesus in the Wilderness

The sweep of biblical narrative allows us to perceive an arc in the story of humanity's struggle with temptation. When the nation of Israel came into Sinai, they faced the same set of temptations that had perennially beset humanity. Their trials and failures in the desert seemed to be a replay of Eden. Adam and Eve were tempted by the fruit because it was "good for food." In a similar way, the people of Israel grumbled and complained when they were hungry and had nothing to eat or drink. Adam and Eve were drawn to the fruit because of its beauty. In the same way, Israel worshiped a visually pleasing idol of gold. Adam and Eve ate the fruit because it would make them like God. In the same way, the people of Israel sought to appropriate power for themselves by appointing their own leaders, instead of those whom God had chosen.[18] Thus all of three temptations that had initially led to the fall of humanity—the urges of the body, the lust of the eyes, and the desire for autonomous control—continued to plague the nation of Israel in the desert.

The forty years that Israel spent in Sinai became emblematic of spiritual trial. Moses had said to the generation entering Canaan: "And

would pour out his holy spirit, so that she would be able to keep the Torah properly, from the heart. (*New Testament*, 301).

17. See Matt 4:1–11; Luke 4:1–12; Mark 1:12–13. The characterization of this episode as a "renewal of the vows" is my own, and one which I have not encountered elsewhere.

18. See Exodus 16, 32; Number 14, 20; Gen 3:6.

you shall remember the whole way that the Lord your God has led you these forty years in the wilderness, that he might humble you, testing you to know what was in your heart, whether you would keep his commandments or not" (Deut 8:2). The generation of the exodus had failed this trial, and even after Moses had renewed the covenant with their children, the people of Israel would continue to fail again and again.

The forty days that Jesus spent fasting and praying in the wilderness of Judah may be read as Israel's opportunity to have a "do-over." Jesus would go out into the desert and face every temptation there that Israel (and Adam and Eve) had experienced. Satan would come at him appealing to the same primordial vulnerabilities. If Jesus could overcome temptation where Israel had failed, his obedience would count as their obedience, and the marriage to YHWH could be restored.

The first temptation that Jesus faced was to break his fast and eat. In response, he quotes from Israel's wedding vows in the book of the Deuteronomy, saying, "It is written, 'Man shall not live by bread alone, but by every word that comes from the mouth of God'" (Matt 4:3). Then Satan appeals to his pride, challenging him to perform a sign and gain the admiration of the people. In response, Jesus again quotes from Deuteronomy, saying, "Again it is written, 'You shall not put the Lord your God to the test'" (Matt 4:7). Finally, Satan appeals to his eyes, showing him the kingdoms of the world and offering them to Jesus in exchange for worship. Jesus says to him, "Be gone, Satan! For it is written, 'You shall worship the Lord your God and him only shall you serve'" (Matt 4:10).[19]

The larger biblical story I am describing allows me to suggest that when Jesus went into the desert, he did so as if he were the personification of Israel. For many generations the Jewish people had been waiting for such a figure to come. Isaiah, for example, had prophesied about the coming of the "servant of YHWH" who would stand in Israel's place and fulfill the covenant on her behalf. This man would be sent by God "to bring Jacob back to him . . . that Israel might

19. See Deut 8:3; 6:13, 16.

be gathered to him" (Isa 49:5). He would be given "as a covenant to the people, to establish the land, to apportion the desolate heritages" (Isa 49:8). Jesus had faced the prototypical temptations himself *and overcame them*. The story suggests that Jesus had fulfilled the covenant on Israel's behalf. That is why Jesus had the confidence to publically proclaim, "The time is fulfilled, and the kingdom of God is at hand; repent and believe in the gospel" (Mark 4:15). Going into the Nazareth synagogue where he had grown up, he read from one of Isaiah's servant passages (Isaiah 61) and then declared to the people, "Today this Scripture has been fulfilled in your hearing" (Luke 4:21). Jesus presented himself as the divinely appointed representative for whom Israel had been waiting.

Redefining Israel and Their Hopes

Having redeemed Israel from their past, Jesus now claimed the right to redefine their hopes for the future. In his day, the people of Israel awaited the "final chapter" of the Deuteronomistic narrative. Certain expectations were in place: her enemies had to be defeated; the tribes had to be brought back to the land; the presence of YHWH had to return to Zion; Israel had to be made pure; and the nations had to come to salvation. When all of these things occurred, then and only then could Israel could say that the purpose of the covenant had been achieved. By the time Jesus ended his ministry, however, it would seem that little had changed: the Romans were still firmly in control; the majority of the Jewish people were still scattered across the earth; the temple system remained corrupt; the Jewish people remained divided and in need of revival; and salvation had not spread to the nations. So how is it that we can we speak of "covenant fulfillment" in Jesus, when on the surface it would seem that his mission had failed?

One way to resolve this dilemma is by understanding that Jesus *redefined* Israel and their hopes for the future. Membership in the renewed Israel was now a matter of sharing in Jesus's faithful obedience to God. He defeated Israel's enemies—but not the ones they thought needed to be overthrown. The *real enemies* of Israel were sin and Satan, and these Jesus overcame. He regathered the tribes, but not in a physical sense. In Jesus's proclamation, the return of the twelve tribes was a metaphor for spiritual revival. Through Jesus, YHWH had returned to Zion and taken possession of his temple, but that temple was the body of Jesus himself. In him, Israel was now ready to exert its influence among the nations. Jesus's final command to his followers was for them to go make disciples throughout the world.[20]

Thus we see in the Lord's Prayer that the restoration of Israel is an event now in progress. Jesus had gone into the desert and obeyed on Israel's behalf. Hope was now restored. The prayer that he taught his followers is the prayer of those who have tasted the first fruits of restoration. Israel is now being exalted and the followers of Jesus now envision the consummation of the age: the salvation of all nations.

The Prayer of the Renewed Israel

As was common among many ancient Jewish prayers, the Lord's Prayer looks backward and forward. As we now look at the seven petitions of the Lord's Prayer, we will do so through the lens of the renewed Israel. We will draw out the meaning of this prayer by exploring how it relates to the covenant that YHWH made with Israel in the book of

---

20. This paradigm of Jesus's ministry that I here present is based on the work of N. T. Wright, *Jesus and the Victory of God* (Minneapolis: Fortress, 1997). Note the following: (1) Wright (p. 430) argues that the national identity of Israel was to be redefined by relationship to him: "Jesus had called for a deep and shocking disloyalty to the human, and nation-defining family, that his hearers knew; it was to be replaced by total devotion and loyalty to Jesus himself." (2) With regard to defining Israel's enemies, Wright (p. 173) notes, "Jesus was affirming the basic beliefs and aspirations of the kingdom: Israel's god is lord of the world, and, if Israel is still languishing in misery, he must act to defeat her enemies and vindicate her. Jesus was not doing away with that basic Jewish paradigm. He was reaffirming it most strongly. . . . He was, however, redefining the Israel that was to be vindicated, and hence was also redrawing Israel's picture of her true enemies." (3) Wright (p. 428) states that the restoration of the land and the return of the tribe is symbolized by "the dramatic restoration of creation, focused on the healing of the sick." (4) With regard to the temple, Wright (p. 435) argues that "for Jesus, part of the point of the kingdom he was claiming to inaugurate would be that it would bring with it all that the Temple offered, thereby replacing, and making redundant Israel's greatest symbol." In sum, Wright (p. 436) states, "Healing, forgiveness, renewal, the twelve, the new family and its new defining characteristics, open commensality, the promise of blessing for the Gentiles, feasts replacing fasts, the destruction and rebuilding of the Temple: all declared, in the powerful language of symbol, that Israel's exile was over, that Jesus was himself in some way responsible for this new state of affairs, and that all that the Temple had stood for was now available through Jesus and his movement."

Deuteronomy. And we will evaluate how it expresses the hopes of Israel as redefined by Jesus.

The Lord's Prayer is built upon two premises: YHWH is the one and only true God, and Israel is the nation that he has chosen to reveal his greatness to all of humanity. There are two parts of this prayer, corresponding to these foundational affirmations. In the first section, the supremacy of YHWH is affirmed: he is the one true God, his name alone is to be honored, his rule is universal, and his will matters more than anything else in the world. The first three petitions of the Lord's Prayer declare these things as true, and they ask God to lead all people toward the recognition of these truths. The second section of the Lord's Prayer is a series of petitions on behalf of Israel. In language that reflects a keen awareness of their past failings, the people of the new Israel pray that they may become the model people that their ancestors had never been. They must be a community that is characterized by their trust in God, repentance, love for one another, understanding of God's heart, and ability to resist evil.

Affirming the Supremacy of the One True God

The prayer (in Matthew's text) begins with the address "Our Father in heaven." This might not seem to us like a theologically loaded way to begin a prayer, but to Jesus it was. This was a bold, yet intimate way for Jesus's followers to address YHWH. Israel was entering into an era of new intimacy with God, and Jesus invited his disciples to address their God in the same way he did: "Father."[21]

Another notable aspect of the opening address is the powerful declaration that the Father is the God who is "in heaven." To us, this

---

21. To address God as "Father" in prayer was innovative but not necessarily unorthodox. Deissler remarks, "The prayers in the Old Testament do not know of the opening *'abh* or *abhinu* (i.e., '[Our] Father'). But Israel knows the title 'father' as appellation for its covenantal God" (Alfons Deissler, "The Spirit of the Lord's Prayer in the Faith and Worship of the Old Testament," in *The Lord's Prayer and Jewish Liturgy*, ed. Jakob Petuchowski and Michael Brocke [New York: Seabury, 1978], 5). Jeremias suggests that in the original Aramaic, the opening address would have been *"abba."* He comments, "In the Lord's Prayer Jesus authorizes his disciples to repeat the word *abba* after him. He gives them a share in his sonship and empowers them, as his disciples, to speak with their heavenly Father in just such a familiar, trusting way as a child would with his father" (Joachim Jeremias, *The Prayers of Jesus* [Philadelphia: Fortress, 1978], 97).

might simply appear as a reference to the place where God dwells. In the ears of the ancient Jews, however, it was much more. Moses had proclaimed to Israel, "Know therefore today, and lay it to your heart, that *the Lord is God in heaven* above and on the earth beneath; there is no other" (Deut 4:39, emphasis added). In 2 Chronicles 20:6, King Jehoshaphat prays, "O Lord, God of our fathers, are you not *God in heaven*? You rule over all the kingdoms of the nations. In your hand are power and might, so that none is able to withstand you."[22] Psalm 115 rails against man-made idols, which have eyes but cannot see and ears but cannot hear. In contrast to false gods, YHWH's status as the one and only true God is proven in this: "Our God is in the heavens" (v. 6). In this light then we understand that "Our Father in heaven" is an affirmation of the absolute kingship of YHWH above all other gods. It is the equivalent of saying, "There is no other god in all of the universe. He is the one God, the only God," much in the same way that the *Shema* (based on Deut 6:4) declares, "Hear O Israel: the Lord our God, the Lord is one."

Thus, Jesus taught his followers to begin their prayers with the same affirmation that is found in the most important of Jewish prayers. Three times a day, the people of Israel were in the habit of declaring, "The Lord our God, the Lord is one." The prayer of Jesus continues in this tradition. His disciples are to affirm the absolute oneness of God, even as they also declare that he is their intimate Father.

The Sanctification of God's Name

The first petition of the Lord's Prayer in English says, "Hallowed be your name." This particular construction of the archaic verb *to hallow* may lead many to think that this phrase is somehow a declaration of the Father's holiness: "Your name is holy." The original Greek, however, expresses something quite different. First we note that the verb *hagiazein* describes the action of making or honoring something as holy. Second, the verb tense (as with all of the first three petitions)

---

22. Emphasis added. See also Josh 2:11; 1 Chron 16:26; Ezra 1:2, 5:11–12; 6:10; 7:12, 21, 23; 9:6; Dan 2:18–19, 28, 37, 44; 4:37; 5:23; Ps 2:4; 96:4–5; 136:26; Isa 14:12–13; 63:15; 66:1; Jer 10:11; Jonah 1:9.

expresses a request, not a declaration of what already is true. Thus, a more accurate translation from the original would be this: "Let your name be honored as holy."

For Jesus and his Jewish contemporaries, the actual holiness of YHWH was never in question.[23] But the *earthly recognition* of that holiness was always in doubt. Who YHWH is as a *person* is something different than his *name*. God's identity in heaven transcends human description. But his *name* describes how he is known down here. Crossan explains, "Your good name is the favorable view that others have of you. Name is your reputation or, in other cultures, your face, your countenance, your honor. The name of God means both God's identity and God's reputation as known externally to human beings in God's world."[24] Thus, as used by people, the name given to God may accurately depict who he is and what he does. Or conversely, the name by which people know him may not accurately reflect what he is like.

When the covenant was made at Sinai, Moses expressed the hope that Israel's obedience would ultimately bring honor to the name of YHWH: "And all the peoples of the earth shall see that you are called by the name of the Lord, and they shall be afraid of you" (Deut 28:10). As the generations passed, this didn't happen. YHWH would later complain that they had done the opposite: they had profaned his name among the peoples of the earth. He said, "But when they came to the nations, wherever they came, they profaned my holy name" (Ezek 36:20). His reputation had been tarnished by Israel's rebellion and disgrace. Consequently, he vowed to act in such a way that would restore his honor on the earth. Ezekiel 36:23 says: "I will sanctify my great name, which has been profaned among the nations, and which you have profaned among them; and the nations shall know that I am the Lord, says the Lord God, when through you I display my holiness before their eyes" (NRSV). The same idea is communicated in Isaiah 29:23: "Jacob shall no more be ashamed, no more shall his face grow

---

23. Cf. Exod 15:11; Lev 11:44–45; 20:7, 26; 21:8; 1 Sam 2:2; 6:20; 1 Chron 16:29; Ps 99:5; Isa 5:16; 6:3; 43:3; Hab 1:12; Zech 8:20.
24. John Dominic Crossan, *The Greatest Prayer: Rediscovering the Revolutionary Message of the Lord's Prayer* (New York: HarperOne, 2010), 52.

pale. For when he sees his children, the work of my hands, in his midst, they will sanctify my name; they will sanctify the Holy One of Jacob, and will stand in awe of the God of Israel."

What we see in these two verses is two different angles on the sanctification of God's name. The passage in Ezekiel states that YHWH will sanctify his own name by displaying his holiness through Israel. Isaiah takes a different approach. Rather than saying that God sanctifies his own name, it states that the people will sanctify his name when they see his works. In either case, the idea is same. God's name is sanctified when he acts and people on earth recognize what he has done.

When the first Jewish followers of Jesus prayed the Lord's Prayer, these verses would have come to mind. "Hallowed be your name" was a request for God to move in such a way that his name would be honored as holy (or sanctified) among the nations. This petition envisioned a chain reaction. First, God would move among his own people, renewing and restoring them to relationship with himself. As a result, the blessings he had promised would come upon them. Then, when Israel's honor was established among the nations, all the peoples of the earth would recognize the power of Israel's God, and YHWH's reputation would be restored. By teaching his followers to pray in this way, Jesus was letting them know that the time had come for the renewed Israel to establish itself as a righteous nation. Through them, God would display his holiness to all the world. When they lived in righteousness and God moved mightily through them, then the Father's name would accurately reflect who he really is, and he would be honored by all the peoples of the earth.

The Kingdom of the One God

When Jesus taught his followers to pray "your kingdom come," he was using a phrase that was uncommon but not indecipherable to the Jews of his day. As an expression of God's kingship and power, this phrase meant nothing new or controversial. But the establishment of God's "kingdom" on earth was not a common theme in ancient

Jewish literature.[25] In this unusual phrase, Jesus was tapping into a deep longing of the Jewish people: to be under the rule of God alone. The daily prayer known as the *Amidah* spoke of this same desire: "reign over us—You alone."

For generations, Israel had been under the authority of foreign rulers due to their failure to keep the covenant. When Israel was in the Sinai desert, God had promised them that if they obeyed his commands, they would remain in their land and enjoy his blessings. The punishment for disobedience, however, was that they would be taken into exile and ruled by others: "The Lord will bring you and your king whom you set over you to a nation that neither you nor your fathers have known." And "you shall be plucked off the land that you are entering to take possession of it. And the Lord will scatter you among all peoples, from one end of the earth to the other" (Deut 28:36, 63–64).

When Moses spoke to the people about to enter the land, he seemed to foresee their future. He described the captivity that would come centuries later, but he also foresaw their restoration. He declared that when Israel returns to the Lord with all their heart and soul:

> Then the Lord your God will restore your fortunes and have mercy on you, and he will gather you again from all the peoples where the Lord your God has scattered you. . . . And the Lord your God will circumcise your heart and the heart of your offspring, so that you will love the Lord your God with all your heart and with all your soul, that you may live. . . . And you shall again obey the voice of the Lord and keep all his commandments that I command you today. (Deut 30:1–8)

As we have mentioned above, God did "pluck" Israel from the land by the hands of the Assyrians and the Babylonians. After seventy years of

---

25. Dunn notes, "In the Scriptures and post-biblical writings of Second Temple Judaism the phrase itself is hardly attested, and though reference is made to God's 'kingdom' or 'kingship,' the theme is not particularly prominent" (James Dunn, *Jesus Remembered* [Grand Rapids: Eerdmans, 2003], 385). Nickelsburg, *Ancient Judaism and Christian Origins* (Minneapolis: Augsburg Fortress, 2003) cites the following examples in Jewish literature:

"The kingdom of God" (Wis 10:10; Pss. Sol. 17:3); "The kingdom (*malkut*) of Yahweh" (1 Chr 28:5; 2 Chr 13:8); "my kingdom" (1 Chr 17:14); "his kingdom" (Ps 103:19; Dan 4:34; 6:26; Tob 13:1; Wis 6:4); "your kingdom" (Ps 145:11–13; Pss. Sol. 5:18); "Kingship (*mamlaka, meluka*)" belongs to God (1 Chr 29:11; Ps 22:28; Obad 2.1); Aramaic *malkuta* (Dan 3:33; 4:34); Latin *regnum* (T. Mos. 10:1).

captivity, some of the people returned to Judah. A second temple was built, and sacrifices resumed. But most of the Jewish people remained scattered throughout the nations. The new temple paled in comparison to what Solomon had built. The land of Israel remained under the rule of foreigners. Restoration had begun, but there was still a long way to go. During this time, the people remembered passages such as Deuteronomy 30, and this was the basis for their prayers. James Dunn notes that there was "a widespread belief that after a period of dispersion among the nations, the outcasts/scattered of Israel would be gathered again and brought back to the promised land, the unity of the twelve tribes reestablished, and the relation of Israel as God's people, and Yahweh as Israel's God, restored."[26] A scattered Israel would repent, and return to YHWH. He would restore their fortunes and bring them back to the land. He would then make them "more prosperous and numerous" than their fathers, renew their love for him, and give them victory over their enemies.

Over time, this theme of "return from exile" became increasingly associated with the promise of David's son.[27] According to Psalm 72, a king would come to restore the fortunes of Israel and give victory over her enemies. This "royal son" would bring justice to the poor and peace and prosperity to the nation, and would establish Israel's place of honor among all nations.

Jesus came as the one who would bring the promised restoration. Through him the kingdom would come. But even as he fulfilled many of the people's expectations, there were others that he sought to redefine. Jews in the Second Temple period had come to see the restoration of their nation as having political and material implications. In this sense, Jesus was perceived by many as a disappointment. The Gospels present him, however, as the fulfillment of Israel's hopes. Wright notes that "Christian kingdom-language has little or nothing to do with the vindication of ethnic Israel, the overthrow of Roman rule in Palestine, the building of a new Temple on Mount Zion, the establishment of

---

26. Dunn, *Jesus*, 393. Wright, *New Testament*, 268–71, 299–301, refers to this theme as the "return from exile."

27. See Dunn, *Jesus*, 395–96.

Torah-observance, or the nations flocking to Mount Zion to be judged and/or to be educated in the knowledge of YHWH."[28] Consequently, in order for Jesus's mission to be seen and proclaimed as having succeeded, these aspects of Jewish hopes had to be expressed in a new way. Jesus accomplished this, according to the Gospels, by redefining the kingdom as righteous living, victory over Satan, and the restoration of the human heart.[29] When Israel's love for the Father and for one another was restored, then God would be their king once again.

Thus, the petition "your kingdom come" was a prayer for heart transformation. It was an invitation to imagine what it would look like for God, and God alone, to rule over Israel. There would be compassion for the poor, justice for the oppressed, and care given to the fatherless and the widow. Evildoers who oppress and exploit the poor would be crushed, and those who steal and prosper by sin would be driven back. All the blessings of the covenant would come to Israel: strong families, abundant crops and cattle, and blessing on the work of each person's hand. All the nations of the world would see the righteousness and spiritual prosperity of Israel, and they would recognize that YHWH is the one true God.

This is what Jesus's followers requested when praying for the coming of the kingdom. It had little to do with politics. The twelve tribes might remain physically dispersed across the nations, but their hearts would be regathered to YHWH. The Romans might maintain military control over their land, but God, and God alone, would be their king. This was a kingdom that would come through repentance, compassion for the poor, a renewed love for YHWH, and a commitment to follow his commands.

The Will of the One True God

The third petition of the Lord's Prayer says, "Let your will be done." The key to understanding this petition lies in its relationship with

---

28. Wright, *Jesus*, 219.
29. Note the correlation in these passages between the "kingdom of God" and the attitude of the heart: Matt 5:3, 19–20; 6:33; 7:21; 12:28; 13:11 (Mark 4:11; Luke 8:10); 13:18–23, 44–47; 18:3–4; 25:34–36; Mark 4:47; 10:14–15; Luke 6:20; 9:2; 11:20.

the opening address: "Our Father in heaven." We noted above that in Psalm 115:3, the expression "Our God is in the heavens" was a way of declaring his absolute power as the only true God. We now look at the entire verse: "Our God is in the heavens, all that pleases him he does." Two ideas are here placed together: *God's absolute power*, and *the accomplishment of what pleases him*. This pairing is seen frequently throughout the OT in various configurations: Psalm 135:5–6, "For I know that great is YHWH, Lord above all gods. All that pleases YHWH he does"; Isaiah 55:11, "My word . . . will do all that pleases me"; and in Jonah 1:14, the sailors declare to God that "all that has pleased you, you have done."[30] There was a perceived connection between *power* and the *ability to do what one pleases*. Thus in Psalm 115:3 the statement "God is in heaven" was naturally followed by "all that pleases him he does."

This pairing, as a liturgical formula, also appears frequently in ancient Jewish prayers.[31] The Lord's Prayer continues in this tradition, but with a twist. The prayer opens with the address "Our Father in Heaven" as a means of highlighting that he is the one and only true God. The third petition then says, "Let your will be done." In the ear of a first-century Jew, this would have sounded more like "Do all that pleases you."[32] Thus, the Lord's Prayer makes use of this standard liturgical expression, but instead of framing it as a declaration, it comes as a petition. Rather than simply stating "You are the God in heaven, you do all that pleases you," this prayer presents a request: "You are the God in heaven, *we ask* you to do all that pleases you." The difference might seem very subtle, but there is a rich theology behind it.

As it is constructed, the Lord's Prayer does not say, "God is sovereign, he will do what he will do," as if the role of the person

---

30. I have translated these verses more literally in order to highlight the phrase under consideration.

31. The basic form of this phrase in Hebrew is *kol asher chafetz asah*. For more examples of this phrase (discernible in the Hebrew) see 2 Sam 15:24–26; Ps 40:9; Eccl 8:1–3. Hurvitz notes:

> The phrase refers either to God (Psalms, Isaiah, Jonah) or to an earthly king (Ecclesiastes) and denotes the unlimited power of the supreme authority which enables him 'to do whatever he pleases.' . . . At first glance, this idiom would seem to be a rhetorical phrase lauding the omnipotent ruler. However, a closer examination reveals that, in fact, this is no empty literary cliché but rather the adoption of a legal formula whose *Sitz im Leben* is to be sought in the domain of jurisprudence. (Avi Hurvitz, "The History of a Legal Formula," *Vetus Testamentum* 32 [1982]: 257–58).

32. See LXX Ps 113:11; 134:6; Eccl 8:3.

praying is merely to recognize his supremacy. Rather, "let your will be done" is a petition asking God to act. The person who prays in this way is inviting him to bring about the *doing of his will* on earth.

Psalm 115 offers insights into the theology of this petition. The text opens by declaring the absolute sovereignty of God and then continues with a series of rants against idolatry. An internal tension is created in this passage: If God is the sovereign ruler of all things, then why does he allow people to worship false gods? This tension is resolved at the end of the passage, where the author declares, "The heavens are the Lord's heavens, but the earth he has given to the children of man" (Ps 115:16). The implication is that people are able to practice evil on earth—such as worshiping false gods—because it is the realm that has been placed under their dominion. They have a free will. YHWH is the absolute ruler of the universe, but on earth he has given people control over their own conduct.

The vision of the Lord's Prayer is that women and men on earth will follow the ways of the God, who is in heaven. This is why the first section of the prayer ends with the words, "On earth as it is heaven." This is a request for what *can be*, not a declaration of *what already is*.

Those who pray this prayer believe that God is able to bring about that which pleases him on earth by changing human hearts. Jeremiah had said that the "new covenant" between YHWH and his people would be this: "I will put my law within them, and I will write it on their hearts. And I will be their God and they shall be my people" (Jer 31:33). Thus, as a petition of covenant renewal, "let your will be done" is a way of asking God to write his laws on human hearts, show people how to do the things that are pleasing to him, and guide our steps toward that which honors him.

In Deuteronomy 6:5, YHWH made clear what he desires from all people: "You shall love the Lord your God with all your heart, with all your soul and with all your might." This is the absolute declaration of God's will. He is the sovereign ruler of the universe, and he has declared that this is the one thing he desires above all else: he wants to be loved by people. Thus, to pray "let your will be done" is to ask God,

"Make that which pleases you happen. Write your laws on our hearts. Teach us your ways, and show us how to love you with all of our heart, all of our soul and with all of our might."

The God of the Covenant

As we look back at the opening address and petitions of the Lord's Prayer, we see that there is an overarching emphasis on the power and authority of God. He is the one and only true God. It is his name that must be honored as holy by all nations. He is the one and only King who must rule over Israel. And it is his will—all that which pleases him—that men and women must do on earth. The first section of the Lord's Prayer clearly outlines who God is and how he is to be honored. It centers on a contemplation of the God who is in heaven.

In the second part of the Lord's Prayer, the gaze is turned exclusively upon the earth. The final four petitions are all about God's people: their material needs, their relationships with one another, their ability to overcome testing, and their triumph over evil. All of these things are important if God is ultimately going to be honored by all nations. In the framework of the covenant, as represented by the Deuteronomistic authors, this never happened because the people of Israel had done such a poor job at keeping his commands. In his vision to establish a new Israel, Jesus taught his followers how to pray for themselves. When they walk in relational dependence on the Father, when there is forgiveness toward one another, righteousness, and victory over Satan—then all of the nations of the earth will realize that Israel's God is the one and only God.

As we now look at the second section of the Lord's Prayer, we find that the backdrop is once again the Sinai desert. During their forty-year journey, Israel had failed to trust YHWH and rebelled against him. Jesus had gone on a forty-day fast and faced Satan in the wilderness as a way of giving Israel a "do-over." He demonstrated what covenant faithfulness would look like. These final four petitions constitute a detailed outline of what it will now look like for the renewed Israel to succeed in the same way.

A Day's Portion Every Day

In the fourth petition of the Lord's Prayer, there is a notable repetition: "Give us today the bread that we need for today." It should have been sufficient to say, "Give us today our bread," or "Give us the bread that we need for today." But the petition as Jesus taught it places particular emphasis on the idea that his followers are to ask for a day's portion every day.[33] The obvious allusion is to the provision of manna in Sinai. In Exodus 16:4 God said to Moses, "the people shall go out and gather a day's portion every day."

There was a reason the people would only be given a measured amount each day. Israel's commitment to the entire covenant would be reflected in their attitude toward their daily provisions. Moses would later explain, "And he humbled you and let you hunger and fed you with manna . . . that he might make you know that man does not live by bread alone, but man lives by every word that comes from the mouth of the Lord" (Deut 8:3).

In the Lord's Prayer, Jesus was trying to instill this same mindset within his followers. By requesting only the amount of bread that they needed for each day, they were affirming their trust in God. It was their way of saying, "Our security in life will not be found in abundance of food, nor in any other material thing—but our security will found in the Father alone." Jesus had given them the example during his own temptation in the wilderness. He had overcome Satan by demonstrating his own dependence on the Word of the Lord. In teaching his followers to pray this petition, he invited them to do the same.

In the wilderness, all the manna that the Israelites collected was gathered in one place and distributed equally among the people. Each person did not take home the precise amount he or she had gathered. The strapping young lad who gathered more than what was needed for one day would take home one day's portion. The little old lady

---

33. Although there has been considerable discussion with regard to the exact meaning of the word *epiousios*, the predominant (and I would assert *correct*) translation in English remains "daily." The term refers to the portion necessary for one day.

who gathered a tiny amount (or nothing) would take home one day's portion. The idea was that each individual saw his or her own intake as God's provision for the group. Everyone worked hard, and everyone brought home the same amount (Exod 16:18).

In the petition "Give us today the bread that we need for today," the group together prays for the provision of all. Jesus didn't teach his followers to say, "Give me the bread that I need for today." The Lord's Prayer is a call to be attentive to the material needs of others. Those who ask for God to provide for others must be willing to share what they themselves have taken in. This was God's intention for the manna and what is expressed in the petition for daily bread.

Forgiveness

When Israel was in the wilderness, YHWH declared to them that one of his greatest attributes was his mercy: "YHWH, YHWH, a God merciful and gracious, slow to anger, and abounding in steadfast love and faithfulness, keeping steadfast love for thousands, forgiving iniquity and transgression and sin" (Exod 34:6–7).[34] Israel's relationship with God had always been dependent on this very same mercy and willingness to forgive.

In the Hebrew mindset, forgiveness was about more than just erasing a debt or overlooking an offense. It was about the restoration of relationships broken by sin. God offered forgiveness to the people of Israel because he wanted to maintain relationship. He expected them to extend this same forgiveness toward one another: "You shall not take vengeance or bear a grudge against the sons of your own people, but you shall love your neighbor as yourself: I am YHWH" (Lev 19:18). This fundamental maintenance of right relationships—both vertical and horizontal—was essential to Israel's identity as a chosen people.

When the first followers of Jesus prayed, "Forgive us our sins as we forgive those who sin against us," they would have had these same principles in mind. The people of the renewed Israel must be known

---

34. In this verse and that from Leviticus cited below, I have replaced the ESV "the Lord" with the tetragrammaton.

for their right relationship with the Father and by their love for one another. Therefore, the regular confession of their sins and the commitment to forgive others were essential.

Lead Us Not into Testing

Even though we are accustomed to the saying the fifth petition as "lead us not into temptation," the first followers of Jesus would have understood this phrase more along the lines of "lead us not into testing." The Greek word typically translated as "temptation" is *peirasmos*, which has the connotation of "testing" or "trial." First-century Jews would have connected *peirasmos* with the experience of Israel in Sinai.

In the Greek text of Exodus 16:4, YHWH said that he fed them on manna so that he might "test (*peirazein*) them" to see whether they would walk in his laws or not. Again in Deuteronomy 8:2, Moses explained that "the Lord your God has led you these forty years in the wilderness, that he might humble you, testing (*peirazein*) you to know what was in your heart, whether you would keep his commandments or not." The OT often talks about the idea of testing in this way. God takes the initiative to create difficult circumstances for Israel because he is not sure what is in their hearts.[35]

Another angle on "testing" refers to the idea of Israel *putting God* to the test. This is seen, for example, in Psalm 95: "Do not harden your hearts, as at Meribah, as on the day at Massah in the wilderness, when your fathers put me to the test and put me to the proof, though they had seen my work. For forty years I loathed that generation and said, 'They are a people who go astray in their heart, and they have not known my ways'" (Ps 95:8–10). In this case, "testing" refers to the attitude of Israel that "tests" God: grumbling, doubt, and hardness of heart.[36]

So the question is: When Jesus's followers prayed "Lead us not into testing," were they saying "don't test us," or did they mean "don't

---

35. See also Exod 15:25; 16:4; 20:20; Deut 4:34; 8:2, 16; 13:3; Judg 2:22; 3:1, 4.
36. See also Exod 17:2; Deut 6:16; 33:8; Isa 7:12; Ps 78:18, 41, 56; 95:9; 106:14.

let us test you"? Given that in the OT the idea of "testing" embraced both possibilities, it seems then that the same is true in the Lord's Prayer. It can mean either testing God or being tested by God. As we look at all the different places that "testing" appears in the OT, we find that both forms of testing occurred when Israel struggled with doubt and sin.[37] Grumbling and rebellion among the people of Israel were characterized as "putting God to the test." At the same time, when YHWH questioned the commitment of the people, he would put them to "the test."[38] Thus, it is seen that no "testing" in any form occurred when the people walked in faithfulness and trust. They weren't testing YHWH, and YHWH saw no need to test them.

Meribah and Massah, the places of testing in the Sinai wilderness, had become metaphors for hardness of heart. In his own wilderness experience, Jesus had resisted Satan's temptation, citing Deuteronomy 8:2, which reads, "You shall not put the Lord your God to the test, as you tested him at Massah." Jesus and the renewed Israel would not repeat the mistakes that Israel had once made. They would avoid testing by remaining committed and faithful. Thus, in the Lord's Prayer, "Lead us not into testing" means "Let us not go back to the sins of our forefathers. Let us be a people whose hearts are fully committed to you, so that we might not test you, and that you may find no need to test us."[39]

---

37. The Hebrew word to which I here refer is *nasah*. It appears in thirty-four verses, with eleven morally "neutral" applications, e.g., 1 Sam 17:39 and 1 Kgs 10:9. There are also two instances in Scripture where the verb is used to describe the testing of the righteous: Gen 22:1 (the testing of Abraham) and Ps 26:2.

38. See Exod 17:7, "And he called the name of the place Massah and Meribah, because of the quarreling of the people of Israel, and because they tested the Lord by saying, 'Is the Lord among us or not?'" And see Deut 8:2, "And you shall remember the whole way that the Lord your God has led you these forty years in the wilderness, that he might humble you, testing you to know what was in your heart, whether you would keep his commandments or not."

39. For a thorough exploration of the fifth petition, see Gibson, *Disciple's Prayer*, 134–60. Gibson places primary emphasis on man putting God to the test, but our conclusions on the meaning of this phrase are similar. He notes, "It follows that if πειρασμός here means 'the testing of God,' then given all that the idea of 'the testing of God' connotes, the request in which the term appears must mean something like 'prevent us, Father, from putting you to the test by doubting your ways and renouncing all that you have deemed fit for us to follow'" (150).

Victory over Evil

In the story of Jesus's forty-day fast in the desert, Satan figures very prominently as his adversary. In the original story of Israel in Sinai, however, this enemy did not appear so clearly. The passages that we have seen above point more to the hardness of the human heart as the source of sin and less to the work of the tempter. So when we look at Jesus's reenactment of the wilderness experience, it's striking to see how he has illuminated the story. One of the primary lessons is that the battle with sin is not only a struggle against the evil inside of us but also against the *evil one*.

Jesus thus revealed the full complexity of the human fight. In the garden of Eden YHWH had declared to the serpent, "I will put enmity between you and the woman, and between your offspring and her offspring; he shall bruise your head, and you shall bruise his heel" (Gen 3:15). From the offspring of Eve would come he who would strike Satan with a mortal blow. This theme is again seen in the Abrahamic promise, where God declared, "Your offspring shall possess the gate of his enemies, and in your offspring shall all the nations of the earth be blessed" (Gen 3:18). The family of Abraham would bring blessing to all nations of the earth, but this process would be marked by conflict with "enemies" over whom YHWH promised victory.

Jesus perceived that part of Israel's problem was their inability to fully recognize who the real enemy was. In his day, the people thought their enemies were the Romans. Before that it had been the Greeks, Babylonians, Assyrians, Egyptians, and so on. Having lived under the oppression of foreign nations for generations, the Jews of first-century Israel longed for freedom and sovereignty. But Jesus came to redefine who the real enemy was. By teaching his followers to pray "deliver us from evil" (or "the evil one"), he turned their attention away from the notion of foreign oppressors and toward the notions of Satan and the power of sin. These were the enemies he had come to defeat. The triumph in the wilderness; the declaration of forgiveness, healing, and deliverance from demonic oppression; and his resurrection and ascension all formed part of Jesus's victory over the evil one.[40]

Thus, when the early disciples prayed "deliver us from evil," they were asking the Father to make them participants in the victory of Jesus. The vision was to triumph over sin, Satan, and ultimately death. Jesus had attained for Israel what she had historically failed to achieve. The people in Sinai had never recognized who the true the enemy was behind all of their troubles. The people of Jesus's day ran the risk of making the same mistake. Jesus demonstrated that the real enemy was not Rome or the Greeks but rather Satan and the internal enemy of sin. He himself had overcome Satan, and he showed the way to live in freedom from sin. In effect, he conquered evil on behalf of his people. The Lord's Prayer was an invitation to share in his triumph.

Reaffirming the Vows

In the framework of the covenant, the excellence of Israel and the salvation of the nations were ideas that went hand in hand. Israel was the one nation chosen by the one true God. He had chosen Israel from among all the nations to be the object of his special attention and affection. When the people of Israel walked in relationship with him and obeyed his commands, they would prosper both spiritually and materially. When all the nations of the world looked at Israel, they would see its power, its internal peace, the fairness of its laws, the joy and peace of its people, and the kindness it showed to foreigners. Comparing all these blessings with the strife and weakness of their own societies, the nations of the world would eventually come to realize

---

40. Wright comments, "Jesus was affirming the basic beliefs and aspirations of the kingdom: Israel's god is lord of the world, and, if Israel is still languishing in misery, he must act to defeat her enemies and vindicate her. Jesus was not doing away with that basic Jewish paradigm. He was reaffirming it most strongly. . . . He was, however, redefining the Israel that was to be vindicated, and hence was also redrawing Israel's picture of her true enemies" (*Jesus*, 173). Wright says further on, "The return from exile, the defeat of evil, and the return of YHWH to Zion were all coming about, but not in the way Israel had supposed. The time of restoration was at hand, and people of all sorts were summoned to share and enjoy it. . . . Jesus was therefore summoning his hearers to be Israel in a new way. . . . In the course of all this, he was launching the decisive battle with the real satanic enemy—a different battle, and a different enemy, from those Israel had envisaged" (ibid., 201).

that the God of Israel must be the true God. Setting aside their idols, they would come to worship YHWH.

This was the vision that Tobit had expressed, and this was the prayer of the Jewish people throughout the Second Temple period. The only problem was that Israel had never quite been able to keep up their end of the bargain. Because they hadn't kept God's laws, they had never yet really prospered as a nation. Consequently, the other nations of the world had little regard for YHWH their God. The people of Israel remained in exile.

Jesus began his ministry by metaphorically going back in time to give Israel a second chance. Going into the wilderness, he faced all of the same temptations, but he succeeded where Israel had failed. What Jesus accomplished in the desert was symbolically a renewal of the vows that God had made with Israel through the Deuteronomic covenant. Having now renewed the relationship with YHWH, Jesus called upon the people of Israel to join him as the community of covenant fulfillment. As the renewed Israel, they could now experience the restoration that had awaited them for so long. YHWH, and YHWH alone, was now their king. He had gathered their hearts. His presence had returned to Zion. The true enemies of sin and Satan were now being defeated. The time had come for Israel to arise and call the nations to salvation.

The Lord's Prayer recapitulates the covenant and gives voice to fulfilled hopes. Here the people of the renewed Israel affirm the oneness and power of their God; they pray for and commit themselves to honor his name, submit to him as king, and do his will. They pray for provision, forgiveness, an attentive ear, a soft heart, and victory over the enemies of sin and Satan. They realize that their God will only be worshiped by the nations when they as a community reflect his glory.

3

Matthew's Vision of Heaven and Earth

It had been said that all worlds must come to an end, and so it was with Narnia. Aslan and the Pevensie children stood at the Doorway and watched their magical country slip backward through time. Once the humans and animals were gone, the land was left to the Dragons and Giant Lizards who rendered its surface barren. These creatures then died and turned to dust, leaving nothing but rock. With a roar, the seas then rose and covered the dry land with water. The sun and the moon died, the face of the deep froze, and Narnia returned to the nothingness from whence it had been created. Aslan gave the command, and the Door was closed.

The children now found themselves in a new world. As they began to explore their surroundings, they realized that it all seemed strangely familiar. The mountains on the horizon looked similar, but they were somehow now more colorful and imposing. The fruit that they were now allowed to eat tasted something like what they had eaten before, but much better. The freshest grapefruit was now, by comparison, dull. "The juiciest orange was dry, and the most melting pear was hard and woody, and the sweetest wild strawberry was sour."[1] The children were coming to understand that everything they had seen and experienced before was only a shadow or copy of this paradise where they now walked. In the previous world, their senses had been awoken, and yet never truly satisfied. All of the things that they were now seeing, tasting, touching, and smelling were, for the first time ever, *satisfying*. "And of course it is different," their uncle explained to them, "as different as a real thing is from a shadow or as waking life is from a dream. . . . It's all in Plato, all in Plato."[2]

This picture of the world's ending and the afterlife is taken from C. S. Lewis's classic children's book, *The Last Battle*. Lewis there presents many difficult concepts in a clear (albeit oversimplified) fashion: death is merely a transition (never mind that the children and their families had died in a violent train accident); falling away from faith is more an issue of distraction than choosing evil (Susan hadn't quite made it to heaven, as her concerns were now with "nylons and lipstick and invitations"); and heaven is tangible and real (what child wouldn't want to go to a place where everything sweet is even sweeter?).

Christian parents have long appreciated the allegorical qualities of the Chronicles of Narnia series. Lewis is at times subtle, and then quite direct in his allusions to Scripture and the Christian worldview. Over the years, the Chronicles have taken on an almost *authoritative* character for many thinkers and theologians.[3] But in spite of the enthusiasm that many Christians have displayed over these works, we must also be aware that Lewis does not always get everything right. In the story we've cited above, there is actually a cause for concern. The world's ending that the children watch through the Doorway is more akin to what we would find in the writings of the ancient Greek philosophers than Scripture. And with regard to the experience of

---

1. C. S. Lewis, *The Last Battle* (New York: HarperCollins, 1956), 172.
2. Ibid., 212.
3. I say this in jest, but in the defense of a certain theological position, Dr. Greg Boyd (whom I deeply respect) dedicates a full four pages to explaining how his view is supported by *The Lion, the Witch, and the Wardrobe* (Gregory Boyd, "Christus Victor Response," *The Nature of the Atonement: Four Views*, ed. James Beilby and Paul Eddy [Downers Grove, IL: IVP Academic, 2006], 99–105). A search on Amazon for "the Bible and the chronicles of Narnia" yields numerous results, including *A Family Guide to Narnia: Biblical Truths in C. S. Lewis's The Chronicles of Narnia, Eternal Truths of Narnia: Bible Studies and Leaders Guide for the Chronicles of Narnia*, and *A Christian Teacher's Guide to the Chronicles of Narnia*.

paradise, what Lewis presents is indeed found "in Plato" but not necessarily in the Bible.

The idea of this physical world coming to "an end" seeped into the Western worldview from Stoic philosophy and has been espoused by many Christians (like Lewis) who have misunderstood the language of Scripture.[4] The idea that this world is a copy or a shadow of the heavenly reality is a theme developed throughout the works of Plato. Many philosophers of the ancient Greek world thought of heaven as an intensification of all that is good in our earthly lives. They saw it as a place where we taste the same foods, see the same landscapes, sleep in the same types of beds—but where everything is *better*. Plato viewed heaven as a "purer earth," a place where our senses experience all things in an untainted form. In his work *Phaedo* he explains that upon death, "those also who are remarkable for having led holy lives are released from this earthly prison, and go to their pure home which is above, and dwell in the purer earth; and those who have duly purified themselves with philosophy, live henceforth altogether without the

---

4. For an overview of the notion of the "end of the world" in Greek, Jewish, and Christian thought, see Pieter van der Horst, *Hellenism—Judaism—Christianity: Essays on Their Interaction* (Leuven: Peeters, 1998), 272–92. He notes that Greek Stoic philosophers upheld the idea of a periodic "global conflagration" (*ekpurosis*) wherein everything in the universe would be consumed by fire and returned to its primordial state. The OT employs the imagery of judgment by fire, but this is not to be confused with the end of the world. Second Peter 3:10–13 is often used as a passage to support the idea of this present physical world coming to an end, but what we actually find here is the use of Stoic imagery to communicate an OT idea. In this passage "the earth and the works that are done on it" are exposed by the fire of God but not obliterated.

It is at a later time in the development of Christian thought that we find a full embrace of the Stoic destruction of the world. We see, for example, in the writings of the third-century theologian Minucius Felix: "Further, in respect of the burning up of the world, it is a vulgar error not to believe either that fire will fall upon it in an unforeseen way, or that the world will be destroyed by it. For who of wise men doubts, who is ignorant, that all things which have had a beginning perish, all things which are made come to an end? The heaven also, with all things which are contained in heaven, will cease even as it began. The nourishment of the seas by the sweet waters of the springs shall pass away into the power of fire. The Stoics have a constant belief that, the moisture being dried up, all this world will take fire; and the Epicureans have the very same opinion concerning the conflagration of the elements and the destruction of the world. Plato speaks, saying that parts of the world are now inundated, and are now burnt up by alternate changes" (Minucius Felix, "The Octavius," in *The Ante-Nicene Fathers*, vol. 4, ed. Alexander Roberts, James Donaldson, and A. Cleveland Coxe, trans. Felix Wallis [Buffalo, NY: Christian Literature Company, 1850], 194; henceforth *ANF* 4). Note how Minucius makes it clear that many Christians of his day were in agreement with the Greek philosophers on this subject.

Many church fathers were concerned about the infiltration of this doctrine into the church. Irenaeus argued that God will renew what he has created, not destroy it (*Adversus Haereses* 5.36.1). And Origen (*Contra Celsum* 4.11–13) argued that the fire of destruction is only a metaphor for the purging of evil from the world.

body, in mansions fairer far than these, which may not be described."[5] It's easy to see why some Christians have viewed some of Plato's ideas as quasi-inspired. Replace the phrase "those who have purified themselves with philosophy" with "those who have believed in Jesus Christ," and the result is a fairly standard confession of faith.

But are these ideas really compatible with what the Bible says? Is the physical world in which we now dwell coming to a fiery end? Is it to be destroyed and sent back primordial chaos as we leave it behind and go to a better place? Is this earth really a "prison," an inferior copy of heaven? Even though this is what many Christians believe with regard to this world and the afterlife, it is not actually what Scripture teaches.

The Gospel of Matthew has a very different concept of heaven and the future of this earth. Its presentation of the Lord's Prayer addresses many of the questions we have asked. Although our present purpose is not to carry out a full-scale study of eschatology and the afterlife, we will find that Matthew's Gospel has a lot to say on these topics. Matthew's vision is summarized in one phrase: "on earth as it is in heaven." In this present chapter we will consider what *heaven* and *earth* meant to him, and how his understanding of these two realms shaped his interpretation of the Lord's Prayer. In Matthew's theology the earth was not on a path toward destruction. Rather, he envisioned a *palingenesia* (literally "genesis again"), which would be a new beginning for earth. The radical renewal and restoration of this planet would come about not about by its obliteration but by its transformation through union with heaven. Matthew saw heaven descending to our world. He does indeed talk about a process of judgment and purging, but once again this is not to be confused with the "end of the world."[6] His vision was for the earth to experience rebirth, and for him this was the central theme of the Lord's Prayer.

Our strategy in this chapter will be to look at the Lord's Prayer from a wider angle. Rather than focusing on each of the seven petitions, we will discuss the broad significance of this one line: "on earth as it in

---

5. Plato, *Phaedo*, in *Six Great Dialogues*, trans. Benjamin Jowett (New York: Dover, 2007), 89.
6. See, for example, Matt 24:29–51; 25:31–46.

heaven." We will see that this idea controls Matthew's understanding of the entire prayer. It is a bridge between the first and second sections that unites them around a single vision: union. For Matthew, the first section of the Lord's Prayer is about heaven. It is the place where God dwells, and it is from there that the Father's plans and purposes for history emanate. The second part of the prayer focuses on earth, the place of need. Those who pray the Lord's Prayer ask not for the earth to pass away or be destroyed. They don't see themselves as "leaving the earth" to spend eternity in heaven. Rather, they pray for the earthly realm to become one with the heavenly realm. It's a cosmological marriage, and not a cataclysmic conflagration.

In order to unpack the fullness of Matthew's theology, certain foundations need to be set in place. First we will explore his understanding of *heaven and earth* (cosmology), which is a major theme throughout his Gospel. Second, we will look at Matthew's view of the church (ecclesiology). And finally, we will see how the vision behind Matthew's cosmology and ecclesiology become reality as the church prays the Lord's Prayer.

The Theology of Matthew

Of all the NT writers, no one talks more about heaven than Matthew. Forms of the Greek word for *heaven* (*ouranos*) appear in Matthew's Gospel eighty-two times, making up over 30 percent of its appearances in the NT.[7] Part of the reason that this word appears so frequently is that Matthew tended to insert *heaven* language into his account whenever he could. Whereas Mark reported Jesus preaching, "Repent for the kingdom of God is at hand" (Mark 1:15), Matthew's rendition says, "Repent, for the kingdom of *heaven* is at hand" (Matt 4:17). Luke reports Jesus saying that the poor are blessed because theirs is the "kingdom of God" (Luke 6:20), whereas Matthew says that theirs is the "kingdom of heaven" (Matt 5:3). Mark recounts Jesus saying that his brothers and sisters are those who do "the will of God" (Mark 3:35),

---

7. Jonathan Pennington, *Heaven and Earth in the Gospel of Matthew* (Leiden and Boston: Brill, 2007), 2.

whereas in Matthew they are those who do "the will of my Father in heaven" (Matt 12:50). These types of differences occur twenty-four times in Matthew, clearly indicating a deliberate effort to direct attention toward heaven.[8]

What did heaven mean to Matthew? Surprisingly, he never refers to it as a place separate from the earth to which believers *go* after death.[9] Rather, for Matthew heaven is broadly conveyed as *the place where things are right*. In this current age, heaven does not have a material existence. Unlike Plato, Matthew does not imagine heaven as the place where those who have died are now drinking *really good* wine and eating *really good* chocolate. It's not a parallel, perfect world or a "purer earth" floating around in some other part of the universe. Heaven represents for Matthew the full authority of God, the full execution of his will, the full expression of his desires, and the full implementation his values.

One of the most important ideas that Matthew wishes to convey about heaven is that it is the place where the Father dwells. Forty-six times Matthew calls attention to the fact that God is the "heavenly Father," or the Father who is "in heaven." Mark and Luke each describe God in this way only one time, and John not at all. What Matthew communicates through the title "Father in heaven" is that God always does *what is right*. We noted in the previous chapter that for the first-century Jews, referring to God as the one who is "in heaven" described his standing as the one and only true God. Matthew expands on this idea demonstrating that he is the one true God who is righteous in all of his ways. Thus for Matthew, "heavenly" is a synonym for *good, righteous,* or *doing what is right*. To illuminate Matthew's thought, we

---

8. Ibid., 71.

9. Of the eighty-three appearances of heaven in Matthew, there are only three instances where something close to this idea may be deduced. In Matt 5:12 Jesus says that the persecuted rejoice "for your reward is great in heaven." Note, however, that the reward is stated as being in the present tense. In Matthew's framework, this denotes simply the idea the reward comes from the Father. The phrase "kingdom of heaven" sometimes has a futuristic orientation, as in Matt 8:11: "I tell you, many will come from east and west and recline at table with Abraham, Isaac, and Jacob in the kingdom of heaven" (see also Matt 5:19–20; 19:23). But in these cases, Matthew is referring to the heavenly kingdom, which will be established on earth, not a spiritual paradise.

will replace "Father in heaven" in various verses with "Father who does what is right."

- "Let your light shine before others so that they may see your good works and give glory to your Father *who does what is right*" (Matt 5:16).

- "You must be perfect, as your Father *who does what is right* is perfect" (Matt 5:48).

- "If you then, who are evil, know how to give good gifts to your children, how much more will your Father who *does what is right* give good things to those who ask him!" (Matt 7:11).

- "Not everyone who says to me, 'Lord, Lord,' will enter the kingdom of heaven, but the one who does the will of my *Father who does what is right*" (Matt 7:21).

- "Every plant that my *Father, who does what is right,* has not planted will be rooted up" (Matt 15:13).

- "So it is not the will of my *Father who does what is right* that one of these little ones should perish" (Matt 18:14).

If the words "in heaven" or "heavenly" are mere descriptions of where the Father lives, their inclusion adds little to our understanding of the above passages. The meaning of each text would be unchanged without them. When we understand, however, that Matthew used "in heaven" and "heavenly" as a means of emphasizing the Father's character, then each declaration becomes much stronger: *Do what is right, because the Father does what is right; the Father who does what is right will answer your prayers; not everyone who calls on the Father's name will be with him, but only those who do what is right;* and so on. Being "in heaven" is not so much about where the Father dwells as it is a description of the Father's *character*.

It follows that when Matthew refers to heaven as a noun (i.e., a place), the meaning he seeks to convey is not about the clouds or the afterlife. Heaven is the place where the Father *who does what is right* rules, and therefore heaven is *the place where things are right*. One of Matthew's favorite phrases (and one that is unique to his Gospel) was the "kingdom of heaven." If we take this phrase and replace it with "the place where things are right," we get a clearer understanding of Matthew's meaning.

- "Repent, for *the place where things are right* is at hand" (Matt 3:2; 4:17). In other words: *Amend your ways, because a new standard of measure is being set in place, and you need to get on board.*

- "Blessed are those who are persecuted for righteousness sake, for *the place where things are right* belongs to you" (Matt 5:10). That is: *Be assured that when you do the right thing and are persecuted for it, God is on your side.*

- "Woe to you scribes and Pharisees, because you shut the *place where things are right* in people's faces. For you neither enter yourselves nor allow those who would enter to go in" (Matt 23:13). That is: *You make it impossible for people to feel that they're good enough. You yourselves live under self-condemnation, and you want to make sure that everyone else feels the same way.*

- "Let the children come to me and do not hinder them, for to such belongs *the place where things are right*" (Matt 19:14). That is: *Children give us an example of the right way of doing things, so let me honor them.*

In this light, the parables of Jesus also tend to make more sense. These short stories were the way he revealed to his disciples "the secrets of *the place where things are right*" (Matt 13:11) or *the mysteries of the righteous life*. He said that the *place where things are right* is like a mustard seed or a little bit of leaven (Matt 13:31–33). When you commit to doing things the right way, you will flourish. Discovering *the place where things are right* is like a man who finds a treasure in the field or a merchant who finds a pearl (Matt 13:44). When you discover the right way of doing things, you find something of great worth.

What we see in all of these instances is that the "kingdom of heaven" is not limited to the idea of future reward or bliss. The *right way of doing things* is offered to us at this very moment. The joy of doing the right thing is attainable now. There is, to be sure, a futuristic element to the "kingdom of heaven" in the sense that the *right way of doing things* will soon be the *only way of doing things*. If you are already following the Lord's ways, you have a bright future. And if you're not aligned to his standard of measure, then you're going to be in trouble.[10] What Jesus teaches is that in the present time we can experience the joys of living a righteous life and the blessings of having the Father's approval and acceptance.

Thus we see that *heaven* in Matthew is not just a casual reference to the place where God lives. And it is definitely not just the place where we go after we die. Heaven denotes a way of doing things, the *Father's* way of doing things. At a future time, it will be *the only way of doing things.* So according to Matthew, heaven is all about how you live your life. It is about understanding the Father's will and heart. And it is about living in the awareness of a future reality. When the time comes for it to be *God's way or the highway*, those who have already aligned themselves to his commands will be rewarded. Those who have been careless and wicked will have regrets.

Heaven and Earth

Because *heaven* was central to his Gospel, Matthew went out of his way to make sure that his readers understood exactly what he meant. In that effort he frequently presented contrasting ideas, or what we will call "oppositions." In modern communication, we also use this method when we want to avoid misunderstandings. To make our intended message clear, we will often provide a contrast to what we actually mean. For example, I might say to my son, "When I say be home at

---

10. We see, for example, in the Beatitudes: "blessed are the meek, for they shall inherit the earth" (Matt 5:6); "blessed are the merciful, for they will be shown mercy" (v. 7); "blessed are the pure in heart, for they shall see God" (v. 8); "blessed are the peacemakers, for they will called sons of God" (v. 9); and so on. Jesus here advocates a present way of living that stands in the light of a future reality. The disciples of Jesus must live in the awareness of God's eventual intervention. Those who do good know that he will come at a future time to reward them. Those who do evil will be taken by surprise. The idea of being ready for the "kingdom of heaven" is conveyed in the parables of Matt 25:1-30. You need oil in your lamp. You need to invest your talents wisely, knowing that you'll have to give an account.

eleven o'clock, I don't mean eleven thirty!" When Matthew wrote his Gospel, he used this technique frequently.[11] Many of Jesus's teachings utilize contrasts. For example, in the Sermon on the Mount, he repeats the phrases, "You have heard that it was said . . . but I say . . .":

- "You have heard that it was said to those of old, 'You shall not murder' . . . But I say . . ." (Matt 5:21–22).

- "You have heard that it was said, 'You shall not commit adultery' . . . But I say . . ." (Matt 5:27–28).

- "It was also said, 'Whoever divorces his wife' . . . But I say . . ." (Matt 5:31–32).

- "Again you have heard that is was said to those of old, 'You shall not swear falsely' . . . But I say to you . . ." (Matt 5:33–34).

- "You have heard that it was said, 'An eye for an eye' . . . But I say . . ." (Matt 5:38–39).

- "You have heard that it was said, 'You shall love your neighbor and hate your enemy' . . . But I say . . ." (Matt 5:43–44).

Further on in the same discourse he uses the practice of hypocrites as his contrast:

- "When you give to the needy, sound no trumpets before you as the hypocrites do . . . But when you give to the needy . . ." (Matt 6:2–3).

- "And when you pray, you must not be like the hypocrites . . . But when you pray . . ." (Matt 6:5–6).

- "And when you fast, do not look gloomy like the hypocrites . . . But when you fast . . ." (Matt 6:16–17).

Time and time again, the meaning of Jesus's teaching is clarified by setting up a contrast with the teaching or practice of others.

This same approach is seen in the way Matthew describes heaven.

---

11. For an excellent overview of the use of oppositions in Matthew, see Daniel Patte, *The Gospel according to Matthew: A Structural Commentary on Matthew's Gospel* (Minneapolis: Fortress, 1986).

In order to help his readers understand what heaven is, he sets up an opposition, or a contrast, revealing what it is not. The opposite of *heaven* is communicated through the idea of *earth*. Some of these contrasts are quite obvious: for example, the disciples are told to not to practice their righteousness before other people (on earth) but rather to seek the reward from their Father in heaven (Matt 6:1–2). They are told, "Do not lay up for yourselves treasures on earth . . . but lay up for yourselves treasures in heaven" (Matt 6:19–20). Other examples are broader and more subtle. In Matthew 23:9 Jesus tells his disciples to "call no man father on earth, for you have one Father, who is heaven." This verse forms part a broader theme in Matthew wherein the character of the Father in heaven is presented as righteous and compassionate, set in contrast to the predominantly negative portrayal of earthly fathers.[12] In all of these instances, all that heaven signifies is enhanced and clarified by its negative counterpart on earth. This does not mean that the earth is inherently evil. But it does mean that on earth there is a certain way of thinking, and a certain way of doing things that stands in contrast to heaven, where things are done the Father's way.

Matthew presents heaven and earth as existing in contrast and tension. These realms, however, are not at war with one another. There will be no cataclysmic end to the physical creation, wherein the spiritual realm of heaven triumphs over the material realm of earth. As we have said before, heaven is not a place to which the faithful "go" to spend eternity after the earth has been destroyed.[13] Rather, Matthew envisions a final union of the two realms. Jonathan Pennington notes,

---

12. Pennington, *Heaven and Earth*, 238, mentions several passages where this negative contrast is either explicit or inferred: a group of brothers leaves their fishing nets in the hands of their father as they begin to follow Jesus (Matt 4:21–22); another man is invited to become a disciple but chooses instead to stay with his father (Matt 8:21); Jesus praises his disciples for leaving their fathers (Matt 19:29); and the day will come when earthly fathers will betray their children because they are followers of Christ (Matt 10:21).

13. Matthew's parable of the seed (Matt 13:24–30, 37–43, a significant expansion of Mark 4:30–32) offers unique insight into Matthew's eschatology. The kingdom's final consummation occurs on earth. In this parable, the "field" is the world (Matt 13:38), where both the good and bad seeds are planted. At the end of the age, the angels "gather out of his kingdom all causes of sin and all law-breakers" (Matt 13:41). Thus, at the parousia the world (i.e., the earth) is referred to as the locus of the kingdom of Jesus as well as the kingdom of the Father (Matt 13:43).

"For Matthew, this tension has an eschatological resolution; heaven and earth will not always stand in contrast . . . the goal of God's redemptive plan in Jesus is not the removal of the earth in the sense of being replaced with a kingdom in heaven, but is instead the eschatological reuniting of the heavenly and earthly realms."[14] We tend to think about heaven as a place of future bliss, where those who have died in Christ live forever. This is what Matthew would have described as the future earth—the world as it will be after the *palingenesia* ("new genesis") (Matt 19:28). Matthew envisioned a coming time when the *right way of doing things* will be practiced on this earth. When this happens, the two become one. It will no longer be just in heaven that things are right, but in heaven and on earth. The future of heaven is to be on the earth, and the future of the earth is to be in heaven.[15]

Identifying the Problem

We now turn our attention to what Matthew identified as the root of the problem. The question he grappled with is: Why are heaven and earth now separated? Or stated another way: Why is it that things are not right? The Jewish people of his day would have explained this problem in different ways. On the one hand, some would say that the root cause is spiritual and can only be addressed by God: the earthly realm has been caught up in a web of supernatural conflict that only God and the powers of heaven can break. On the other hand, some would say that the problem is human: people make bad choices and disregard the Father's ways; this rebellion against God has driven a wedge between God and man, heaven and earth, and can only be resolved when people choose to change their ways.

Martin de Boer has summarized how this "duality" found expression

---

14. Pennington, *Heaven and Earth*, 210.
15. One might ask, What is the state of those who have died and are now with Christ? Alcorn refers to the place where they are as the "intermediate heaven." It is a "paradise" but not the final dwelling place of those who are in Christ. See Randy Alcorn, *Heaven* (Carol Stream, IL: Tyndale House, 2004), 41–66.

in the literature of Second Temple Judaism.[16] He notes that in many texts, the problem is presented in spiritual terms:

> The created world has come under the dominion of evil, angelic powers in some primeval time, namely in the time of Noah. . . . God's sovereign rights have been usurped and the world, including God's own people, has been led astray into forms of idolatry. . . . God will invade the world under the dominion of the evil powers and defeat them in a cosmic war. Only God has the power to defeat and to overthrow the demonic and diabolical powers that have subjugated and perverted the earth. God will establish his sovereignty very soon, delivering the righteous and bringing about a new age in which he will reign unopposed.[17]

But other texts acknowledged that this supernatural aspect of the problem doesn't explain things completely. People are also to blame, and people have to be part of the solution. De Boer explains that from this perspective, "the emphasis falls on free will and individual human decisions. Sin is the willful rejection of the Creator God (the breaking of the first commandment), and death is punishment for this fundamental sin. God, however, has provided the law as a remedy for this situation, and a person's posture toward this law determines his or her ultimate destiny."[18] In his analysis of Matthew's Gospel, John Riches has come to the conclusion that Matthew moves back and forth between these perspectives. Neither side could fully explain the human situation, and thus the two perspectives were held in dialogue and tension. Riches describes the dilemma that Matthew faced:

> Some account of human responsibility for sin and its overcoming is necessary, if human beings are not to be reduced merely to puppets in the hands of the gods, good or evil. On the other hand, were all responsibility for the present condition of the world to be loaded onto human beings, it would seem to destroy any basis for hope in a future purged of evil. If humanity were in and of itself so corrupt, what possible basis could it provide for a new world freed of sin? Only if some angelic agency is

16. Martin de Boer, "Paul and Apocalyptic Eschatology," in *The Encyclopedia of Apocalypticism,* ed. J. J. Collins (New York: Bloomsbury Academic, 1999) points to various texts from 1 Enoch., 2 Baruch., 4 Ezra, Testament of Moses., and Psalm of Solomon as examples of the apocalyptic eschatology being formed during this period.

17. Ibid., 358–59. He goes on to cite 1 Enoch 1–36 and Testament of Moses 10 as examples of this cosmology.

18. Ibid., 359. He cites *4 Ez.* and *2 Bar.* as examples.

invoked, which can also shoulder the responsibility for the world's ills and which can be overcome by divine intervention, can a view of the future be constructed which provides hope for a restored humanity.[19]

As we take a closer look at Matthew's Gospel, the "supernatural" perspective is easy to discern. He portrays evil as a present reality. Satan has a kingdom and asserts his authority over the kingdoms of the world; evil spirits seek to destroy human lives; it is predicted that evil men will prosper and live their lives without being held to account; the disciples will be persecuted and betrayed, wickedness will increase, wars will be on the rise, false prophets will appear, and abominations will occur.[20] The problem of evil will not be ultimately resolved until the "end of the age," when the Son of Man returns to "weed out of his kingdom everything that causes sin and all who do evil" (Matt 13:41).

But in Matthew's Gospel, the human, moral side of the problem is also clearly illustrated. The idea of righteousness (being good) is a major theme of his narrative: Jesus promises reward for those who hunger and thirst for righteousness; the kingdom belongs to those who are persecuted for sake of righteousness; the righteousness of Jesus's followers must surpass that of the Pharisees; the disciples are called to seek first the kingdom and its righteousness; salvation is not simply for those who call Jesus Lord, but only for those who do the will of the Father.[21]

Thus, as Riches suggests, the supernatural and human perspectives are both validated in Matthew's narrative. The genius of his Gospel is found in the way he presents a solution that addresses both sides of the problem. Matthew's fundamental argument is that if people live with the awareness of the coming supernatural intervention, then they will choose to live moral lives. As we have noted above, the coming of the kingdom of heaven means that very soon, God will make things right. He will punish the wicked and reward the righteous. Given that the time is drawing near, women and men are called to amend their lives

---

19. John Riches, *Conflicting Mythologies: Identity Formation in the Gospels of Mark and Matthew* (Edinburgh: T&T Clark, 2000), 53.
20. See Matt 12:26; 4:8–9; 12:45; 13:24–29, 37–43; 10:17–24.
21. See Matt 5:6, 10, 20; 6:33; 7:20–21.

and align themselves with the Father's ways. "Repent, for the kingdom of heaven is near!" *Get your life in order, because God will now set about making things right.*

This idea of living today with an awareness of God's intervention is clearly seen in the Beatitudes: "Blessed are the meek, for they shall inherit the earth" (Matt 5:6); "blessed are the merciful, for they will be shown mercy" (Matt 5:7); "blessed are the pure in heart, for they shall see God" (Matt 5:8); "blessed are the peacemakers, for they will be called sons of God" (Matt 5:9); and so on. Jesus advocates a present, earthly way of living that stands in the light of a supernatural reality. The disciples of Jesus must live in the awareness of God's present and future intervention.

To sum up Matthew's understanding of the problem—why heaven and earth are in conflict—we remember that he embraces two explanations that were common in his day. On the one hand, it's a supernatural problem; on the other, it's a human problem. Matthew believes that God will intervene. He will come to make things right. But Matthew also believes the human awareness of that coming intervention should drive people to amend their lives. God is going to address the problem of evil. He will close the gap between heaven and earth. But if people start changing their lives now, if they repent and do good, then in a sense the union of heaven and earth begins now.

The Role of the Church

We have seen above that the push toward the "new genesis" will be driven by both humanity and God. God is making things right presently and will continue to do so in the future. Jesus invites people to get on board with what God is doing. Matthew thus sees human history as standing in a time of transition. The process of uniting heaven and earth has begun. People are repenting and believing, and the kingdom of heaven is taking root on earth. It's like a mustard seed or a bit of leaven. It's here, and it's growing. And yet Matthew realizes that the full consummation of the kingdom of heaven will only occur when the bridegroom returns, when the master comes back from his journey.

Hence, the followers of Jesus find themselves living in this tension between "the now and not yet." It's not the end, but it is the beginning of the end.

During this time of transition, Matthew sees the church playing an important role. The followers of Jesus are the agents of God's present intervention. They have been endowed with a supernatural power and the authority to act on God's behalf. The church is God's transitional government on earth. Everyone knows that the permanent ruler, the king, is coming soon. But during the interim period, he has appointed his servants to be in charge of the house and to get things in order before he arrives.

One way that Matthew describes this transitional authority is through the idea of "binding and loosing." What he is trying to convey is the idea that any decision made by the transitional government in this present age will be upheld by the king when he arrives. They are given authority to act on his behalf. Two passages in which we see this dynamic are Peter's declaration of faith in Matthew 16:13–20 and the instruction on proclaiming forgiveness in Matthew 18:18–20.

In the first passage, Peter demonstrates how to bridge the gap between heaven and earth. Jesus begins the discourse by addressing a human, moral issue. *People are saying a lot of things about me, but what's your decision? Who do you say that I am?* Peter responds, "You are the Christ, the Son of the living God" (Matt 16:16). Illustrating the tension that exists between heaven and earth, Jesus then explains that this revelation is not from "flesh and blood" (i.e., from the earth) but from the Father *in heaven* (v. 17). Heaven is manifest on earth through Peter's declaration. Jesus then goes on to say that he will build his church upon "this rock" and that the gates of Hades will not overcome it (v. 18).

Thus in Peter's declaration we see the merging of heaven and earth. He's making a moral choice—professing his faith in Jesus—but this choice is not made in a vacuum. The Father had taken the initiative to reveal the truth to Peter, and Peter has responded in faith. Jesus then says that exactly this kind of collaboration is necessary for the building of his church on earth. "I will build my church," Jesus declares (Matt

16:18), *but I will not build it alone. My church will be built upon your faith, your decision to believe in me.* Peter has demonstrated that he is a reliable agent for the Father to use in the establishment of heaven on earth. For this reason, Jesus makes his role official: "I will give you the keys of the kingdom of heaven, and whatever you bind on earth shall be bound in heaven, and whatever you loose on earth shall be loosed in heaven" (Matt 16:19).

The church is the transitional authority that Jesus sets in place. When the kingdom of heaven comes in its fullness, everything they have determined will be honored. Whatever they bind now is bound and will remain so when the king returns. Whatever they loose will remain so. Jesus is communicating to his disciples that he trusts them to start setting things in order now.

A similar description of the church's authority is found in Matthew 18:15–20. The primary issue in this passage is the internal purity of the community. Jesus teaches his followers how to deal with the problem of "sin in the camp," giving them authority to banish the unrepentant. In Matthew 16:13–20, Jesus had only addressed Peter. In Matthew 18:15–20, he speaks to all of his disciples, "Truly, I say to you, whatever you bind on earth shall be bound in heaven, and whatever you loose on earth shall be loosed in heaven" (Matt 18:18). What follows is a reiteration of the church's authority to act as the transitional government: "Again I say to you, if two of you agree on earth about anything they ask, it will be done for them by my Father in heaven. For where two or three are gathered in my name, there am I among them" (Matt 18:18–19). Here, Jesus is speaking about prayer, and he broadens the teaching beyond the simple notion of binding and loosing. He says that *whatever* they will agree upon on the earth will be accomplished by the Father in heaven. This will be possible because he will be in their midst. Through his presence among them, heaven will be manifest on earth.

Throughout Matthew, we have seen his emphasis on the distinction between heaven and earth as two realms living in tension and in contrast. However, in Matthew 16:19 and 18:18–19, heaven and earth are brought into union through the active mediation of the church. The church on earth is a transitional authority. The decisions that they make now stand and will not be undone when the king returns to make things right. What this means is the process of uniting heaven and earth—*making things right*—has begun now. The church is given the authority to carry out the will of the Father because Jesus is in their midst. This authority is exercised through prayer.

The Lord's Prayer in Matthew

We are now at the place where we can explore what all of these observations have to do with the Lord's Prayer. In review: (1) We have discussed the meaning of *heaven* in Matthew, noting that it denotes the place where things are right. (2) We have observed that Matthew frequently sets heaven in contrast to the earth. In this present age, he viewed them as being unnaturally separate. And (3), we have seen that Matthew envisioned the church playing a meditative role, bridging the gap between the two realms by her prayers.

Tension between Heaven and Earth

The contrast between heaven and earth, seen clearly throughout Matthew's Gospel, is also found in the Lord's Prayer. The first three petitions of this prayer illuminate the abundance of heaven, whereas the final four petitions call attention to the poverty of the earth. The characteristics of each realm stand in tension and contrast. The meaning of heaven is made clear because it is *different* from the earth and vice versa. But despite the sharp distinction that exists between these two places, the Lord's Prayer holds out the hope that this tension can be resolved, and the two can become one.

Looking at the first section of the prayer, we find that everything that rightly belongs to God finds its source in the realm of heaven. He is addressed as "our Father in Heaven," *our Father who is in the place where things are right*. It continues with three petitions that all relate to him: "hallowed be your name"; "your kingdom come"; "your will be done." In heaven, all of these things are already happening. God's name is hallowed by those in his presence who cry "holy, holy, holy."[22] In heaven he sits on a throne, and his kingdom is firmly established (Matt 5:34; 23:22). And all who dwell in heaven obey the Father's will. Psalm 103:19–21 says, "The Lord has established his throne in the heavens, and his kingdom rules over all. Bless the Lord, O you his angels, you mighty ones who do his word, obeying the voice of his word! Bless the Lord, all his hosts, his ministers, who do his will!" The purpose of the opening section of the Lord's Prayer is to draw those who pray into the heavenly realm, where they can envision what it looks like in the place where everything is right.

Standing in sharp contrast to the rightness of heaven is the desperate situation of the earth. The last four petitions—"give us this day our daily bread," "forgive us our debts," "lead us not into temptation," and "deliver us from evil"—all convey the idea of *human need*. On the earth we see humanity's vulnerability: we need bread every day, we are prone to sin, we find it difficult to forgive others, we fail when we are tested, and we are susceptible to the powerful influence of evil. Throughout his Gospel, Matthew has depicted each of these needs as things that distract us from the kingdom of heaven. Worrying about clothing and food for the next day is characterized as the anxiety of gentiles (see Matt 6:25–34). Unrighteous people find it difficult to forgive others (see Matt 18:22–35). Jesus rebukes the people of "the world" for their weakness in temptation and their proclivity toward evil.[23] Everything that is found in heaven, the place where things are right, is painfully lacking down here on earth.

There is reason for hope, however. Throughout his Gospel Matthew has set forth the idea that heaven and earth will be brought into union. The tension that stands between these two realms and the hope of its resolution are encapsulated in the Lord's Prayer. The core vision of this

---

22. Isaiah 6:3. Matthew does not make explicit reference in his Gospel to this passage, but his Jewish readers would no doubt have made this association. The continuity of this tradition is attested by Rev 4:2–11, where John describes a vision very similar to that of Isaiah, where angels around the throne pronounce the *trisagion*.

23. See Matt 18:7 ("Woe to the world for temptations to sin!") and Matt 7:11; 9:4; 12:34, 39; 15:19; 16:4.

prayer is that the fullness of heaven will supply the need of the earth. The two realms will become one.

As in Heaven, so on Earth

For Matthew, the most important line in the Lord's Prayer was "on earth as it is in heaven" (Matt 6:10). These words incorporate everything that Matthew has said about heaven and earth, and they articulate his vision for the future. We will explore the meaning of this phrase from various angles.

First, let us look at the grammar. The Greek phrase *hōs en ouranō kai epi gēs* is most commonly rendered as "on earth as it is in heaven." But this is only one of the various ways that it can be translated. Literally, it says, "as (*hōs*) in (*en*) heaven (*ouranō*) also (*kai*) upon (*epi*) earth (*gēs*)." The two key words in this phrase are *hōs* and *kai*. In *Koine* Greek, these two words together in a sentence express the idea of equality or similarity.[24] Thus, alternative translations include, "both in heaven and on earth," "as on earth, so in heaven," and "as in heaven, so on earth."[25] The meaning of "on earth as it is in heaven" is that heaven and earth must become the same.

Next, let us look at the relationship of this phrase to the first three petitions of the Lord's Prayer. Even as most people think that "on earth as it is in heaven" corresponds only "your will be done," this is not the case. There is nothing in the grammar that ties "on earth as it is in heaven" to the third petition. Rather, "on earth as it is heaven" stands alone between the first and second sections of the prayer.[26] It is a bridge between the two "worlds" addressed in this prayer.

---

24. Cf. Matt 6:12; 20:14; 24:38–39; Acts 11:17; 13:33; 17:28; 1 Cor 7:7; 9:5; Eph 5:23; 2 Tim 3:9; Heb 3:2; 2 Pet 2:1; Rev 3:21; 18:6.

25. G. Thompson, "Thy Will Be Done in Earth as It Is in Heaven (Matt 6:11): A Suggested Re-Interpretation," *Expository Times* 70 (1959): 379–81.

26. There is nothing in the grammatical construction of this phrase that ties it to the third petition. Crossan argues that the phrase "as in heaven so on earth" is a hinge between two sections of the prayer that creates a "poetic parallelism." He combines the last two petitions of the prayer into one, thus presenting three petitions on each side of this phrase. He notes, "The first half of the prayer is framed by a phrase about heaven and the next half opens with a mention of the earth" (John Dominic Crossan, *The Greatest Prayer: Rediscovering the Revolutionary Message of the Lord's Prayer* [New York: HarperOne, 2010], 48–49).

The first three petitions of the Lord's Prayer illuminate the glory of the Father who is heaven. The second set of petitions portrays the plight of humans on earth. Set between these realms is the phrase "on earth as it is in heaven." To clarify, let us imagine what the Lord's Prayer might look like as a drawing. On the left side, the illustrator depicts heaven: God is on the throne being worshiped and honored by everyone present. On the right side, the artist draws the earth: chaos, poverty, and conflict. But there is a bridge that stands between the right and left sides of the drawing. Over the bridge is written, "On earth as it is in heaven." This prayer brings the two realms together.

Heaven is the place where things are right, and earth must become that kind of place as well. Matthew sees the current separation between heaven and earth as something that is unnatural and wrong. As Jonathan Pennington notes,

> For Matthew, the current tension or contrast between heaven and earth is not part of God's creative and redemptive plans. The great Christian prayer is that the disjuncture between the two realms will cease to be: God's Name will be hallowed, his will done, and his kingdom manifested not only in the heavenly realm but also in the earthly. This is important because when emphasizing the contrast between heaven and earth it would be a mistake to understand this as a permanent and divinely designed state. The contrast between heaven and earth is a result of the sinfulness of the world and is thus unnatural. The eschatological goal, according to 6:9–10, is that this unnatural tension will be resolved into the unity of God's reign over heaven and earth.[27]

"On earth as it is in heaven" is a prayer within a prayer. It stands in the middle as summary of everything that the Lord's Prayer envisions: *May things be made right on earth just as they are right in heaven.*

The Role of the Church

There is one more detail that needs to be added to the picture we are painting. In our imagined drawing of the Lord's Prayer—with heaven on the left side, the earth on the right, and a bridge standing in the

27. Pennington, *Heaven and Earth*, 155.

gap between them—we saw the words "on earth as it is in heaven." The illustrator now slightly modifies his drawing. Around this phrase he now draws a balloon, making it a caption. Below he draws a picture of Christians praying. Now imagine that this drawing becomes animated and is given sound. Christians stand on the bridge and pray the Lord's Prayer out loud. As they pray, the left side (heaven) and the right side (earth) start moving toward one another. The people continue to pray, and heaven and earth begin to merge around them. When they finally meet, neither looks exactly the same. Their union has transformed them both. God is still on the throne, and he is still surrounded by people worshiping him. But he is surrounded by scenes from the earth. Now there are trees and lakes and mountains and people (and yes, grapefruits—C. S. Lewis was right). The violence and poverty and chaos are gone, and everything is beautiful and right. The old earth wasn't destroyed. This is the *palingenesia* that Matthew envisioned. This present world doesn't "come to an end." Rather, it is transformed.[28]

One thing that Matthew would stress in this picture is the people on the bridge. It is the church that stands in the gap between heaven and earth. As the church exercises its authority in prayer, heaven and earth move closer together. When the church prays, heaven rumbles and creaks and is slowly pulled toward earth. When the church prays, the earth groans and heaves as it is drawn toward heaven. We have seen in Matthew 16:19 and 18:18 that what the church binds on earth is

---

28. Much of the confusion around heaven and the future of the earth stems from a misunderstanding of Revelation 21:1–5. Verse 1 says, "Then I saw a new heaven and a new earth, for the first heaven and the first earth had passed away, and the sea was no more." This is often understood to mean that the current world is annihilated and replaced by a newly created heaven and earth. It is more appropriate, however, to interpret these words as representing renewal and transformation rather than obliteration. Using similar language, Paul said that "if anyone is in Christ, he is a new creation. The old has passed away; behold, the new has come" (2 Cor 5:17). He was not saying that the physical body disappears and is replaced. Rather, he is saying that we are transformed. It is in with this understanding that we can correctly interpret Rev 21:2–5: "And I saw the holy city, new Jerusalem, coming down out of heaven from God, prepared as a bride adorned for her husband. And I heard a loud voice from the throne saying, 'Behold, the dwelling place of God is with man. He will dwell with them, and they will be his people, and God himself will be with them as their God. He will wipe away every tear from their eyes, and death shall be no more, neither shall there be mourning, nor crying, nor pain anymore, for the former things have passed away.' And he who was seated on the throne said, 'Behold, I am making all things new.'" The earth isn't destroyed; it is made new. Those who have been resurrected in Christ don't leave the earth and go to heaven; the New Jerusalem descends, and God makes his dwelling place here on earth forever.

bound in heaven, and what the church loosens on earth is loosened in heaven. What these verses indicate is that the church has the ability to generate movement in both places. Through prayer, heaven is pulled toward the earth, and the earth is pulled toward heaven. What the church does on earth has an effect in heaven, even as the activity of the Father in heaven also has an effect on earth.

With the Lord's Prayer, Jesus was inviting his followers to be players in the unfolding of the Father's plan. The progress of human history is not driven by God alone. It's an act of collaboration between God and humanity. Jesus promised that after his departure, he would be in our midst when we gather. Heaven would be present on earth, and the church on earth will make its presence felt in heaven. This community of empowered believers prays the Lord's Prayer and straddles heaven and earth. The church mediates the tension, pulling both realms toward the goal of their transformative union.

How the Lord's Prayer Works

The final question that we need to consider is, For Matthew, what makes the Lord's Prayer effective? In other words, how does it work? Did he see the power of this prayer lying in its ability to change human behavior? Or was this prayer powerful because it could move God into action?

As we have mentioned above, in Matthew's worldview there were two basic problems: (1) evil forces are at work opposing the purposes of God, and (2) people on earth make bad choices. The combination of these two issues keeps heaven and earth in separation. Thus, if heaven and earth are ever going to come together, then both problems have to be addressed. On the one hand, God needs to wage war against the powers of evil and defeat them. And on the other hand, people need to stop sinning and start doing what is right.

In Matthew's view, the Lord's Prayer dealt with both of these issues. First and foremost, the Lord's Prayer moves heaven. It is a prayer addressed to God, and God answers prayer. Matthew does not conceive of the Lord's Prayer merely as recitation of doctrine nor mere assent to what God will do *with or without* our prayers. He has made it clear throughout his work that prayer moves God to action: "if two of you agree on earth about anything they ask, it will be done for them by my Father in heaven" (18:19); "ask and it will be given to you; seek, and you will find; knock, and it will be opened to you" (Matt 7:7).

For Matthew, the Lord's Prayer was a way of asking God to go to war against the powers of evil that opposed the Father's way of doing things. His will is to feed all of creation, but sin and evil have led to hunger and scarcity. "Give us this day our daily bread" is the church's way of asking God to overcome all forces opposing his generosity and send bread to his people. The Father's will is for everyone to have clean hearts and live in healthy relationships. Satan is at work to destroy people's lives. He tempts them and ensnares them in sin. He plants seeds of unforgiveness and provokes people to test God. But as the church prays the Lord's Prayer, the Father wages war against Satan's activities in the lives of his people. He forgives our sin and helps us forgive others. He gives us strength to resist Satan, and he drives him away from us. There is a strong element of the supernatural in the Lord's Prayer. It is effective because it moves the Father to action.

But for Matthew, there was another element of the Lord's Prayer, wherein its effectiveness was based upon its ability to shape human behavior. Not everything is dependent on God's action. People must also take responsibility for their choices. The Lord's Prayer shows them how to live. Everything that the church envisions for the world—as stated in the first three petitions of the Lord's Prayer—must be practiced in people's own lives. Whatever we ask God do to in the world must first be lived out by us. This is evident in the first three petitions of the prayer. We can't ask for God's name to be honored as holy if we do not honor him with our choices. We cannot ask for the kingdom to come if we ourselves do not seek righteousness. And we cannot ask for the Father's will to be done on earth if we ourselves do not put it into practice. Matthew's point is that heaven must be manifest in our own lives before it can take its hold on the earth.[29]

29. See Matt 5:16: "In the same way, let your light shine before others, so that they may see your good

This imperative to live out what we pray is even more clear in the second section of the prayer. We can't just ask God to wage war against the "spirit of unforgiveness"; we must make the choice to forgive one another.[30] We can't just ask the Father to feed our brothers and sisters; we must feed them if we have the means.[31] We can't just ask God to protect us from Satan; we must commit ourselves not to test God. In all these things, the demand for human action is clear. Ulrich Luz notes that "the Lord's Prayer is a prayer of active and obedient men and women, not of those who let their hands rest in their laps and direct their gaze humbly upward. Matthew's main concern is not only that 'Need teaches to pray' . . . but equally that 'Action teaches to pray.'"[32]

In sum, Matthew presents the Lord's Prayer as being effective both in heaven (to move God) and on earth (to move people). It envisions God and people working together to bring about his kingdom on the earth. Crossan concludes that

> God's kingdom did not, could not, and will not begin, continue, or conclude without human collaboration. It will not happen by divine intervention alone—neither to start, continue, or conclude. That is why Matthew's Abba Prayer has two even parts with the divine "you" in the first half and the human "we" in the second half. And those two parts are correlatives. They come together or never come at all. They are like two sides of the same eschatological coin.[33]

Thus, the union of heaven and earth that Matthew envisions will not come about by the activity God alone, nor by humans alone. The power of the Lord's Prayer lies in the fact that it draws both God and humans into collaborative interaction.

works and give glory to your Father who is in heaven"; Matt 6:33, "But seek first the kingdom of God and his righteousness, and all these things will be added to you"; Matt 7:21, "Not everyone who says to me, 'Lord, Lord,' will enter the kingdom of heaven, but the one who does the will of my Father who is in heaven"; and Matt 12:50, "For whoever does the will of my Father in heaven is my brother and sister and mother."

30. This notion is then reiterated in Matt 6:14–15.
31. God's provision to one was his provision for all. Ayo notes, "We might say: Give us our daily bread as we give daily bread to others. May we receive the love of God so that we may love our neighbor as ourselves" (Nicholas Ayo, *The Lord's Prayer: A Survey Theological and Literary* [Notre Dame: University of Notre Dame Press, 1992], 66). Matthew 25:35 also reiterates the fundamental obligation of the community members to share their bread with one another.
32. Ulrich Luz, *The Theology of the Gospel of Matthew* (Cambridge: Cambridge University Press, 1995), 50.
33. Crossan, *Greatest*, 94.

Conclusion

Matthew is by far the most theologically complex interpreter of the Lord's Prayer that we will encounter in this book. He presents an intricate system of ideas that requires both close scrutiny and broad analysis. In order to appreciate the handiwork behind a mosaic, a magnifying glass is a useful tool. The only problem is that when we look too closely, it's difficult to see the image. It's only when we stand back that we can see how all of the unique stones come together to make a picture.

In this chapter, we have looked at many stones in the mosaic of Matthew. We have seen that Matthew thought of heaven as the place where things are right. The earth, in contrast, is the place where things are not quite as they should be. Matthew saw heaven and earth as being out of sync, and this state of affairs is not what God had intended. He understood the root of the problem as being both spiritual and moral. War was being waged in the spiritual realm, and in some ways, only God could combat the forces that kept heaven and earth apart. But people are also to blame. Humanity's choice to sin had also contributed the problem. Matthew thus envisioned a partnership between God and humanity to restore the unity that existed in the beginning. Leading the way would be the church, which God had appointed as an authority on earth to move both heaven and earth toward union.

All of these diverse components contribute to Matthew's understanding of the Lord's Prayer. The first section of the prayer is about heaven. The second section of the prayer is about the earth. Bridging these two parts of the prayer is the vision that everything would come to be "on earth as it is in heaven." And that is the summary of what the Lord's Prayer meant for Matthew: may this earth and heaven become one. When the church prays this prayer, it comes to pass.

In the previous chapter we looked at the Lord's Prayer through the lens of narrative theology. The meaning of the prayer was drawn from its place in the history of Israel. In contrast, what we have seen in this chapter is what we might call a "systematic theology" of the Lord's Prayer. Matthew is concerned less with history and more with cosmology and ecclesiology: the order of the created world and the order of the church. Narrative theology and systematic theology will each shed light on some different characteristics of the Lord's Prayer, even as many of the conclusions reached by each methodology will be the same. What is important to note at this stage is the fact that even in the first century, there was not one single way to interpret the Lord's Prayer. Multiple approaches to this text led to multiple interpretations. Even during these earliest stages of the Christian movement, there was an understanding that the same prayer could mean different things to different people. This didn't mean that any interpretation was accepted, but an author like Matthew surely felt the freedom to convey what it meant *to him.*

In the next leg of our journey we will look at how still another first-century community interpreted the Lord's Prayer. We will visit a group of Christians held together by their adherence to a discipleship manual known as the *Didache.* They prayed the Lord's Prayer just as Matthew's readers did. In many ways, its meaning was the same. But the circumstances and priorities of the *Didache* community were unique. For them, the Lord's Prayer wasn't so much about history or theology. It was about how to "do life" in Christian community. To that story we now turn.

4

Order and Chaos in the *Didache*

For many years I have worked for an organization that consistently resists any efforts to define it. Known as Youth with a Mission (YWAM), the name itself is a bit of an oxymoron. With regard to the first part of our title, we call ourselves "youth," when in actuality we are an odd mixture of authentic young people and a bunch of old people in denial. And what exactly constitutes our "mission" is increasingly difficult to explain. Our programs include missionary training schools, maternity shelters, food distribution, church planting, home construction, and evangelistic outreaches. We think we have twenty thousand members, but no one knows for sure. Workers toil in 160 nations, and yet we have no headquarters and no single leader. It's somewhat surprising that YWAM would even refer to itself as an *organization*. When experts have been asked to characterize us, the best description they have come up with is that we are a *chaordic* entity. That is to say, we embody a strange amalgam of chaos and order. Those of us in leadership often feel like the mythological king Sisyphus, who spent eternity repeatedly trying to roll a boulder up a hill only to watch it crash back down each time he neared the top. We are a group of poor souls charged with the creation of an organized system that will, in fact, never exist.

I have always assumed that YWAM was an anomaly within Christianity. Other missionary groups and denominations have seemed so structured and ordered. YWAM is just *different*. From a historical perspective, however, I have been encouraged to discover that YWAM is not the first group with these characteristics. *Chaordic* communities—those holding the tension between order and chaos—have a long history within Christianity. In this present chapter our attention will be focused on one such community (or group of communities) that existed nearly two thousand years ago.

The document known as the *Didache* (pronounced *DID-ah-kay*) opens the window on a first-century group of Christians that most likely lived in Syria. What we uncover is a bit surprising. In some ways their community life was very ordered, to judge from the document. They had a liturgical order of worship, established leaders, rules for testing prophecies and prophets, and policies governing daily life. Yet they also had their fair share of chaos: their worship locations constantly changed; itinerant prophets and teachers would show up without warning; the charismatics could get weird; and many of their rules were subject to personal interpretation. Amid the back and forth between order and chaos, we may imagine that one of the "rudders" by which they managed to stay on course was the Lord's Prayer. In a world that often seemed disordered, this prayer gave them a sense of sanity. Whereas the forces of chaos always threatened to destroy their community, the Lord's Prayer helped keep them together.

Our present purpose is to explore how the daily practice of saying the Lord's Prayer accomplished this task. What we will discover is that the Lord's Prayer mattered to these Christians primarily as a tool for discipleship. In previous chapters, we have seen that other early interpretations of the Lord's Prayer emphasized its significance to the narrative history of Israel or the theological cosmology of heaven and earth. The followers of the *Didache* were perhaps a bit more "down to earth." These weren't scholars and theologians. They were normal families trying to figure out what it looked like to follow Jesus in a world gone mad. The main issue for them was what the Lord's Prayer *did* for their life in community. Above all, it was a functional prayer.

The people that followed the *Didache* embraced what can be called a *spirituality of the road*. They viewed themselves as a people moving toward perfection, with a long path in front of them. They experienced moments of messiness and chaos. Yet they believed that the way of life had been clearly set before them. God was in their midst, and he was making them holy. When they said the Lord's Prayer, they were reminded of who they were and what they stood for. This prayer summarized the foundational elements of their worldview and values: the holiness of the community, the coming restoration, the moral commitment to be righteous, the responsibility to share, the need for ongoing confession and mercy, and the call to overcome evil and sin.

As we now look at what the Lord's Prayer meant to this ancient community, our study will be broken into two parts. First, we will look at the community life of these particular Christians, focusing on their values, beliefs, and approach to discipleship. Then, in the light of what we've learned about their community life, we will try to discern the unique perspective on the meaning of the Lord's Prayer.

Introduction to the *Didache*

The *Didache* was most likely written in the first century CE as a discipleship manual for training new believers. While it didn't make it into the official list of New Testament books, it was nonetheless highly regarded in many Christian circles until at least the fourth century. We should not think of the *Didache* as a spurious or heretical document. The doctrines and practices described in it fully fall within the boundaries of orthodox Christianity. What we see here is a manual that was useful to many Christians for a season in history but eventually fell "out of fashion." The text was eventually lost and almost forgotten until its rediscovery at a library in Turkey in 1873. Since that time, this document has been the subject of numerous books and articles, all of which recognize its value in displaying the wonderful diversity of early Christianity. There can be a tendency today to think that the only "true" Christians in the first century were those communities described in the New Testament: Jerusalem, Rome, Corinth, Ephesus, and so on. We often think of Christianity as defined by Paul as the only "orthodox" or "original" faith. But the *Didache* demonstrates that in the early stages of the church, there were other "real" Christians who had a different approach to living out their faith.

The *Didache* does not specifically name any teacher or apostle as its author. The title by which it was anciently known, *The Teaching of the Lord to the Gentiles by the Twelve Apostles* (*Didachē Kyriou dia tōn Dōdeka Apostolōn tois Ethnesin*), indicates that the framers of this document saw it as a continuation of Christ's teaching to the Twelve. To be sure, there are many similarities with New Testament texts: the language at times resembles that of John, the sayings of Jesus are among those also recorded by Matthew, and many of the concerns addressed within the *Didache* were shared by Paul.[1] Yet there is no conclusive indication that the *Didache* was somehow based on a New Testament book or the teaching of a particular apostle. It was obviously dependent on many of the same oral traditions other authors used (particularly Matthew), but the *Didache* describes a very unique expression of the Christian life.[2] The teaching of the *Didache* finds its roots in Jewish discipleship communities that existed before the Jesus movement began. It is for this reason that this text tells us just as much about first-century Judaism as it does about early Christianity.

Various Jewish groups in the Second Temple era actively sought converts throughout the Mediterranean region.[3] When successful, the task before them was to train these gentile "God-fearers" in the ways of the covenant. A series of teachings was formed that came to be known as the "Two Ways." This instruction was an adaptation of the

---

1. See Arthur Voobus, "Regarding the Background of the Liturgical Traditions in the Didache: The Question of Literary Relation between Didache IX.4 and the Fourth Gospel," *Vigilae Christianae* 23, no. 2 (1969): 81–87; Jonathan Draper, "The Jesus Tradition in the Didache," in *The Didache in Modern Research*, ed. Jonathan A. Draper (Leiden: Brill, 1996), 91; David Flusser, "Paul's Jewish-Christian Opponents in the Didache," in Draper, *Didache in Modern Research*, 194–211.

2. See Aaron Milavec, *The Didache: Faith, Hope, and Life of the Earliest Christian Communities, 50–70 C.E.* (New York: Newman, 2003), 695–739.

3. Jesus noted that the scribes and Pharisees would cross "land and sea to make a single convert" (Matt 23:15).

Hebrew Scriptures formulated to teach gentiles the basic requirements of serving the God of Israel.

As many of the Jewish communities using the Two Ways teaching came to believe in Jesus as the Messiah, certain adjustments had to be made. The core teaching now had to be supplemented to incorporate the teachings of Jesus. And new practices had to be set in place to reflect the customs of the burgeoning Jesus movement. These expansions of the Two Ways teaching ultimately resulted in the document that we now know as the *Didache.*

The first chapter opens with the declaration, "There are two ways: one is the Way of Life, the other is the Way of Death; and there is a mighty difference between these two ways."[4] The first six chapters of the text then closely follow the traditional Two Ways teaching. It is in chapters 7–16 that we find material that was added to the Jewish tradition. In these chapters are found Christian teachings that had been passed down orally, traditional prayers, and some content written by the community leaders themselves.[5]

What must be emphasized in our understanding of these communities is that they never abandoned their commitment to Jewish spirituality and the Jewish way of life. For this reason, the *Didache* can at times seem very different to what we read in other New Testament texts. It has little in common with Paul's doctrine of the law and grace, and it shows no awareness of the Jerusalem council described in Acts 15. These Christians still believed that the law should be kept in full, and they made the righteousness defined by the law their goal. The authors of the *Didache* were Jewish followers of Jesus who embraced him as "the servant" of God who had come to reveal

4. *Didache* 1.1. Unless otherwise noted, all texts from the *Didache* will be taken from Thomas O'Loughlin, "The Teaching of the Lord Given to the Gentiles by the Twelve Apostles," in *The Didache: A Window on the Earliest Christians* (London: SPCK, 2010), 161–71.

5. It is generally accepted that the *Didache* reached something very close to its current form no later than the end of the first century. It is important to note that the composite character of the *Didache* in no way diminishes the overall coherence of its message. Sandt and Flusser have noted that "the Didache must not be treated . . . as a fragmented collage of materials only, for since as a whole it is a community rule, intended to regulate the behavior of the community, the manual deserves to be considered as a coherent systematic unity as well" (Huub van de Sandt and David Flusser, *The Didache: Its Jewish Sources and Its Place in Early Judaism and Christianity* [Minneapolis: Fortress, 2002], 31).

the true path to life and knowledge.[6] Even though they had separated themselves from the synagogue, they still held on to many of the practices of first-century Judaism.

The main concern of the *Didache* is discipleship, that is, how to live life on a daily basis in accordance with the teachings of Jesus. Even as these Christians were very idealistic in their aspiration to keep the law of Moses, they were at the same time very practical. They understood that establishing order was not an overnight process, especially when dealing with people who had come from "rough" backgrounds. Certainly there were many members of the community who had grown up in good Jewish families and who had spent their lives reading the Scriptures. But many—if not most—new members of the community were coming out of pagan culture. Sacrifices to idols, astrology, curses, spells, magic potions, and orgies had all been part of their life experiences. These were people emerging from chaotic lifestyles. The suggestion that they should immediately put into practice all of the law's commands was an unrealistic expectation. Thus the leaders of the *Didache* community had to find a compromise. They had to come up with a way for the group as a whole to remain true to its Jewish heritage while still making room for the newly converted gentiles. The arrangement that they devised is as follows: "Now if you are able to bear the whole of the Lord's yoke, you will be complete. However, if you are not able [to bear that yoke], then do what you can. And concerning food regulations, bear what you are able. However, you must keep strictly away from meat that has been sacrificed to idols, for involvement with it involves worship of dead gods" (*Did.* 6.2–3). What the discipleship manual says here is that each person can decide what aspects of the law to keep. Certain things are prohibited for everyone (meat sacrificed to idols), but beyond that, no one would be criticized for choosing not to keep all of the rules. The *Didache* encourages everyone to keep the whole law; this was the path to being

---

6. *Didache* 9.3: "We give thanks to you, our Father, for the life and knowledge which you have made known to us. Through Jesus, your servant, to you be glory forever."

"complete." At the same time, they could be flexible. *Try to keep the law, but if you find it too difficult, then just do your best.*

In practice, this approach no doubt led to a lot of chaos. Perhaps some ate pork, others abstained; some circumcised their children, others chose not to; some strictly observed the Sabbath, others took a more "laid back" approach; some ate sausages made with blood, and others could never think of eating something so disgusting. (One can imagine how stressful their church potlucks must have been!) There was a potential for total disorder. Yet the underlying assumption of the *Didache* is that as they prayed and continued in the community discipline, the Father would lead them toward perfection. A bit of chaos was tolerated because they knew that God was internally at work in their lives to create order.

What we see in their approach to the law is that there was "flexibility within boundaries." This same mindset characterized the way they practiced baptism, communal prayer, and hospitality, as the following passages reveal:

- In the section that teaches on baptism (*Did.* 7.1–4), we find elements of both order and chaos. There was one strict requirement: baptism had to be done in the name of the Father, Son, and Holy Spirit. But in other aspects there was flexibility: there was no set place; the water could be running (in a river) or still (in a container); there was no set person to baptize; it could be done by immersion or sprinkling; and even though people were supposed to fast along with the person being baptized, the text doesn't really say who this should be.

- *Didache* 9–10 contains various liturgical, orderly prayers that were to be said in the worship service. But in addition to these prewritten prayers, spontaneity was also encouraged. Once the formal prayers were concluded, they were to "permit the prophets to give thanks in whatever manner they wish" (*Did.* 10.7). This adjustment was made, no doubt, because the prophets needed to pray "as the Spirit led."

- *Didache* 11–13 gives guidelines for the practice of hospitality. Every apostle, prophet, or teacher who wanted to stay among them had to be received. Yet boundaries were established. A limit was set with regard to how long an apostle could stay. When he left, he couldn't ask for excessive provision for his trip. If a prophet came to stay, the community members had to make sure that he didn't use his prophetic gift as a means of getting special meals or other "perks" for himself. The text gave guidelines as to how the community could know if these apostles and prophets were true or false. If it turned out that they were self-seeking and manipulative, they were to be kicked out.[7]

In all of these cases we see that the *Didache* community could be idealistic and practical at the same time. They believed that eventually they would achieve perfect harmony, yet they accepted the fact that getting there would be a process. As long as new converts from paganism kept coming in, as long as rivers ran dry, as long as prophets would insist on "doing their own thing," and as long as guests would overstay their welcome—the community would have to accept the reality of an imperfect world. What gave them hope in all of this disorder was their confidence in the work of the Holy Spirit, who was at work in their midst leading them toward wholeness. Not everyone would reach this perfection at the same time. Their unity was not based on uniformity but rather on their common hope. As long as they all believed that someday everyone would arrive at the place the Spirit was leading them to, a certain degree of disarray was tolerable.

This ability to navigate order and chaos is part of what makes the *Didache* such an ingenious manual of discipleship. The community did not compromise its goals. The way of life was a path toward perfection. Yet they understood that they would walk that road in patience, hope, and forgiveness.

The Role of the Lord's Prayer

Communities and families are held together by common values and beliefs. Anthropology describes how these exist in an interdependent

7. See *Did.* 11.3–12; 12:5; 13.1–2.

relationship.[8] For example, many children are taught about the value of forgiveness. What parents discover, however, is that this value cannot stand alone. It needs to be undergirded by a rationale. As a child grows, he or she may ask *why* forgiveness is important. At this point, the parents might explain that Jesus forgave us and commands us to forgive others. If the child accepts the parents' explanation, *value* (that forgiveness is important) is then supported by a *belief* (that God forgives and commands us to forgive.) A cycle is thus created in which values are undergirded by beliefs, and beliefs lead to the acceptance of new values.

Even as this cycle is common to cultures across the ages, it is fairly easy to disrupt. Particularly when a religious group finds itself in a context that is contrary (or even hostile) to its values, it is important to engage in rituals and practices that remind the community of what they hold to be true and what things in life really matter. When beliefs and values are not reinforced, some members might eventually slip away from the group, following the path of least resistance and reverting to the mindset of the prevailing culture.[9] People need constant reminders about what they believe and why.

Liturgical prayers accomplish this task by declaring what the community holds to be true and then "praying out" the values that make sense in light of their beliefs. This is exactly the function that the Lord's Prayer played among the followers of the *Didache*. This prayer was important because it both declared what they believed to be true about God and served as a daily reminder of the things that really mattered in light of their beliefs. The Lord's Prayer gave them a sense

---

8. Clifford Geertz notes that the role of religious symbols (such as prayer) is to "formulate an image of the world's construction and a program for human conduct." He continues, "Such symbols render the world view believable and the ethos justifiable, and they do so by invoking each in the support of the other. The world view is believable because the ethos, which grows out of it, is felt to be authoritative; the ethos is justifiable because the worldview, upon which it rests, is held to be true" (Clifford Geertz, *The Interpretation of Cultures* [New York: Basic Books, 1973], 97).

9. In describing societies Berger notes that "continuing reality, both objective (as common, taken-for-granted facticity) and subjective (as facticity imposing itself on individual consciousness), depends upon specific social processes, namely those processes that on-goingly reconstruct and maintain the particular worlds in question. Conversely, the interruption of these social processes threatens the (objective and subjective) reality of the worlds in question" (Peter Berger, *The Sacred Canopy: Elements of a Sociological Theory of Religion* [New York: Anchor, 1967], 45).

of order within the confusion of everyday life. In a world dominated by idolaters and hypocrites, they needed a daily reminder of who they were, what they believed, and what they held to be important. Their practice of saying this prayer every morning, afternoon, and evening served to bring their attention back to their faith and their community. Wherever they were and whatever they were doing, they would pause to pray at these times. And in so doing, they remembered that they were not alone. Their scattered brothers and sisters—across the village, in the city, or working in the fields—were also praying with them. They were part of a family of people that shared their needs, struggles, and vision. Each day would bring its fair share of chaos, but in saying the Lord's Prayer the world once again made sense.

One might argue that any prayer could have served some of these same purposes. The simple idea of pausing three times a day would no doubt be of benefit to most Christians. But the *Didache* makes it clear that the prayer to be said each day has to be the *Lord's Prayer*. This prayer, above all others, reinforced everything that the community stood for, valued, and believed. It wasn't just a spiritual formula to get a blessing. Each word meant something; each word counted; each word would help them through the day. Theirs was a "spirituality of the road." They knew that they had a long way to go before reaching perfection. The Lord's Prayer kept them on the path. In its words they reaffirmed their commitment to righteousness, willingness to share, need to forgive and receive forgiveness, and desire to overcome the evil and sin in their own lives. This prayer reminded them of the destination: the common goal of purity and wholeness to which they all aspired.

Looking at the internal evidence of the text, we will now explore what each petition of the Lord's Prayer meant to the followers of the *Didache* and how it kept them on the way of life.

The Name of God

We begin by reflecting on the idea of God's name. Each of us received the surname of our parents at birth. I was born into the family known by the name of Clark. Those of us who are the descendents of our illustrious progenitors—men such as Buck, Dude, and Jim Clark—share not only common blood but a common history. The Clark name gives us a sense of who we are and to whom we owe allegiance.

For the followers of the *Didache,* the name of God served a similar purpose. Faith in Christ meant birth into a new family, and it was important to identify the name by which they were identified. The *Didache* teaches that the name they inherited—conferred upon them at baptism—was the name of God himself (*Did.* 7.1).

All who bore the "name of God" were members of an exclusive group. Participation in the Lord's Supper was restricted only to those who had been "baptized in the name of the Lord" (*Did.* 9.5). There was an understanding that if a stranger arrived in need of housing, "anyone coming in the Lord's name should be made welcome" (*Did.* 12.1). It was their common sharing in the "name of the Lord" that gave them their identity and defined their loyalties.

When they prayed, "Our Father in Heaven, hallowed be your name" (*Did.* 8:1), they were first and foremost reaffirming the fact that God had shared his identity with them. He had given them his name, and now they were his children. There was an exclusivity to this understanding. God had not shared his name with all of humanity, and therefore not everyone had the right to call him "Father." Their identity as God's children was a special privilege they had received through Jesus.

These disciples also believed that the privilege of bearing God's name brought responsibility. As they said "hallowed be your name," they understood that the fulfillment of this petition was, in part, dependent upon them. The honoring of his name on earth was intertwined with the way they lived their lives.

There is another liturgical prayer in the *Didache* that illuminates how they would have understood the Lord's Prayer. *Didache* 10.2–3 is a post-communion prayer, which reads as follows:

> We give you thanks, holy Father, for your holy name which you have made to dwell in our hearts, and for the knowledge and faith and immortality

which you have made known to us. Through Jesus, your servant, to you be glory forever. You are the mighty ruler of all who has created all for your name's sake, and you have given food and drink to human beings for their enjoyment so that they might give thanks to you. But to us, from your generosity, you have given spiritual food and drink, and life eternal, through your servant. Above all things we give thanks to you because you are mighty: to you be glory forever. Remember, Lord, your church, deliver her from evil, make her complete in your love, and gather her from the four winds into your kingdom you have prepared for her, for yours is the power and the glory forever. May grace come and may this world pass away. Hosanna to the God of David. If anyone is holy, let him advance; if anyone is not, let him be converted. Maranatha. Amen.

We see in the opening line of this prayer that the name of the Father is regarded as holy and that he has made his name to dwell in their hearts. The imagery here created hearkens back to the Jerusalem temple. Referring to that building, YHWH had once said "My name shall be there" (1 Kgs 8:29). It was the dwelling place of his holy presence on earth. Now that the temple was gone, the followers of the *Didache* saw themselves as the dwelling place of YHWH. The Father's name was in them, and through them he revealed his holiness to the world.

This same post-communion prayer presents the idea that everything God does is for the sake of his sake of his name and receiving honor. God wants all of humanity to give thanks to him. Toward this end, he has given all people food and drink, and to his church he has given *spiritual* food and drink. The material provision for all and the spiritual provision for the church are given for the same reason: that all people "might give thanks." With the extra measure of blessing that the church has received comes an extra measure of responsibility. They have received much, and now much is required of them. It is for this reason that they ask God to make them holy: "Remember, Lord, your church, deliver her from evil, make her complete in your love."

What we see in this post-communion prayer is the simple idea that the Father had shared his holiness with his children, and it was now their responsibility to display that holiness to the world. This same understanding applies to the way they would have understood "hallowed be thy name." In these words they were committing themselves, with God's assistance, to live lives that would bring honor to him. They knew that apart from their own sanctification, the name of God could not be sanctified on earth. As their Father, his very identity was intertwined with theirs. The world would never see the righteous character of the Father unless it was seen in his children. Their request was for assistance in living lives that would result in the honoring of his name among the nations.

The Coming Kingdom

In the second petition of the Lord's Prayer, the *Didache* communities prayed for the coming of the Father's kingdom. As we have noted previously, first-century Jews would have understood the kingdom of God to signify the restoration of Israel. For these disciples, however, the "kingdom" no longer meant the literal return of the twelve tribes to the land of Israel nor the defeat of its political enemies. They were now a Christian community made up of both Jews and gentiles. The land and politics of Palestine were no longer a primary concern.

But this is not to say that they had abandoned the symbolic imagery of Israel's restoration. The followers of the *Didache* believed that they were heirs of YHWH's promises to Israel. They had been made part of the "holy vine of David" through Jesus, the servant of the Father (*Did.* 9.1). All of the promises once made to Israel were now theirs. YHWH had told the Jewish people that he would regather them from the nations. Isaiah had once predicted that God would "assemble the banished of Israel, and gather the dispersed of Judah from the four corners of the earth" (Isa 11:12). In this same way he would now regather them. The communion prayer of the *Didache* implores, "Just as this broken bread was scattered on the mountains and then was gathered together and became one, so may your church be gathered together from the ends of the earth into your kingdom,"[10] and "remember, Lord, your church, deliver her from evil, make her

---

10. *Didache* 9.4 (Michael Holmes, "The *Didache*," in *The Apostolic Fathers: Greek Texts and English Translations*, trans. Michael W. Holmes [Grand Rapids: Baker Academic, 2007]).

complete in your love, and gather her from the four winds into your kingdom you have prepared for her" (*Did.* 10.5).

For the gentile members of these communities, the imagery of literally being "regathered" from the four winds, or from the ends of the earth, might have seemed a bit strange. This was the symbolic language of the kingdom. In the same way that the twelve tribes of Israel had languished in exile, hoping that their nation would be restored, the church now struggled against sin. She was "scattered on the mountains" in disarray, beset by the forces of evil and in need of purification. The hope of the kingdom was the hope of being brought to wholeness and being made perfect in the Father's love. The petition "let your kingdom come" was a request for their own spiritual restoration.

The antithesis of the kingdom was division. Being scattered, separated, and plundered by the forces of evil was their darkest fear. Each and every day the threat of division in the community loomed large. The diversity that characterized these fellowships at any moment could collapse into outright conflict. The kingdom for which they prayed daily was a place of harmony and peace. To be sure, they were on a progressive path toward perfect unity. The fullness of the kingdom was something they would only experience at a future time. But there was also a present reality to the kingdom. On any given day they could get a foretaste of what was to come by walking in unity and peace.

The Will of the Father

What exactly is meant by the "will of God" was a subject of debate in the first century, just as it is today. Among the Jewish communities that formed the backdrop of the *Didache*, there was a diversity of perspectives. Some believed that if God is sovereign and his power is absolute, then his will is always accomplished. Whatever happens is essentially God's will because nothing occurs that is contrary to his desires or plans. According to this view, human will is subject to God's divine direction. His ultimate purposes cannot be resisted by humanity.[11] An alternative approach was to think of God's will as an expression of that which he *desires* to happen. This is to say that sometimes things happen on earth that are contrary to his will. Proponents of this second belief system argued that even though it pains God when people don't act according to his will, this is the price that must be paid if women and men are to be free to make choices for themselves.

The question we must now consider is: What did the followers of the *Didache* believe about the will of God? When they prayed "let your will be done," did they think of God's will as an immutable decree of what he had predestined to occur? Or did they think of it in terms of a choice that people must make? To find the answers, we must consider the history of the Jewish teachings that went into the formation of the *Didache*.

As we have mentioned above, the *Didache* was based upon a tradition known as the Two Ways. There are other versions of the Two Ways teaching predating the *Didache* that point toward a theology of predetermination. One example is found among the Dead Sea Scrolls (1QS 3:13–4:26). Referring to the way of life, one section of this text states, "And in the hand of the Prince of Lights is dominion over all the sons of justice; they walk on paths of light." Then, in reference to the way of death it says, "And in the hand of the Angel of Darkness is total dominion over the sons of deceit; they walk on paths of darkness."[12] This portrayal of the two spirits, according to Sandt and Flusser, "is closely connected with this notion of predetermination . . . the Prince of Lights is synonymous with the Spirit of Truth and the Angel of Darkness is equivalent to the Spirit of Deceit. The function of the two spirits is to control all people for good and evil and men are assigned to one or the other spirit as a result of the will of God."[13] In this system of

---

11. Sandt and Flusser note, "Dualistic beliefs in terms of predetermination are found in various Jewish writings which, although not sectarian in character, probably belonged to the wider Essene movement such as Jub. 10:1, 9, 11; 15:31b–32a; Sir. 42:24–25; T. Asher 1:8–9; 3:3; 6:2, and 6:4–6" (*Didache*, 151).

12. 1QS 3:20–21 (Florentino García Martínez and Eibert J. C. Tigchelaar, *The Dead Sea Scrolls Study Edition* [Leiden: Brill, 1997-1998], 2:75).

13. Sandt and Flusser, *Didache*, 150.

thought, whether one walks on the Way of Life or the Way of Death is ultimately not a personal choice. The life one lives is simply a reflection of the ruling spirits that control one's destiny.

Similar versions of this predeterministic Two Ways teaching were passed down in Greek. A reconstructed rendition reads, "There are two ways in the world, one of life, the other of death, one of light, the other of darkness; upon them two angels are appointed, one of righteousness, the other of iniquity, and between the two ways there is a great difference."[14] This version of the Two Ways teaching is very similar to that which the framers of the *Didache* used when writing the first chapter. But there is one notable difference between this "original" version and the final product. *Didache* 1.1 reads, "There are two ways: one of life and one of death, and there is a great difference between these two ways."[15] What is to be noted here is the absence of the two controlling angels. It is clear that the description of these two figures was deliberately snipped out.

What this bit of editing tells us is that even though the framers of the *Didache* embraced the idea of the Two Ways, they did not believe that the fates of women and men were predetermined. In other words, they believed in free will.[16] Tom O'Loughlin notes that in the *Didache* "there is no place . . . for cosmic fatalism such as the notion that our destiny is written in the stars. In this vision our destiny is in our own hands: we must positively choose good and deliberately avoid evil."[17] The Two Ways represent the life-and-death decisions that men and women must make. The path that any individual walks upon is a matter of free choice, not the predetermination of God. Men and women are not under the power of an angel of light who controls their right conduct, nor are they under the power of a dark angel who compels them to do evil. God does not predetermine the fate of each person on earth. He

---

14. Ibid., 128.
15. Holmes translation.
16. On this point most scholars agree. See also John Kloppenburg, "The Transformation of Moral Exhortation in Didache 1–5," in *The Didache in Context: Essays on Its Text, History and Transmission*, ed. Clayton N. Jefford (Leiden: Brill, 1995), 88–109.
17. O'Loughlin, *Didache*, 30. See also Sandt and Flusser, *Didache*, 141–52.

invites all to choose the path of life and desires that no one would walk on the path of death.

Thus, the followers of the *Didache* understood the doing of God's will as a matter of free will. They might say, "Do God's will by walking on the path of life, or reject God's will by walking on the path of death." How to walk on the way of life is made clear in the first four chapters: love God; love others; bless those who curse you, pray for your enemies; give to whoever asks of you, and so on. What it looks like to walk on the way of death is made clear in the fifth chapter: cursing, murder, adultery, lust, robbery, fornication, and so on. The entire premise of the *Didache* is that God's will has been made clear to all, and everyone must choose which path to walk.

When the followers of the *Didache* prayed "let your will be done," they were praying for themselves and for all humanity. This is a request for assistance: *help us, and all people, to choose your will. Help us to walk on the path of life.* These disciples acknowledged that obedience was difficult. The world was a hostile place. Being a Christian meant being persecuted and hated, abused and exploited (see *Did.* 1.3–4). They were taught that a time of testing was coming when there would be a great falling away fueled by betrayal and a concentrated effort to destroy the faith (see *Did.* 16). "Let your will be done" was the church's way of crying to God, "Help us to be faithful to you."

Before we close the discussion on this petition, we must mention one more aspect of doing God's will. The *Didache* describes the ways of life and death as unambiguous declarations of what is morally right and wrong. Because these paths are clearly revealed, the doing of God's will is also revealed. But the *Didache* also acknowledges the fact that sometimes the will of God is not clear to the disciple. Not every decision in life comes down to a choice between the paths of life and death. Not every decision affecting us is under our control. When the disciple doesn't know which way is best or doesn't have control over the decisions of others, "let your will be done" is an invitation for God to intervene in our circumstances and direct our path according to his desires. "Let your will be done" is a means of submitting one's own preferences and choices to God, acknowledging the human incapacity to make right choices in every situation. This petition asks God "to have his way."

It is for this reason that *Didache* 3.10 states, "Accept as good the things that happen to you, knowing that nothing transpires apart from God" (Holmes trans.). This is to say: *Once you have prayed and asked God for the doing of his will, you can be confident that God will act according to his purposes. Accept and be at peace with whatever happens.* When the path before them was unclear, the followers of the *Didache* could pray "let your will be done" and then trust that God would move. To accept whatever happens in the knowledge that "nothing transpires apart from God" was the proper response of a person who had prayed and entrusted his or her path to God. The authors of the *Didache* wanted their followers to know that they could be secure in God's response to their request for the doing of his will.[18]

In sum, the petition "let your will be done" was a way of saying, "Help us, and all humanity, to know and to choose the path of life." It reinforced their personal commitment to righteousness, even as they acknowledged their need for God's assistance. It was also an act of surrender—a way of releasing their choices, preferences, and understanding—to the will of the Father. Amid the chaos of daily life, the good way—the right way—was not always easy to follow or discern. They believed that the ultimate responsibility for their choices was theirs, but they sought to exercise their freedom in a spirit of dependence and submission to their heavenly Father.

---

18. An alternative way of interpreting *Did.* 3.10 ("Accept as good the things that happen to you, knowing that nothing transpires apart from God") would be to explain this verse deterministically. That is: *whatever happens in your life is God's will, so accept it.*

The aphorism this verse repeats appears in various texts. In many non-Christian writings, it did have a more deterministic meaning. Niederwimmer cites the following examples: Cleanthes's Hymn to Zeus declares, "No work on earth takes place without you, O deity" (SVF 1.122.11); the Roman philosopher Seneca argued, "It is best to suffer what you cannot change, and commit yourself to god, who is the author of all things, without complaint" (*Epistulae Morales* 107.9); and the Dead Sea Scrolls say, "All that is, he governs according to his plan, and without him nothing occurs" (1QS 11.11) (Kurt Niederwimmer, *The Didache: A Commentary*, ed. Harold W. Attridge, trans. Linda M. Maloney [Minneapolis: Fortress, 1998], 102).

We have seen that the *Didache* has sided against this type of fatalism. It would be difficult to explain the purpose of *asking* God to do his will if our prayers can't make a difference either way.

On Earth as It Is in Heaven

One thing that becomes very clear to any reader of the *Didache* is that these Christians did not have a very positive image of the world. Even though this document is relatively short, it probably tells us more about the types of sin being committed in the first century than any other text from the period. Among the transgressions listed in chapters 2–3 and 5 are murder, adultery, pedophilia, sexual immorality, theft, divination, magic, abortion, infanticide, perjury, lying, speaking evil, holding grudges, fickleness, deceit, avarice, greed, hypocrisy, spite, disdain, evil plotting, hatred, anger, being argumentative, jealousy, lust, obscene speech, a roaming eye, astrology, vanity, grumbling, blasphemy, arrogance, bad-mindedness, and haughtiness. The world was full of people who persecuted the righteous, hated the truth, loved lies, committed themselves to evil, loved worthless things, had no mercy for the poor, murdered children, corrupted creation, oppressed the afflicted, and sided with the wealthy instead of the poor. In sum, it was not a good place.

For the followers of the *Didache*, there did not seem much hope for global transformation in the present age. These Christians were among those who set their hope on the "end-time" intervention of God. As part of their regular prayers, they would cry out, "Maranatha" and "May grace come and may this world pass away" (*Did.* 10.6). As we have mentioned above, *Didache* 16 speaks of a coming time when the entire earth would be delivered into the hands of "the deceiver of the world." This man would appear as a "Son of God," but he would commit abominations unlike those ever seen before. All of the earth would be put to the test, and many would fall away and die. This terrible tribulation would only to come to an end when the Lord himself returned on the clouds of heaven.

The followers of the *Didache* viewed their program of discipleship as a way of preparing themselves for the coming test. They did not want to be caught unprepared. They were instructed to gather frequently and build one another up in the awareness that "all the time you have believed will be of no use to you if you are not found perfect in the last time" (*Did.* 16:2, Holmes).

For these Christians who believed that they were living in the "last days," the expression "on earth as it is in heaven" expressed an eschatological hope. In the Lord's Prayer they prayed for the honoring of God's name, for the coming of his kingdom, and the doing of his will. They believed that in their own midst, these things could all be a present reality. But because the world was on the brink of falling into chaos and evil, they did not seem to think that their hopes would be universally fulfilled prior to the return of Christ. They put no limitations on what God could do among them. In this sense, all of the "end time" promises were already being fulfilled. They were the heirs of all that God had promised to Israel. Knowledge, faith, and immortality had been given to them through Jesus. The way of life showed them how to live in a way that was righteous and pleasing to God. Yet at the same time, they seemed to have little hope for the world as a whole. It was on a path toward destruction. Thus, even as they prayed for all humanity to honor God's name, receive his kingdom, and do his will, there was no expectation that this would ever happen on a large scale before the return of Jesus. The community seemed to take a more defensive posture. Their orientation was directed more toward the preservation of their own sanctity in a hostile world and less toward its transformation.

Daily Bread

Throughout the history of the Lord's Prayer, "give us this day our daily bread" is the one petition that seems to produce the most embarrassment. Many theologians have thought it "unspiritual" to ask God for material things in such a direct manner, and they consequently tended to "spiritualize" the meaning of bread. This is seen, for example, in the writings of the third-century theologian Origen, who thought it would be uncharacteristic for a prayer dealing with "heavenly and great matters" to occupy itself with something so "earthly and petty" as real bread. In his view, the only true bread could be Jesus himself.[19]

The followers of the *Didache* weren't quite as extreme as Origen, but they did have the tendency to distinguish between "material bread" and "spiritual bread." It is very clear which one was more important. In their communion prayer, for example, they said, "You, almighty Master, created all things for your name's sake, and gave food and drink to humans to enjoy, so that they might give you thanks; but to us you have graciously given spiritual food and drink, and eternal life through your servant" (*Did.* 10.3). There is a general provision of material food and drink to all of humanity. But this blessing is inferior to the greater gift of the "spiritual food and drink" that they had received through Jesus.

We have mentioned above that for the followers of the *Didache*, any blessing they had received brought with it certain responsibilities. In their minds, if they had received the superior blessing of "spiritual bread," then there should be no hesitation to share with anyone and everyone the material bread that they had also received. *Didache* 4.8 declares, "You shall not turn away from someone in need, but shall share everything with 'our brother or sister, and do not claim that anything is your own. For if you are sharers in what is imperishable, how much more so in perishable things!"

This responsibility to share extended beyond the family of faith: "Give to everyone who asks you, and do not demand it back, for the Father wants something from his own gifts to be given to everyone."[20] Although these guidelines do not ignore the possibility for abuse, the fundamental teaching is that the members of the community should view all of the material blessings they had personally received as God's way of providing for all. In other words, they were just the conduits through which God blessed others.

In this light, "give us this day our daily bread" was a way of asking

---

19. See Allistair Stewart-Sykes, *Tertullian, Cyprian, Origen: On the Lord's Prayer* (Crestwood, NY: St. Vladimir's Seminary Press, 2004), 175–86.
20. *Didache* 1.5. Additionally, *Did.* 5–8 sets forth principles for dealing with the materially disadvantaged, and chaps. 11–13 provide guidelines for visitors in need of assistance.

God to provide for anyone and everyone who had need. Whatever God provided for the group was for all to share. The members of these communities knew that when they had personal needs, their brothers and sisters would be looking out for them. At the same time, they knew that any material provision they had personally received was not theirs to claim. They had to be attentive to the needs of those around them.

In sum, what we thus see in the *Didache* is a tendency to distinguish between "spiritual" and "material" bread. There is no embarrassment about asking God for material provision. They viewed "daily bread" as *real* bread, or any other material need that they might have. The way they avoided any perception of materialism or selfishness in this request was by standing firm in their commitment to share with others.

Forgiveness

The followers of the *Didache* took confession and forgiveness very seriously. Each day, as part of the Lord's Prayer, they prayed, "Forgive us our debt as we also forgive our debtors." This was one among many spiritual disciplines they practiced in relation to confession and forgiveness. Peace and reconciliation were among the most important values they had.

As we have stressed throughout this chapter, these Christians viewed the world as a fundamentally chaotic place. Outside of the church, people lived in hatred and strife. And within the church, their social and cultural diversity might ignite a conflict at any time. It is for this reason that the *Didache* contains numerous instructions on how to maintain peace.

First, the *Didache* teaches that having enemies is a matter of personal choice. People become enemies when they choose to hate one another. But if one party chooses not to hate, then the enmity dies. The text states, "But you must love those who hate you, and you will not have an enemy" (*Did.* 1.3, Holmes). The simple choice to love and forgive anyone and everyone gives us all the opportunity to live without enemies.

The text is rich with advice on how to live in peace with others. "If someone strikes your left cheek, then turn the right cheek towards him also, and you will be perfect"; "you should be patient and merciful and without guile and quiet"; "do not be someone who creates factions, rather work for reconciliation between parties" (*Did.* 1.4; 3.8; 4.3). The underlying idea in all of these verses is that strife can only be perpetuated by two or more willing parties. When one person (or group) will not hold onto their anger or bitterness, the conflict comes to an end.

Along with this willingness to forgive others, the text instructs its followers to regularly confess their sins. This might occur in formal or informal settings. *Didache* 4.14 states, "You should acknowledge your transgressions in the church; and you should not set out on your prayers when you have a bad conscience." What this passage seems to describe is not a formal ritual but personal confession between members of the community. Another, more structured ritual of confession occurred on the Lord's Day:

> On the day which is the Day of the Lord gather together for the breaking of the loaf and giving thanks. However, you should first confess your sins so that your sacrifice may be a pure one; and do not let anyone who is having a dispute with a neighbor join until they are reconciled so that your sacrifice may not be impure. For this is the sacrifice about which the Lord has said: "In every place and time let a pure sacrifice be offered to me, for I am the great king, says the Lord, and my name is feared among the nations." (*Did.* 14:1–3)

What is seen here is that these fellowships viewed their worship as a form of spiritual sacrifice. As the reference to Malachi 1:11 makes clear, they believed that their offerings had to be pure. Any unconfessed sin would contaminate the sacrifice. For this reason, the community had to be vigilant with regard to conflicts in their midst. Members of the church who had not reconciled were not allowed to participate in communion. Furthermore, if there were any members of the group who refused to repent of a known sin, they were to be shunned. *Didache*

15.3 states, "And when someone does wrong against his neighbor, let no one speak to him, indeed he is not to hear anything from you until he repents."

As these fellowships navigated the tension between order and chaos, confession and forgiveness were essential to maintaining order. Thus, when they prayed "forgive us our debt, as we also forgive our debtors," they were affirming what were already the foundational values of the community. This petition reminded them each day that there was chaos crouching at the doorway. The only way to keep it out was to confess their sins and release those who had offended them.

Testing and Evil

When the *Didache* talks about the idea of evil, the emphasis is on the choices that people make. We have noted above that earlier versions of the Two Ways teaching (upon which *Did.* 1–6 is based) depicted an evil spirit governing over the lives of the wicked, driving them to sin. The *Didache* strenuously avoids the doctrine that moral choices are beyond the control of the individuals making them. The foundation of the entire discipleship program is that every human being is given a free will. Every person has the ability to choose right and wrong. To choose the good is life. To choose sin is death. It is on this basis that they defined their idea of evil. "But the way of death is this: first of all, it is evil" (*Did.* 5.1, Holmes).

Whereas the followers of the *Didache* did believe in Satan and unclean spirits, evil had no power over those who made the choice to reject it. The text instructs its readers to "flee from evil of every kind and from anything resembling it" (*Did.* 3.1, Holmes). To resist and overcome evil was to attain the wholeness and purity to which they were called. In their communion prayers, the church asked God "to deliver it from all evil and to make it perfect in your love" (*Did.* 10.5, Holmes). This perfection was something that they must obtain through their daily choice to walk on the path of life. Yet they could not do this alone. The petition "deliver us from evil" constituted an honest recognition of their own inclination to sin and their desperate desire for God's help. It was their way of saying: *help us to make right choices.*[21]

Resisting evil was a daily task in a world full of sin and sinners. But as we have mentioned above, these Christians also believed that a time would come when this testing would intensify. Chapter 16 describes a coming time of tribulation: "Then all humankind will come to the fiery test, and many will fall away and perish; but those who endure in their faith will be saved by the accursed one himself" (*Did.* 16.5, Holmes). When they prayed "lead us into temptation," they were not asking for exemption from the coming time of tribulation. They knew that it was inevitable. Rather, this was a petition for God to help them persevere in the coming trial.[22]

The fact that the followers of the *Didache* lived in anticipation of the coming tribulation is not to say that the petition "lead us not into temptation" had an exclusively futuristic meaning. It had a present application as well. Many modern theologians who describe the Lord's Prayer as an "eschatological prayer" argue that for the early church, each petition of the Lord's Prayer had an exclusively futuristic fulfillment: the kingdom was a future kingdom; forgiveness was to be granted on judgment day; testing referred only to end-time tribulation; and so on. In this interpretation, the Lord's Prayer would essentially be a prayer asking Jesus to come back soon.[23]

---

21. We should note here that in the Greek, *alla hrysai hēmas apo tou ponerou,* can translate "deliver us from evil" or "deliver us from the evil one." I am here arguing that the former understanding is more suitable to the mindset of the *Didache*.

22. E. F. Scott compares this petition of the Lord's Prayer to an ancient Jewish prayer that reads, "Give me a portion of thy Law and lead my feet into the power of thy commandment, and lead not my feet into the power of a transgression. Bring me not into the power of a sin, nor into the power of a temptation, nor into the power of evil" (E. F. Scott, *The Lord's Prayer: Its Character, Purpose and Interpretation* [New York: Charles Scribner's Sons, 1951], 49).

23. Aaron Milavec is one scholar among many who argues for an eschatological interpretation of the Lord's Prayer. In defense of his interpretation, he makes much of the aorist subjunctive that is used throughout the prayer. Milavec notes:

> The aorist tense is reserved for 'one-time' events. Linguistically, therefore, just as the calling for the sanctification of the name and the arrival of the kingdom are one-time events, so, too, asking for the loaf using the aorist imperative presupposes that it will be given only once. All six petitions of the Lord's Prayer are framed in the aorist imperative. All six, therefore, anticipate a one-time fulfillment. The kingdom comes once. The loaf is given once. Our debt is forgiven once. We are preserved from failing 'in the trial' once. (*Didache*, 329).

I disagree with this assessment and find the argument from the Greek grammar particularly weak. Stagg notes, "The fallacy of 'theology in the aorist tense' stubbornly persists, even in the writings

When the followers of the Didache prayed the Lord's Prayer, they thought about both the present and the future. They believed in a coming season of testing, but they also had to learn how to resist temptation and evil in the present time. The wanted to make it through the future tribulation, and they prayed for the strength to do that. But they could only resist evil *then* if they could resist it *now*. Thus we do not see in this petition (as in all petitions of the Lord's Prayer) a choice between a present or futuristic interpretation. It entails both.

The Final Doxology

Many Christians are unaware of the fact that the traditional ending of the Lord's Prayer, "For yours is the kingdom and the power and the glory, forever and ever, amen," is not found in the oldest and most reliable manuscripts of Matthew's Gospel.[24] Matthew's original version of the Lord's Prayer simply ended with "Deliver us from evil." Luke's version of the Lord's Prayer (11:1–2) also ends without this doxology. It thus seems likely the Lord's Prayer, as taught by Jesus, simply ended with the words "deliver us from evil."

That said, the addition of a concluding doxology is very old, dating back to the first century, as the *Didache* bears witness. In the *Didache* the Lord's Prayer concludes with the words "for yours is the power and the glory forever." The history of this and other similar doxologies is thought to have its beginning in the prayer that David prayed in 1 Chronicles 29:11: "Yours, O Lord, is the greatness and the power and the glory and the victory and the majesty, for all that is in the heavens

---

of distinguished scholars." It is commonly understood that the aorist refers to "punctiliar" action. He clarifies that this tense is to be understood as "a-oristic," i.e., undetermined or undefined (Frank Stagg, "The Abused Aorist," *Journal of Biblical Literature* 91, no. 2 [1972], 222–23).

Thus, the presence of the aorist in the Lord's Prayer does not signify that such action occurs *once and only once*. The aorist imperative appears in the *Didache* eleven times outside the Lord's Prayer. On three occasions, a reasonable case may be made for an eschatological, singular action: "may your church be *gathered*" (*Did.* 9.4); "may grace *come*" and "may this world *pass away*" (*Did.* 10.6). In the other eight appearances, however, there is no implication that the these events occur once and only once, nor that they are futuristic: "let your gift *sweat*" (*Did.* 1.6); "*fast*" (*Did.* 7.4); "let no one *eat* or *drink*" (*Did.* 9.5); let apostles and everyone "*be welcomed*" (*Did.* 11.4; 12.1); "*earn his keep*" (*Did.* 12.3); and "let no one *join*" (*Did.* 14.2).

24. In that form, this doxology doesn't appear in Matthew's text until copies dating from the fourth and fifth century. See Bruce Metzger, *A Textual Commentary on the Greek New Testament* (Stuttgart: Deutsche Bibelgesellschaft, 2002), 13–14.

and in the earth is yours. Yours is the kingdom, O Lord, and you are exalted as head above all." Similar declarations are interspersed throughout the prayers of the *Didache*. These Christians would frequently punctuate their prayers with exclamations such as, "to you be the glory forever"; "for yours is the glory and the power through Jesus Christ forever"; and "for yours is the power and the glory forever" (see *Did.* 9.2–3; 10.2, 4–5). Even as these declarations were part of the formal, liturgical prayers, there is reason to believe that they would also be proclaimed spontaneously. Christians from a variety of traditions today will often support their prayer leader with proclamations such as "amen," or "yes, Lord," or "hear our prayer." For early Christians, "to you be the glory forever" (or similar declarations) served this same purpose.

In this light, it is quite possible that when the followers of the *Didache* prayed the Lord's Prayer, they didn't just recite it from start to finish, as it is recorded in the text. Rather, it may be that the seven petitions of the Lord's Prayer served as a template for a prayer *session* that contained both structured and spontaneous elements. Each petition introduced a theme upon which the participants in the prayer were free to amplify. "For yours is the power and the glory forever" would have served as a marker between each of the petitions.

What we learn here is that the followers of the *Didache* weren't locked into a single structure. There were times when they might just say the "short version" exactly as it was written. But the inclusion of the doxology here and in other prayers indicates that they were also using the Lord's Prayer as a template for longer, more spontaneous prayers. Freedom in the Spirit was an important value, and they could experience this with the Lord's Prayer.

Conclusion

As we conclude our reflections on the interpretation of the Lord's Prayer in the *Didache*, I am reminded once again of the similarities between these ancient fellowships and my experience in Youth with a Mission. One night many years ago, just as I was embarking on my journey with YWAM, I had a dream. I saw myself on a raft peacefully floating down a river. Suddenly the curl of a massive wave was hanging over my head, and I cringed in expectation its imminent collapse. But in this dream, the curl of the wave never fell. It just hung over my head. And then (as it happens with all dreams) I woke up.

I've always thought of this dream as having a somewhat prophetic quality. There have been many moments over the years when I've felt that everything was about to come crashing down. And yet somehow, in each situation, the pending doom that I anticipated never materialized. Somehow, some way, in the midst of all our chaos and dysfunction, we managed to "keep on keepin' on."

As I have studied the *Didache*, I can't help but to think that these Christians had a similar experience. With the potential for so much disagreement from within and so much pressure from outside, there were surely moments when they felt that everything was about to fall apart. Yet somehow they persevered. Their success was due to the genius of their discipleship strategy. The leaders of these communities realized that maintaining the tension between order and chaos was an art. People could tolerate a certain degree of chaos if their hope remained set on a coming time of order. Theirs was a spirituality of the road. There was a willingness to persevere along the difficult path of life as long as they knew that arrival at the final destination would bring the peace and wholeness for which they longed.

The Lord's Prayer played a crucial role in keeping these communities on the way of life. This prayer recognizes the realities of the Christian life: we sin against each other, stumble, make bad choices, and tend to think about ourselves before others. The Lord's Prayer does not ignore the chaos. And yet the Lord's Prayer also points toward order: when we forgive each other, pray together, and ask for God's help to live lives that please him, we can push back the forces of chaos and experience unity and peace. It speaks of the coming day when the Father's name will be honored by all, his kingdom will be established on earth, and all humanity will live in submission to his will.

The Lord's Prayer was effective because it is a prayer that reveals humanity's deep dependence on God. For the followers of the *Didache*, the Lord's Prayer was not a *self-fulfilling* text. God's name was not honored simply by the simple recitation "hallowed by your name." God's will wasn't accomplished by merely mouthing the words "let your will be done." Daily bread wasn't disbursed by the magical formula "Give us this day. . . ." For these believers, every petition of the Lord's Prayer spoke of an action they must take. They had to make the choices that honored the Father's name and fulfilled his will. Daily bread was given to all only when they made the decision to share with one another. Nothing in the Lord's Prayer could be fulfilled apart from their right choices, and no right choice could be made apart from the help of God.

5

Luke on Prayer

August 24 of the year 79 CE began as just another ordinary day for
the people of Pompeii. As the sun rose, household slaves set about
their chores, tradesmen opened shop, and small children were taken
off to school. After several hours of work and the mid-day meal, most
of the upper class passed the heat of the day with a brief siesta. They
were just making their way to the baths when, all of a sudden, it
happened. Without warning, Mount Vesuvius exploded. As the massive
black cloud that hung over the city began to rain down debris, many
tried to take refuge in their homes. Others decided to run for the fields.
But there was nowhere they could hide, and no place to which they
could escape. Over the next eighteen hours, as the volcano continued
to surge, ten thousand people were slowly buried under twenty feet of
ash and pumice.[1]

For seventeen hundred years the city rested in silence, the
commotion of its activities frozen in time. Then, as if by chance, a

------

1. My description is drawn from the following sources: Bruce Longenecker, *The Crosses of Pompeii:
Jesus Devotion in a Vesuvian Town* (Minneapolis: Fortress, 2016); Enrica D'Orta, *How to Visit Pompeii:
Guide to the Excavations with a General Plan* (Pompeii: Falanga Edizioni Pompeiane, 2006); Phillip
Matyszak, *Ancient Rome on Five Denarii a Day* (London: Thames & Hudson, 2007); and *Pompeii: The
Last Day,* dir. Peter Nicholson, 2003, DVD.

construction crew digging a tunnel happened upon an inscription. As they continued to scrape away the rock, it soon dawned upon them that a lost and forgotten city had been found. A flurry of archeological excavations soon followed, and by the mid-nineteenth century, the people of Pompeii had emerged from their stony graves.

Modern visitors to Pompeii are afforded a glimpse unlike any other of what the ancient world looked like. We walk past the market stalls where vendors once sold their goods. At street intersections we are careful to walk on the elevated stones that once saved the sandaled feet of Pompeii's inhabitants from the raw sewage and muck below. We stroll past the Temple of Jupiter, the public saunas, the brothel, the laundry, and the training compound of the gladiators. What most brings this city to life, however, is the graffiti. Scrawled on walls and columns, it is here that we hear the voices of the ordinary people of Pompeii. Some of it is advertising: "Twenty pairs of gladiators provided by Quintus Monnius Rufus are to fight at Nola May First, Second, and Third, and there will be a hunt"; or, "Inn for rent. Triclinium [dining room] with three couches." Some of it is political: "Vesonius Primus urges the election of Gnaeus Helvius as Aedile, a man worthy of public office"; or, "The worshipers of Isis as a body ask for the election of Gnaeus Helvias Sabinus as Aedile." Other inscriptions are mocking: "The sneak thieves request the election of Vatia as Aedile"; and, "The whole company of late risers favor Vatia." There is philosophy: "the smallest evil if neglected, will reach the greatest proportions"; and even awkward romance: "Health to you, Victoria, and wherever you are may you sneeze sweetly."[2]

But among the most enigmatic of the inscriptions found at Pompeii is what has come to be known as the "Rotas Square." This particular graffito was first discovered in 1925 in the house of Paquius Proculus, and then again in 1936, scratched on a pillar in the public area known as the Grand Palaestra. It was written as follows:

2. Taken from *Readings in Ancient History: Illustrative Extracts from the Sources*, ed. William Davis (Boston: Allyn and Bacon, 1912–13), 2:260–65.

```
R   O   T   A   S

O   P   E   R   A

T   E   N   E   T

A   R   E   P   O

S   A   T   O   R
```

Archeologists had seen this particular configuration of letters (known as a palindrome) in several places before, from Turkey to Egypt to Great Britain. But its appearance at Pompeii was by far the most ancient. So what does it mean?

Over the years scholars have made attempt at various explanations. Some have tried to make sense of the Latin, but to no to avail. Others have looked to Jewish Kabbalism or astrology for answers. But one of the oldest and most plausible explanations is that the Rotas Square was a secret symbol designed to identify the presence of Christians. German scholars Grosser and Agrell discovered that the twenty-five letters of this palindrome could be configured in the shape of a cross, reading *Pater Noster* ("Our Father") on the horizontal and vertical axes. Two remaining letters, "A A" and "O O," correspond to a Greek title for Jesus, "Alpha and Omega."[3] The result looks like this:

```
                    P

                    A

        A           T           O

                    E

                    R

P   A   T   E   R   N   O   S   T   E   R

                    O

                    S

        A           T           O

                    E

                    R
```

3. See Carlo Giordano and Isidoro Kahn, *The Jews in Pompeii, Herculaneum, Stabiae and in the Cities of Campania Felix* (Rome: Bardi Editore, 2001), 75–83.

For many years there has been great skepticism concerning the suggestion that there were Christians at Pompeii. Whereas it was acknowledged that this symbol had some religious significance, many scholars doubted that Christianity could have spread so far so soon. Recent studies, however, have made it all but certain that as the gospel was taking hold across the Mediterranean, Christians were among the many victims of Mount Vesuvius' eruption.[4]

As a mere artifact demonstrating the presence of Christianity in Pompeii, the Rotas Square is of enormous value. But what we find even more fascinating is the content of this symbol. "Pater Noster" is a Latin title for the Lord's Prayer. What this means is that just as the written Gospels of Matthew and Luke were being circulated throughout the Roman Empire, the Lord's Prayer was becoming a central symbol of the Christian faith.[5] It was by this prayer that Christians encapsulated their beliefs, and it was by this prayer that they made themselves known to one another.

Perhaps the first New Testament author to recognize the power of the Lord's Prayer as a universal symbol of the Christian faith was Luke. As he wrote his Gospel and the book of Acts, it was Christians just like those in Pompeii whom he had in mind. Luke understood that the time had come to "translate" the story of Jesus for Greco-Roman culture. The teachings and parables of Jesus, the symbolism of his sacrifice, and his resurrection had all begun as the "intellectual property" of the Jewish people. The Jews understood the metaphors and the meaning of the prophecies. But Pacquius Proculus, living with his family off of the via dell'Abbondanza in Pompeii, might not have understood what was meant by Jesus as the "Passover Lamb" or the "shoot of Jesse." We may imagine that his fundamental aspirations consisted of the forgiveness of his sins and protection against the evil spirits that had harassed him

---

4. See Longenecker, *Crosses of Pompeii*.
5. It would seem that the Christians in Pompeii knew the Lord's Prayer even before Luke's Gospel arrived there. Note that Luke's prayer in Latin begins simply with "Pater."

all of his life.[6] He had come to believe in Jesus, and for him the Lord's Prayer was the summary of everything he needed to know.[7]

As we now study the Lord's Prayer within Luke's writings, we will think of Luke-Acts as a two-part stage drama. The theater audience consists mostly of gentiles. We know that the playwright was keenly aware of those who would be coming to the show and we understand that he presents his story in a way that makes sense to them. There will be many characters with whom they can identify, who speak in terms that they understand.

As we study this stage drama, we will pay attention to the playwright's use of backdrops. We know that the background scenarios in a play have an enormous impact on how the action at the front of the stage is interpreted. (For example, a young couple locked in an embrace, set against the backdrop of a sunny blue sky creates one impression; the same couple embracing against the backdrop of dark and stormy clouds creates another.) As a historian retelling the story of Jesus and the early church, Luke did not necessarily determine what was happening at the front of the stage. But as a creative interpreter of the events that he recounted, his use of backdrops gave him the opportunity to shape the way that those stories affected his audience.

The backdrops that we will study in Luke's writings do not concern the physical settings in which events take place. Rather, our focus will be on thematic backdrops. There are recurring motifs, key words, ideas, and actions that appear again and again. There is a worldview—a certain understanding of how life works—behind his story. By various means, Luke shaped the presentation of his narrative so that his audience would interpret the world in the same way he did. The use of these thematic backdrops was a mechanism that Luke employed to craft the story according to his own unique agenda. Thus, even though both Luke and Matthew contain the Lord's Prayer, it is only when

---

6. For a discussion on cultural concepts of protection from evil spirits in Pompeii and the implications for the Christians who may have lived there, see Longenecker, *Crosses of Pompeii*, 133–44.

7. I should note that I am making a liberal association between Pacquius Proculus and Christianity. Whereas the Rotas Square was indeed found written on a wall in his home, it cannot be established with certainty that he and his family were Christians.

we study the thematic backgrounds each author placed behind this prayer that we understand exactly what each man wanted to say. To be sure, in some ways the prayer meant the same thing to both of them. But because Luke was writing to a different audience than Matthew's, and because he had different theological priorities, what he wanted to communicate through this prayer was, in many ways, unique.[8]

One of the most pervasive themes in Luke-Acts is prayer. Thus, we will imagine in the backdrop of every scene a banner in bold letters reading "Pray!" Luke firmly believed that the advance of the kingdom of God on earth was fueled by prayer, and he did everything in his power to persuade his readers that they must never stop calling on God to act. Luke wrote at a time when Christians were starting to feel discouraged. Some were losing heart about the fact that Jesus hadn't returned as soon as they had thought. Consequently their vision for the continuing expansion of the church was starting to falter. Luke needed to persuade them that the "glory days" of the Christian movement were far from over. There was still a tremendous amount of work to be done, and it was only through prayer that the gospel would continue to expand.

The Lord's Prayer played a key role in the fulfillment of Luke's theological agenda. He gave a tight, concise, no-nonsense version of

---

8. There is an entire field of biblical studies devoted to the comparison of the three "Synoptic" Gospels: Matthew, Mark, and Luke. These Gospel accounts tell many of same stories and record many of the same teachings, but each author managed to shape the meaning of the story according to his own purposes. So, for example, Matthew presented Jesus as teaching the Lord's Prayer as part of the Sermon on the Mount (Matt 6:9–11), whereas Luke set the teaching of the Lord's Prayer within a completely different context. In his presentation, Jesus had just spent the night praying, and upon returning, his disciples asked him to teach them how to pray (Luke 11:1–4). Matthew and Luke each had different goals that they wanted to accomplish with the teaching on this prayer, and the way they framed its presentation was aligned with those objectives.

There are diverse possibilities as to why the accounts between Matthew and Luke are different. Strictly speaking, it may be possible that both accounts happened just as the authors describe. Another possibility is that one (or both) Gospel authors created the setting for the presentation of this prayer. Whereas modern historians might object to this type of augmented reality, by the standards of the first century, such a practice was acceptable. The fact that each Gospel author framed the story in his own way should not be interpreted as a "contradiction" between accounts. Rather, we simply accept that each author interpreted the story of Jesus in a different way. Each author had different priorities as to what he wanted his audience to take away. For a good discussion on this issue, particularly as it relates to Luke, see I. Howard Marshall, *Luke: Historian and Theologian* (Exeter: Paternoster, 1970), 21–76.

this text. In contrast to the Jewish interpreters that had gone before him, he had less concern for narrative theology, spiritual cosmology, or discipleship in community. For him, the Lord's Prayer was all about one thing: the advancement of the gospel to the ends of the earth. If Christians would commit themselves to pray the Lord's Prayer and put into practice, the kingdom of God would continue its advance upon the earth. It was that simple.

As we now enter into the stage drama of Luke-Acts, various details of the production will call for our focused attention. We will pay close attention to the clues that confirm our thesis regarding a Greco-Roman audience. And we will thoroughly explore the thematic backdrops against which his story unfolds. Our analysis is divided into three sections. First, we will evaluate the clues that reveal Luke's target audience. Second, we will look at Luke's "theological agenda." And finally, we will look at Luke's interpretation of the Lord's Prayer.

Luke's Audience

There are many books of the New Testament that clearly state for whom they were written and why. For example, we have two letters that Paul wrote to the church in Corinth, and in each he discusses many of the details surrounding his occasion for writing. The dual work of Luke-Acts is a bit different in this regard. On the surface, Luke wrote to a person named "Theophilus" because it "seemed good" for him to do so. His aim was that this mysterious figure might "have certainty" concerning the things that he had been taught (see Luke 1:1–3). Few scholars believe, however, that Luke would go to all that work for just one person. Theophilus may have been a real or fictional character—but it is generally agreed that Luke had a much larger audience in mind. The question is, who?

In order to discover who Luke's intended audience was, we need to do a bit of detective work. He doesn't plainly tell us who they are, but there are many clues to be found throughout Luke-Acts. Some of these are helpful in the process of elimination, by which we can identify who he was *not* writing to. Others give us a clear hint about the people that he *did* have in mind. We will look at some of these clues in succession.

Clue 1: He was not writing to Aramaic speakers. To illuminate how we know this, I will provide an illustration: when I lived in a Mayan village in southeastern Mexico, most of my neighbors spoke both Spanish and Mayan. I didn't understand "pure" Mayan, but I soon learned that even when communicating in Spanish, several Mayan words found their way into the mix. Most of these terms were related to body parts and food (don't ask me why). A navel was not an *ombligo* (Spanish) but a *tuuch*. The armpit was not a *sobaco* but a *sheek*. A curly-haired kid was *moolish* (not *risado*), and my favorite dish was called *poke-chuuk* (not *carne al carbon*). Anyone who lives in a small town in the Yucatan is obligated to learn this kind of Mayanized Spanish.

The same thing happened in first-century Israel. People understood Greek, but when they spoke it, they tended to sprinkle in a bit of Aramaic. For example, Jesus said, "Anyone who says to his brother, 'Raca,' is answerable to the Sanhedrin" (Matt 5:22). Mark, telling the story of a healing, wrote, "Taking her by the hand he said to her, 'Talitha cumi'" (Mark 5:41). And both Matthew and Mark had no hesitation in quoting Jesus's cry in Aramaic, "Eli, Eli, lama sabachthani!" (Matt 27:46; Mark 15:34). What the inclusion of these phrases indicates is that their readers understood both Greek and Aramaic. But Luke, for some reason, never included any Aramaic words in his text, even when the sources he was using did.

Clue 2: Luke clipped out of his account many arcane arguments about the Torah that other Gospel writers (Matthew and Mark) chose to include. For example, Matthew 5:21–48 is a lengthy discussion about how Jesus redefines Jewish law, and Mark 7:1–23 describes a tense interaction that Jesus had with the scribes and Pharisees over the traditions of the Jewish elders. Whereas the three "Synoptic" Gospels (Matthew, Mark, and Luke) tend to share a lot of material in common, Luke chose not to include most of this material in his text.

Clue 3: Luke generally assumed that his readers were unfamiliar with the geography of Israel. It was for this reason that he included references that people living in Palestine would have found unnecessary, such as the remark that the "city of David" is Bethlehem (Luke 2:4) or that Gerasenes is across from Galilee (Luke 8:26). He was clearly writing to people who were unfamiliar with the territory in which these events took place.

Clue 4: Luke's use of the Greek language reflects regional vocabulary that was not used in Palestine. For example, in Luke 5:19 he refers to a roof as "tiles" (*keramōn*) even though the structure he describes actually would have been covered in thatch. Or in Luke 8:24, he uses the word *epistata* for "Master." It would have been very unusual for a person living in Israel to use this particular administrative title (*kyrios* and *didaskalos* were more common).

All of this detective work leads to one conclusion: Luke was not writing to a group of people living in small villages along the Sea of Galilee. His readers were gentiles scattered throughout the Roman Empire who were predominantly living in cities. Now one might say, "That's a lot of fuss about a minor point," but this is actually a very significant issue. Wayne Meeks has noted that "within a decade of the crucifixion of Jesus, the village culture of Palestine had been left behind, and the Greco-Roman city became the dominant environment of the Christian movement."[9] This rapid expansion of the Christian faith into the cities of the Roman Empire shapes everything about the way we interpret Luke's works. Understanding the target audience is essential. If I were writing this book for my old friends in the Mayan village of Oxkutzcab, it would be significantly different than a book written for millennials living in Minneapolis. In order to fully understand what Luke said, why he said it, and why he *didn't* say certain things, we must understand the world of the people sitting in the theater.

When we think of Luke's audience, we envision a rapidly expanding group of house churches located within a sophisticated and cultured city somewhere in the Mediterranean region. Much like our cities today, the urban setting was colored by a multiplicity of languages,

---

9. Wayne Meeks, *The First Urban Christians* (New Haven and London: Yale University Press, 1983), 11.

religions, social classes, and levels of education.[10] These Christian house groups were a cross-section of their society: rich and poor, slaves and masters, Jews and gentiles from various ethnicities.[11]

Paquius Proculus of Pompeii was not a fisherman. He didn't own any sheep. He had not grown up reading the Torah. He had never been to Jerusalem. As we imagine him, he was an upper-class Roman who still owned slaves. He and the other men and women of his house church still sat together naked in the public baths, talking about politics.[12] They all knew their Zodiac sign and were trying to figure out how it was that the stars had nothing to do with their future. They still enjoyed a good gladiator show.[13] They held onto many trappings of their culture, and yet were fully committed to following Jesus. They cast out demons and prayed for healing. They were bold in telling others about Jesus. And they saw new people coming to faith every day.

What we must understand is that Christianity in the first-century Roman Empire was something rather different than what we know today. In many ways, Christians were more radical than us, more committed, more willing to share the gospel, and more ready to die for their faith. Yet they were less doctrinally pure. They didn't have the

---

10. Meeks notes, "As a consequence of Rome's entry into the East and her active interest in the Cities, urban society became somewhat more complex than it had been even during the Hellenistic age. For a very long time groups of foreigners had gathered in each city: merchants and artisans following the armies or in search of better markets or better access to transportation, persons enslaved and displaced by war or piracy and now set free, political exiles, soldiers of fortune" (*First Urban Christians*, 13).

11. See Meeks, *First Urban Christians*, 73.

12. In Greco-Roman cities, it was the general custom for men and women (Christians included) to bathe together nude in the public baths. This matter was eventually addressed at the Synod of Laodicea (343–381 CE), where it was decreed, "None of the priesthood, nor clerics [of lower rank] nor ascetics, nor any Christian or layman, shall wash in a bath with women." ("The Seven Ecumenical Councils," in *A Select Library of the Nicene and Post-Nicene Fathers of the Christian Church*, ed. Phillip Schaff and Henry Wace, trans. Henry Percival (New York: Charles Scribner's Sons, 1900), 14:129.

13. Whereas the writings of the church fathers clearly show that attending gladiatorial matches was not acceptable Christian behavior, Tertullian's work *De spectaculis* reveals that many believers still enjoyed a good contest. Trying to persuade them against this custom, he wrote, "And with his eye fixed on the bites of bears, and the sponge-nets of the net-fighters, can he be moved by compassion? May God avert from His people any such passionate eagerness after a cruel enjoyment! For how monstrous it is to go from God's church to the devil's—from the sky to the stye, as they say; to raise your hands to God, and then to weary them in the applause of an actor; out of the mouth, from which you uttered Amen over the Holy Thing, to give witness in a gladiator's favour; to cry 'for ever' to any one else but God and Christ" (Tertullian, "De Spectaculis," in *The Ante-Nicene Fathers*, vol. 3, eds. Alexander Roberts, James Donaldson, and A. Cleveland Coxe, trans. S. Thelwall [Buffalo, NY: Christian Literature Company, 1885], 89–90; henceforth *ANF* 3).

benefit of a complete New Testament, seminaries, creeds, or theology textbooks. They were still in the process of figuring things out. It was these people in particular to whom Luke wrote.

Luke's Agenda

There are many passages in the New Testament that probably gave first-century readers the impression that the end was near. In Matthew 24, for example, Jesus describes a coming time of catastrophe: famines and earthquakes, false prophets, false christs, and signs in the heavens—all to be followed by the appearance of "the Son of Man coming on clouds" (v. 30) to gather the elect. He told his disciples, "Truly, I say to you, this generation will not pass away until all these things take place" (Matt 24:34). Elsewhere, Paul was comfortable referring to himself and other believers as those "on whom the end of the ages has come" (1 Cor 10:11) And he described the return of Jesus as the day when "we who are alive . . . will be caught up . . . in the clouds to meet the Lord in the air" (1 Thess 4:17).[14] In reading passages like these we understand why many Christians in the first century believed that they would be alive to see Christ's return.

Luke seemed to recognize that perhaps the teachings of Jesus needed to be interpreted in a different light. He understood that the thrust of Jesus's teachings regarding the "second coming" (or parousia) was not necessarily that it would be *soon* but rather that it would be *sudden*. He was concerned that an uninformed expectation of the parousia might have two negative consequences: (1) Christians might get discouraged if it didn't happen as soon as they hoped, and (2) they might decide that missionary expansion was no longer necessary because there wasn't time to advance the gospel any further.

It was with these two concerns in mind that Luke carefully crafted his theology for the church and its mission in the world. At the heart of Luke's worldview was the idea that the age of the church had begun with the outpouring of the Holy Spirit. The amazing signs and wonders

---

14. See also Mark 9:1; 13:28–30; Matt 10:23; 1 Thess 1:10; 4:13–18; 1 Cor 7:29–31.

that the apostles had witnessed didn't signal the end of the world. Rather, for Luke, these were the signs of the beginning. The era had now begun when all of the nations living in darkness would have the opportunity to hear about Jesus. In his view, this was not the time for Christians to feel discouraged about the delay of the parousia. To the contrary, it was time for them to take courage and continue in the work that Paul and the apostles had initiated. In Luke's view, the best was yet to come.[15]

Luke's theology of the church and its present mission is progressively developed throughout his Gospel and into the book of Acts. First, we take note of the particular way that he talks about the parousia. As we have mentioned above, other NT writers tended to give their readers the sense that Jesus might come back at any moment. Luke gently reworked this idea in three ways. First, he took the cataclysmic "end of the world" passage of Mark 13 and retooled it to highlight the fact that the events Jesus described there would not happen all at once but rather over an extended period of time (see Luke 21). Second, Luke tended to treat the return of the Lord as a more distant event.[16] And finally, he made it clear that the apocalyptic events described in Joel 2:28–32 were fulfilled on the day of Pentecost, and not at the world's ending.[17]

In Luke's reworked vision of the *last days*, the church became enormously important.[18] Christians everywhere were to be on active

---

15. The champion of this view was a German theologian named Hans Conzelmann. In his classic work *The Theology of Saint Luke* he noted that in Luke's Gospel "the outpouring of the Spirit is no longer itself the start of the Eschaton, but the beginning of a longer epoch, the period of the Church." The Spirit is given to the believers "to exist in the continuing life of the world and in persecution, and He gives the power for missionary endeavor, and for endurance." What results is a change in the understanding of eschatology that "can be seen in the way in which Luke, by his description of history, depicts the nature of the Church, its relation to the world, and the course of the mission in its progress step by step, and in the way which he repeatedly describes the Spirit as power behind this whole process" (Hans Conzelmann, *The Theology of St. Luke* [London: Faber and Faber, 1960], 95–96).

16. See Luke 12:38, 45; 19:11–27; Acts 1:6–8.

17. See Acts 2:14–21. Cf. Conzelmann, *Theology of St. Luke*, 95–136, and James Dunn, *Unity and Diversity in the New Testament* (Philadelphia: Trinity Press International, 1990), 343–48. Although the notion of a near parousia is not altogether removed in Luke-Acts, it is diminished. Holmas notes "the significant number of references suggesting imminence (e.g., Luke 9:27; 12:54–56; 18:7–8; 21:28, 32–33)" (Geir Holmas, *Prayer and Vindication in Luke-Acts: The Theme of Prayer within the Context of the Legitimating and Edifying Objective of the Lukan Narrative* [London: T&T Clark, 2011], 118).

18. Dunn remarks that Luke "was in effect interposing a whole new epoch between the resurrection/

mission. They weren't to be sitting on their hands and killing time. They had work to do. The gospel had to be preached to every nation on earth, and it was their job to make that happen.

Another one of Luke's strategies was to create a sense of progression in the advancement of the gospel. He sought to emphasize, particularly in the book of Acts, the idea of *outward movement*. The gospel had moved from the Jews (the first followers of Jesus) to God-fearers (gentiles like Cornelius, who were discipled by Jews) to the nations. In a similar pattern, the missionary expansion started in Jerusalem, then went to Judea and Samaria, to the outskirts of the Roman Empire, to Rome itself, and then to the ends of the earth.

This theme of progression culminates in Acts 28. In the last fifteen chapters of this book, there had been plenty of Jews and gentile God-fearers who came to faith. But the audience was still left waiting for the revival to happen among the pagans. There had been almost no accounts of ordinary Greco-Romans accepting the gospel.[19] Then, in chapter 28, the "good part" seemed to draw near. This last chapter was full of prophetic foreshadowing. As Paul made his way to Rome, he was shipwrecked on the island of Malta, where the gentile inhabitants treated him kindly. Then, when he made it to Rome and started preaching to the Jews, they rejected his message. He told the Roman Jews plainly, "Therefore let it be known to you that this salvation of God has been sent to the gentiles; they will also listen" (Acts 28:28). The audience had the sense that Paul's mission was about to break loose. The turning point had come: the Jews were recalcitrant in their rejection of his message, but the pagans seemed to be interested in what he had to say. Paul was in the capital of the world, surrounded by

---

ascension of Jesus and the parousia. Jesus' death and resurrection could no longer be regarded as the beginning of the End, the (final) eschatological climax, as Jesus and the first Christians had understood it, but rather as the mid-point of history, with an epoch stretching forward into the future on one side as well as one stretching back into the past on the other" (Dunn, *Unity and Diversity*, 348).

19. Cf. Phillip Esler, *Community and Gospel in Luke-Acts* (Cambridge: Cambridge University Press, 1987), 38–42. He notes that subsequent to the story of Cornelius, there are an additional twenty conversion accounts in Acts. Almost all are Jews and God-fearers, and none explicitly relates the conversion of an idolater.

people from virtually every known nation on the earth, and thousands of people were about to get saved! And then Luke ended the story.

The abrupt conclusion of Acts has long been a topic of discussion, but the prevailing assessment is that this was a strategic device. Luke was trying to convey that the advance of the gospel to the nations was not in the hands of Paul alone. As Paul exited the stage in an inconclusive manner, Luke was passing on the torch to his audience. The gospel had crossed the frontier of the city, which symbolized the "ends of the earth." Now their work would begin in earnest.

The world was not coming to an end; it was laid out before them waiting to be conquered. But Luke knew that if his audience were to experience the same success that Paul and the apostles had achieved, they would need the same tools. And this brings us to the next item on Luke's agenda: prayer. Luke was fully persuaded that the gospel had advanced thus far on the wings of intercession. And thus, in addition to being a champion of the missionary church, he was an ardent advocate for prayer. In fact, he was obsessed with it.

Luke's Theology of Prayer

No other NT author talks more about prayer than Luke. The words "pray" or "prayer" (from the Greek word *proseuchomai)* appear thirty-five times in Luke-Acts (out of eighty-six total in the NT). If we include other descriptions (not using the word *proseuchomai*), we find that Luke mentions prayer fifty-seven times.[20] When reading through Luke-Acts, it's difficult to flip more than a few pages without finding an account of somebody at prayer. We find at prayer the godly Jews who await the Messiah's coming; Jesus; the early disciples; the Jerusalem church; Peter; Paul; the elders in Ephesus; the Christians in Tyre; Cornelius; and the church in Antioch.[21] We also discover that Luke "inserts" prayer

20. See Stephen Smalley, "Spirit, Kingdom and Prayer in Luke-Acts," *Novum Testamentum* 15, no. 1 (1973): 59.
21. For Jews in prayer, see Luke 1:10, 46, 68; 2:38; for Jesus, see Luke 3:21; 5:16; 6:12; 9:18; 10:21–22; 11:1; 22:41; for the disciples, see Acts 1:14, 24; 3:1; 6:4, 6; for the Jerusalem church, see Acts 2:42; 4:31; 12:12; for Peter, see Acts 9:40; 10:9; for Paul, see Acts 9:11; 14:23; 16:25; 22:17; 28:8; for Ephesus, see Acts 20:36; for Tyre, see Acts 21:5; for Cornelius, see Acts 10:2; for Antioch, see Acts 13:3.

where other Gospel authors left it out. For example, all three Synoptic authors tell the story of Jesus's baptism, but only Luke says that Jesus was praying when the Holy Spirit descended on him.[22] Mark mentions the occasion of Jesus choosing his disciples, but only Luke says that this was preceded by prayer.[23] All three Synoptics describe the transfiguration of Jesus on the mount, but only Luke says that Jesus was praying while it happened.[24]

Throughout his writings, Luke developed a detailed and profound theology of prayer. His doctrine was tightly bound to his understanding of salvation history. For Luke, God's progressive plan to redeem humanity took place in three stages: (1) the period of Israel ("the Law and the Prophets"); (2) the period of Jesus; and (3) the era of the church.[25] In each of these stages, prayer played a key role in the progression of God's purposes on earth.

With regard to first stage (Israel), Luke was keen to demonstrate that God was hearing the prayers of Israel. Certain Scriptures from the OT suggested that in seasons of anger, YHWH would not respond to the people's prayers. God had spoken through Isaiah declaring, "When you spread out your hands, I will hide my eyes from you; even though you make many prayers, I will not listen" (Isa 1:15; see also 59:2). But in the opening chapters of his Gospel, Luke wanted to communicate that this was not a time of wrath but rather one of favor for the Jewish people. Isaiah had also spoken of a time when God would say, "You shall call, and the Lord will answer; you shall cry, and he will say, 'Here I am'" (Isa 58:9).[26] Luke believed that Israel was living in such a time. God was moving in a special way, and Luke sought to demonstrate this by highlighting how godly Jewish people were seeing answers to their prayers. The Jews outside the temple prayed as Zechariah offered the sacrifice; Mary prayed when she visited Elizabeth; Zechariah prayed and prophesied at John's birth; Simeon and Anna both prayed when

---

22. Compare Luke 3:21–22; Mark 1:9–11; Matt 3:13–17.
23. Compare Luke 6:12–13 to Mark 3:13–14.
24. Compare Mark 9:2–4; Matt 17:1–2; Luke 9:28–29.
25. Conzelmann, *Theology of St. Luke*, 150.
26. See also Isa 65:17, 24; 56:6–7; Mal 1:11.

they embraced the boy Jesus.[27] Throughout the course of Luke's narrative, each and every one of these prayers was somehow answered. Luke wanted his audience to understand that as the first stage of salvation history was drawing to an end, the transition into the next stage would be marked by God's special attentiveness to the prayers of his people Israel.[28]

As Luke shifted the focus to Jesus (stage two), prayer took on an even more significant role. Luke made a special effort to highlight how often Jesus prayed: in prayer he launched his public ministry, received the Holy Spirit, and was transfigured; he prayed before choosing his disciples, and it was in prayer that he undergirded their training. He prayed before his crucifixion, and he even prayed on the cross.[29] At every major turning point, in the midst of each crisis, and before every "move of God," Jesus was praying.

Once Jesus has established the pattern, the disciples (stage three) followed his example: they prayed in Jerusalem, and the Holy Spirit fell upon them; it was in prayer that they stood firm amid persecution and found boldness to proclaim the message; Stephen prayed as he was martyred; Paul's commissioning as an apostle came as he prayed; it was because of Cornelius's prayers that salvation came to his house; it was in prayer that Peter received the revelation of God's plan for the gentiles; and it was in prayer that Paul and Silas were commissioned as missionaries.[30] Once again, Luke wanted to show that God was on the move because people were at prayer.

Luke's theology was simple: God's divine plan of salvation is driven forward by the prayers of Jesus and his followers.[31] Luke went to great lengths to model prayer, to teach on prayer, and to document prayer being answered because he believed that God shapes the world by means of prayer. This was Luke's theology. He did not present every

27. See Luke 1:10, 46, 68; 2:29–32, 38.
28. These insights are from Harvie Conn, "Luke's Theology of Prayer," *Christianity Today* 17 (1972): 290–92.
29. See Luke 3:21–23; 4:1–13; 6:12; 9:28–36; 10:21–22; 11:1–2, 5–13; 22:39–44; 23:34, 46.
30. Acts 1:14; 2:1–4; 4:24–30; 7:59–60; 9:10–19; 10:4, 9–16; 13:2–3.
31. Plymale notes that for Luke, "Prayer is God's way of guiding and implementing the accomplishment of His will" (Steven Plymale, *The Prayer Texts of Luke-Acts* [New York: Peter Lang, 1991], 105). See also Smalley, "Spirit, Kingdom and Prayer."

detail of human history unfolding according to a divinely written script. Rather, he believed that men and women must pray in order for God's purposes to come to pass in this world.[32]

A corollary to Luke's theology of prayer is his insistence on perseverance. Luke believed that because there is opposition to the accomplishment of God's purposes on earth, it is sometimes necessary to pray again and again if one desires to see prayer answered. This point was made forcefully in two parables found only in Luke. In Luke 11:5-13, Jesus told the story of a man who wouldn't stop bothering his neighbor until he gave him some bread. And again, in Luke 18:1-8, Jesus told a parable concerning a helpless widow who wouldn't stop bothering a judge until he gave her legal protection. In this second passage, Luke made a point of telling his audience the application point: "that they ought always to pray and not lose heart" (18:1). Persistence in prayer is necessary in order for God's will to be done. The problem is not God's unwillingness to answer. Rather, both of these stories allude to the fact that there are forces that oppose the accomplishment of God's purposes. The human heart can be hardened, there is evil in the world, and discouragement can set in. All these are obstacles that must be overcome by persistent prayer.

Luke envisioned prayer as a collaboration between humanity and God. The initiative of salvation belongs to God. He set the process of salvation in motion. He made the plan by which the human race could be redeemed. But due to the freedom of the human will and the presence of evil in the world, persistent prayer is necessary in order for people to come to salvation. This conviction of necessity drove Luke's presentation of prayer.

The foundation is now in place for us to move forward. We have identified Luke's audience as consisting primarily of gentiles who worshiped in the context of urban house churches. We have noted that they were battling discouragement, and that Luke wanted them to continue boldly with the missionary expansion of the church. We have followed Luke's documentation of godly Jews, Jesus, and the early

32. For a further discussion on Luke's theology of prayer and free will, see Clark, *Lord's*, 146–48.

church as they prayed and saw God respond in powerful ways. Luke persuaded his audience that God's plan of salvation had advanced thus far on the wings of prayer, and he exhorted them to persevere in prayer so that the fullness of God's plan could become reality. These are the backdrops that Luke employed. With this understanding, we can now focus our attention on center stage, where Luke is teaching his readers the meaning of the Lord's Prayer.

The Lord's Prayer in Luke-Acts

As we begin our discussion of the Lord's Prayer in Luke, many of our comments will make reference to the fact that Luke's version of this prayer is considerably shorter than what we've seen in Matthew and the *Didache*. We will devote an entire section to this topic further on, but at the present time we note the simple fact that even the opening address in Luke is more concise. Whereas the other versions are addressed to "*Our* Father," Luke's prayer simply calls him "Father" (Luke 11:2).

Some, but not all, of these differences have an explanation. In our chapter on Matthew, we noted that this Gospel author generally presented a negative image of earthly fathers, and it may be for that reason that Matthew preferred the designation *our* as a way of creating a contrast between (inadequate) earthly fathers and the (perfect) heavenly Father. Luke saw no need for such a distinction. This may be because all of the actual fathers in his narrative are good men: Zechariah is filled with Holy Spirit and prophesies; Joseph is a godly figure; the father of the demon-possessed boy is compassionate and caring; and in the parable of the prodigal son, the father is loving and merciful.[33] In light of the fact that Luke generally liked the fathers in his story, it is not surprising that he includes a teaching on prayer wherein Jesus points to the goodness of earthly fathers as a reflection of how the heavenly Father cares for his children. Jesus asks, "What father among you, if his son asks for a fish, will instead of a fish give

---

33. See Luke 1:67; 2:33; 9:38; 15:12–32.

him a serpent; or if he asks for an egg, will give him a scorpion?" (Luke 11:11–12). Of course no dad would ever be that mean! He then goes on to say that if the goodness of earthly fathers trumps the evil of humanity, "how much more will the heavenly Father give the Holy Spirit to those who ask him" (Luke 11:13). Luke's premise is that there is indeed fatherly goodness on earth, and this goodness reveals the character and generosity of the heavenly Father.

Luke wanted his audience to understand that the Father's goodness is manifest in the things that he does. Toward this end, he enlists the characters in his story to make declarations about God's goodness that find their fulfillment in the narrative. For example, Jesus declares in Luke 6:36, "Your Father is merciful," and then throughout the narrative people find forgiveness (e.g., Luke 5:20; 7:47). Jesus says, "How much more will the heavenly Father give the Holy Spirit to those who ask him" (Luke 11:13), and then on the day of Pentecost, the Spirit is given (Acts 2:4). Jesus instructs his disciples not to seek things such as food or drink "because your Father knows that you need them" (Luke 12:30). Later on in the church, "There was not a needy person among them" (Acts 4:34). Jesus said that it is the "Father's good pleasure to give you the kingdom" (Luke 12:32), and then, "To you it has been given to know the secrets of the kingdom of God" (Luke 8:10). Everything that Luke presents as a sign of the Father's goodness becomes "real" in his tangible dealings with people.

The clearest manifestation of the Father's character, however, is Jesus himself. He said, "All things have been handed over to me by my Father, and no one knows who the Son is except the Father, or who the Father is except the Son and anyone to whom the Son chooses to reveal him" (Luke 10:22). Jesus is here saying that the Father can only be known through him. He stands in special relationship to the Father, and he extends this relationship to those who follow him. Luke in this way gave his audience clear access to the Father. To know Jesus and to follow his teachings was to know the Father.

Thus, we see in Luke's writings that fathers are good. Earthly fathers are portrayed as loving, merciful, and attentive to the needs of their children. Luke assures his readers that the positive experiences they have had with their fathers could be transposed to their understanding of God. Yet this was not the full extent of the revelation. The ultimate embodiment of the Father's character was Jesus himself. Anyone who had known Jesus could know the Father. Luke wanted his readers to have a sense of certainty with regard to this God to whom they prayed. They could be confident that he heard them, and they could be confident that he was good.

The Sanctification of God's Name

As we have noted previously, the sanctification of God's name in the OT was a two-part process. First, YHWH revealed his power, and second, people responded by giving him honor. In Ezekiel 36:23, he declares, "I will sanctify my great name" (NRSV), and in Isaiah 29:23 it says that then "they will sanctify my name." YHWH wanted his name to be honored, and he displayed his grandeur to the nations so that they would worship him accordingly.

Luke's gentile audience may not have been intimately familiar with these finer details of the OT narrative, but Luke found a way to communicate this idea nonetheless. The first petition in Luke's Lord's Prayer says, "Hallowed be your name" (Luke 11:2). Luke presented the theme of sanctifying God's name in this same pattern that is observed in the OT. First, God makes his name holy by demonstrating his power, and then the people make his name holy by recognizing his deeds.

Luke particularly wanted to demonstrate that the mighty deeds of God were performed through Jesus. The Father's initiative to sanctify his name was now realized in his Son. Consequently, when Jesus was recognized by the people as the one who was sent by God and the man through whom God revealed his power, God's name was sanctified. Ultimately, to sanctify the name of Jesus was to sanctify the name of YHWH.

The idea of sanctifying (or hallowing) God's name first appears in the prayer of Mary (Luke 1:46–55). In this strategically placed passage, Luke accomplishes two goals. First, he establishes the fact that the sanctification of God's name requires both an action of God's and a human response. Second, Mary's prayer was essentially a preview of all that the audience was going to see happen in the life of Jesus.[34]

On the first point, Mary sanctified God's name because of what he does: "My soul magnifies the Lord . . . my spirit rejoices in God . . . *because* he has looked upon the lowliness of his servant" (Luke 1:46–48, my translation). And again, "Because the Mighty One has done great things for me, even so his name is holy" (Luke 1:49, my translation). Verses 50–54 then declare his deeds: he shows mercy; he demonstrates his strength; he scatters the proud; he exalts the humble; he feeds the hungry; he sends away the rich; he helps Israel. Luke recognized that for his audience, the holiness of God may have been a somewhat abstract idea. Therefore, he wanted to be sure that they could see a clear connection between God's holiness and his actions.

On the second point, Mary's prayer foreshadowed all that was to come in the life of Jesus. All of the actions for which Mary sanctified God's name were fulfilled through Jesus: he had mercy on the ten lepers; he sent away the rich young ruler; he condemned the rich and powerful; he publicly praised the poor widow; and he fed the multitude.[35] All of the greatness of the mighty One, for which Mary sanctified God's name, was tangibly revealed in the life of Jesus. In this way, Luke successfully helped his audience make a crossover. To honor the name of Jesus was to honor the name of the Lord because all God's mighty acts were accomplished through his son.

Luke introduced this idea to his audience in a progressive fashion. At the beginning of the narrative, it was only YHWH's name that was sanctified in Mary's very Jewish prayer. In the first part of Luke-Acts, the name of Jesus was generally not presented as a source of saving power.[36] It was only in the last chapter of the Gospel, after Jesus had died and rose again, that the name of Jesus became the focal point of

34. Cf. I. Howard Marshall, "The Interpretation of the Magnificat: Luke 1:46–55," in *Der Treue Gottes Trauen: Beiträge zum Werk des Lukas*, ed. Claus Bussmann and Walter Radl (Freiburg: Herder, 1991), 181–96.

35. See Luke 6:24–26; 9:12–17; 17:11–14; 18:18–25; 21:1–4.

36. Cf. Luke 9:48 (receiving children in his name); Luke 9:49; 10:17 (casting out demons in his name); Luke 21:8 (false prophets in his name); and Luke 21:8, 17 (persecution in his name).

salvation: "repentance and forgiveness of sins should be proclaimed in his name to all nations" (Luke 24:47). From that point on, throughout the book of Acts, "the name of Jesus" was the indispensable marker of God's saving deeds.[37] The church asks the Father, "Grant to your servants to continue to speak your word with all boldness, while you stretch out your hand to heal, and signs and wonders are performed through the name of your holy servant Jesus" (Acts 4:29–30). Jesus is the agent of the Father. He is the one through whom God's deeds are manifest on earth.

Thus, Luke led his readers through a process in which the holiness of YHWH's name, as initially proclaimed by Mary, found its fulfillment in the person of Jesus Christ. For Luke, the petition "hallowed be your name" was a way of asking the Father to make his name holy by revealing the saving power that is in Jesus. This request also expresses the hope that as people see the mighty deeds of God, they would give him the recognition that he deserves. They will sanctify his name by worshiping him for what he has done.

Your Kingdom Come

The next petition in the Lukan text is "your kingdom come" (Luke 11:2). "The kingdom of God" was something of a "stock" phrase for Luke, and he often used it as a broad summary of the gospel message.[38] The features by which he characterized the kingdom were consistent with what is seen throughout the other Gospels. For example, the kingdom is both a present reality and a future event (e.g., Luke 11:20; 22:18). The tension between the "now" and the "not yet" found expression in Luke's writings just as it did throughout the New Testament.

But if there is a "special message" that Luke wanted to communicate

37. In Acts, there are two references to the "name of the Lord" that are not explicitly referring to Jesus (Acts 2:21; 15:17), and both are quotations from the OT. Every other reference to the power of God's name is explicitly connoted by the name of Jesus. See "the name of Jesus" in Acts 2:28; 3:6; 3:16; 4:10; 4:12; 4:18; 4:30; 8:12; 10:48; 16:18; 26:9; and "the name of the Lord Jesus" in Acts 8:16; 15:26; 19:5; 19:13; 21:13.

38. E.g., Acts 19:8: "And he entered the synagogue and for three months spoke boldly, reasoning and persuading them about the kingdom of God." See also Acts 1:3; 8:12; 20:35; 28:23, 31.

about the kingdom of God, it would be the connection that he saw between the kingdom and the work of the Holy Spirit. James Dunn calls attention to the corollary relationship between the Spirit and the kingdom, evident in Acts 1:3–8.[39] In a deliberately confusing pattern, Jesus speaks to the disciples about the kingdom in verse 3, then in verses 4–5, he instructs them to wait for the Spirit. In verse 6, they ask when the kingdom will come, and then in verses 7–8, Jesus tells them that it is not for them to know the times, but that they will receive Spirit. Hence, in response to their question regarding the kingdom, Jesus replied speaking of the Spirit. Dunn paraphrases Jesus's response in this way: "Do not concern yourselves about the *when* of the kingdom; as to the *what* of the kingdom, that which concerns you is that you shall receive power when the Holy Spirit comes upon you."[40] The kingdom of God was to be ushered in by the work of the Spirit. If the disciples were eager to see the kingdom, then they must seek the Spirit.

Stephen Smalley has taken Dunn's observations one step further. He notes that in Luke-Acts there is a three-way relationship between the Spirit, the kingdom, and prayer. He notes that "Luke . . . regards petitionary prayer as the means by which the dynamic power of God's Spirit is historically realised for purposes of salvation. Luke's theological understanding, moreover, is such that he also views the activity of the Spirit among men and the arrival of the kingdom of God as aligned if not synonymous."[41]

Jesus had said that the Holy Spirit was the ultimate goal of prayer: "If you then, who are evil, know how to give good gifts to your children, how much more will the heavenly Father give the Holy Spirit to those who ask him!" (Luke 11:13). Matthew's version of this statement was a bit different. His text reads, "How much more will your Father who is in heaven give *good things* to those who ask him!" (Matt 7:11; emphasis added). Luke changed this phrase because he wanted to communicate the idea that the Holy Spirit is the summary of every good thing that the Father gives. The Holy Spirit is everything people are seeking

39. James Dunn, *The Christ and the Spirit: Pneumatology* (Grand Rapids: Eerdmans, 1998), 2:133–41.
40. Dunn, *Christ and the Spirit*, 137.
41. Smalley, "Spirit, Kingdom and Prayer," 68.

through prayer. There is no desire, need, or problem that doesn't somehow find its answer through the Holy Spirit. Thus, to ask the Father for the Holy Spirit is to ask him for everything that we want or need in life. It is with this idea in mind that Jesus tells his disciples to seek the Spirit when they asked him about the kingdom.

We conclude that for Luke, the petition "your kingdom come" was a request for the fullness of the Holy Spirit. Prayer for the Spirit and prayer for the kingdom were one and the same. Several decades after the original "publication" of Luke's Gospel, some copyists took this connection so much to heart that they changed the wording of the Lord's Prayer. In their manuscripts, "let your kingdom come" was replaced with "let your Holy Spirit come upon us and cleanse us."[42] It is fascinating to see how these people (who were perhaps later disciples of Luke) expressed their longing for the kingdom in this way. For Luke and his disciples, "your kingdom come" was just another way of saying "your Spirit come," because they believed that the Holy Spirit was the fulfillment of everything that people could ever want or ask in prayer.

The Provision of Bread

After the request for the kingdom, the prayer in Luke continues with "Give us each day our daily bread" (Luke 11:2). Luke's framing of this petition places particular emphasis on the idea that we ask the Father to *keep on* giving us bread day after day. There is a special emphasis on the repetitive, daily nature of this request.[43] Luke's gentile readers may not have been familiar with the story of the manna, and that may

---

42. See Bruce Metzger, *A Textual Commentary on the Greek New Testament* (Stuttgart: Deutsche Bibelgesellschaft, 2002), 130–31. Harnack, Leaney, and Ott are among the scholars who have argued for the authenticity of this reading, although the majority characterize it as later liturgical modification. For a survey of the opinions, see Shawn Carruth and Albrecht Garsky, *Documenta Q: Reconstuctions of Q through Two Centuries of Gospel Research*, vols. Q 11:2b–4 (Leuven: Peeters, 1996), 4–18.

43. We note that in the Greek grammar there is a slight variation between Luke's rendition of this petition and what we have seen in Matthew and the *Didache*. In both Matthew and the *Didache*, the petitions read, *ton arton hemon ton epiousion dos hemin smeron*, where the verb *didomi* (to give) is in the aorist tense (signifying punctiliar action) and the indication of frequency is simply *smeron* (today). In the Lukan reading, the petition is *ton arton hemon ton epiousion didou hemin to kath hemeran*. The verb *didomi* is conjugated in the active form (signifying continual action), and the indication of frequency is *to kath hemeran* (every day). On this last point, Meier notes that Luke has similarly changed the instruction on carrying the cross from "today" (Mark 8:34; Matt 16:24) to

be the explanation as to why Luke wanted to emphasize the idea of *repetition* by means of grammar. Beyond the lack of historical reference, however, there were other aspects of this petition, and of Christian prayer in general, that would have been problematic for Luke's Greco-Roman audience. Prayer was being depicted in a way that they had never seen before. What would have stood out more than anything was Luke's emphasis (throughout his writings) on prayer as an expression of relationship.

Before becoming Christians, Luke's gentile readers would have been in the habit of making different kinds of petitions to different gods. For instance, if the need was victory in war, the prayer would be directed to Mars. If the need was health, then Isis was the goddess to go to. In every case, prayer was a way of bargaining with the deities. The supplicant had to offer something in return for the favor requested. This is seen, for example, in Cato's prayer to Mars: "Father Mars, I pray and request, that you be willing and propitious to me, my house and family. Therefore I have commanded this offering of a pig, sheep and ox. May you prevent, ward off, and turn away diseases visible and invisible, sterility and destruction, accident, brackish water and inclement weather. And you allow the fruits and grains and vines and shrubs to grow and turn out well."[44] Others among Luke's audience may have been a bit more sophisticated in their theology of prayer. Those who had been trained in Greek philosophy would have conceived of the Supreme Being as being too far removed from humanity to bargain with people or to be influenced by their prayers. Many philosophers had taught that the highest God could not be changed, persuaded, or influenced by prayer or any other human activity. Thus we see, for example, that Cleanthes's *Hymn to Zeus* is not so much a series of petitions as it is a declaration of his absolute sovereignty and power:

So I will hymn you and sing always of your strength,
For all the cosmos, as it whirls around earth,

"everyday" in Luke 9:23 (John P. Meier, *A Marginal Jew: Companions and Competitors* [New Haven and London: Yale University Press, 2001], 355).
44. C. Robert Phillips, "Cato the Elder," in *Prayer from Alexander to Constantine: A Critical Anthology*, ed. Mark Kiley et al. (London: Routledge, 1997), 130–31.

Obeys you, wherever you lead, and it is willingly ruled by you.
For such is the power you hold in your unconquerable hands . . .
Nothing is accomplished in this world save through you, O Spirit
Neither in the divine, heavenly, ethereal sphere, nor upon the sea . . .
For thus you have fit together into one all good things with the bad
So that they become one single, eternal harmony.[45]

In this case, prayer is rendered to Zeus because it is honorable for people to acknowledge him. But Cleanthes's prayer contains no requests. All the universe obeys Zeus and operates according to his designs.

In book 12 of his work *Metaphysics*, Aristotle presents God as the "unmoved mover," the ultimate power that acts upon all things but is affected by nothing. He is unchangeable, unmovable, unpersuadable, and self-sufficient in all ways. God is pure activity, and everything that humanity perceives as reality is simply the projection of his thought. Aristotle spoke of God as being wholly *other*, with no need of anything outside of himself: "One who is self-sufficient can have no need of the service of others, nor of their affection, nor of social life, since he is capable of living alone. . . . Clearly, since he is in need of nothing, God cannot have need of friends, nor will he have any."[46] In the Greek worldview, God's provision for humanity in no way came as a result of their prayers or petitions. Rather, God's goodness was like the benevolence of the sun, which blesses all the earth with its rays and yet remains unaffected by those who receive its warmth.

This far-removed, transcendent, immutable, impassible God is someone completely different than the God whom Luke presents to his audience. Luke's God is engaged and present, waiting to hear from his children every day so that he can respond in love to their every need. For Luke, the daily petition for bread corresponded to the relationship between God and his people. Asking the Father for bread was not just a formula for covering material needs. Luke saw it as an expression of the loving interaction that takes place between a father and his

---

45. William Cassidy, "Cleanthes' Hymn to Zeus," in Kiley et al., *Prayer from Alexander to Constantine*, 136.
46. Aristotle, *Eudemian Ethics* 7, 1244b. Cited by Abraham Heschel, *The Prophets* (New York: Harper Collins, 1962), 300.

children: "What father among you, if his son asks for a fish, will instead of a fish give him a serpent; or if he asks for an egg, will give him a scorpion?" (Luke 11:11–12). In Luke's mind, the Father wants his children to come back to him every day because he takes pleasure in provision and in the relationship.

There is a conditional element in Luke's understanding of petition. Jesus said, "Ask, and it will be given to you; seek, and you will find; knock, and it will be opened to you. For everyone who asks receives, and the one who seeks finds, and to the one who knocks it will be opened" (Luke 11:9–10). The corollary to this teaching was that those who *don't* ask, seek, and knock will not see the Father respond. Luke wanted his readers to pray because he firmly believed that God was waiting for them to ask before he took action.

What Luke presented to his gentile audience was a much more Jewish understanding of the relationship between God and humanity. Abraham Heschel has described the God of Israel as the God of *pathos*, that is, a God who has passions, feelings, emotions, and who is affected by what people do. Heschel notes that in OT thought, "Man is not only an image of God; he is a perpetual concern of God. The idea of pathos adds a new dimension to human existence. Whatever man does affects not only his own life, but also the life of God insofar as it is directed to man. The import of man raises him beyond the level of mere creature. He is a consort, a partner, a factor in the life of God."[47] The Lord's Prayer as presented by Luke is pregnant with this Jewish worldview, and he wanted his readers to understand the deeper theological message. Whereas the Greek worldview saw all of reality as simply the monologue of the Supreme Being, Luke saw the human experience as a dialogue between people and God. He saw a God who is supremely relational. Consequently, even for something so simple as the daily need for bread, Luke's God wants interaction with people. He is not willing to be like the sun, distantly and indifferently sustaining human life. He wants people to come to him each and every day and *ask*. It is their initiative to pray that moves him to action.[48]

47. Heschel, *Prophets*, 292.

On a more practical level, Luke made it very clear what the provision of daily bread would look like. First, Luke did allow for the idea that God, out of his enormous love and mercy for all of humanity, gives general sustenance to all humanity. Paul told his Athenian listeners that it was God who "gives to all mankind life and breath and everything" (Acts 17:25). But even with this idea of universal provision, Luke's greater concern was to show that God provides for his children through human generosity.

Students of Luke-Acts are well aware of the fact that Luke had a deep concern for the poor. We remember from Mary's prayer that God exalts the humble and fills the hungry with good things, while he sends away the rich empty-handed (Luke 1:52–53). Jesus said that he came to proclaim good news to the poor, liberty to the captives, recovery of sight to the blind, and liberty to those who are oppressed (Luke 4:18). Luke went out of his way to emphasize that as a result of Jesus's ministry, "the blind receive their sight, the lame walk, lepers are cleansed, and the deaf hear, the dead are raised up, the poor have good news preached to them" (Luke 7:22). Luke showed how this same concern for the poor continued in the life of the early church. Christians in the book of Acts were characterized by their sacrificial generosity toward one another. They shared their food and wealth to such an extent that no one had need among them (Acts 2:43–47; 4:34–35).

What all of this tells us about the petition "give us each day our daily bread" is that Luke wanted his audience to understand the relational aspects of the Christian faith in both vertical and horizontal dimensions. His emphasis on the need to come back again and again reminded his audience that their God wanted to hear from them and would respond to their requests when they asked. This need for persistence also spoke to the fact that there are forces standing in opposition to the doing of God's will. God wants to provide bread for his children, but persevering prayer is necessary for this to happen.

---

48. See also Michael Brown, "'Panem Nostrum': The Problem of Petition in the Lord's Prayer," *The Journal of Religion* 80, no. 4 (2000): 610.

And finally, we see in Luke's understanding of this request that every person who prays "give us each day our daily bread" must be willing to be the answer to his or her own prayer. Luke saw God's provision as happening through people, and he made no allowance for the idea that a believer would withhold a surplus of bread from another person who had need.

Forgiveness

The next petition in the Lukan Lord's Prayer is "and forgive us our sins," which is followed by the clause, "for we ourselves forgive everyone who is indebted to us" (Luke 11:4).[49] The forgiveness of sins is an important theme in Luke's writings. Throughout his narrative he made the effort to move it from an abstract idea to a tangible, experiential reality. He told several stories that had the effect of making forgiveness real. Three examples found exclusively in Luke are: the woman anointing Jesus's feet in the house of Simon the Pharisee; the story of Zacchaeus; and the parable of the prodigal son.[50] In these three accounts, Luke sought to emphasize the emotional dimensions of forgiveness. The image of a woman wetting Jesus's feet with her tears and oil and then drying them with her hair has an almost sensual feel to it. Jesus showed a peculiar tenderness toward Zacchaeus the "son of Abraham" as he went to his home to share a meal. And the story of the prodigal son evoked tears of joy as a father received back a son he had once counted as dead.

In all of these accounts, Luke was trying to drive home the idea that forgiveness is an emotional experience. We cite Heschel once again, who notes that the God of Israel

does not reveal himself in an abstract absoluteness, but in a personal and

---

49. There are slight variations between these clauses as they appear in Luke and their presentation in Matthew and the *Didache*. These differences reflect the style more than the theology of the respective authors. Luke's characterization of sin as *hamartia* ("missing the mark") would have been familiar to a Greek-speaking audience, as opposed the Aramaism *ofeilema* ("debts") found in the texts of the *Didache* and Matthew. However, Luke uses the debt metaphor in the second clause, in the participle form *panti ofeilonti hemin* ("all those owing us").
50. See Luke 7:36–50; 15:11–32; 19:1–10.

intimate relation to the world. He does not simply command and expect obedience; He is also moved and affected by what happens in the world, and reacts accordingly. Events and human actions arouse in him joy or sorrow, pleasure or wrath. He is not conceived as judging the world in detachment. He reacts in an intimate and subjective manner, and thus determines the value of events. Quite obviously in the biblical view, man's deeds may move Him, affect Him, grieve him or, on the other hand, gladden and please Him. This notion that God can be intimately affected, that He possesses not merely intelligence and will, but also pathos, basically defines the prophetic consciousness of God.[51]

As Luke talked about forgiveness, he wanted his readers to know that this was the God with whom they were dealing.

To illuminate the second clause of this petition, "for we ourselves forgive everyone who is indebted to us," Luke gave numerous examples of what interpersonal forgiveness looked like: Jesus pleaded for the Father to forgive those who crucified him even as they callously cast lots for his clothing (Luke 23:34); amid a shower of stones pelting his body, Stephen fell to his knees and with his last breath implored, "Lord, do not hold this sin against them" (Acts 7:60). By giving account of the highest form of forgiveness—the forgiveness of one's murderers —Luke set a standard for his readers to follow. That is, if Jesus and Stephen could release those who were taking their lives, what offense could Christians justifiably cling to?

We note one final aspect of forgiveness that Luke sought to emphasize: the necessity of repentance. In Luke's view, if people were truly repentant over their sins, an outward expression of change and remorse was necessary. It is only in Luke's account that John the Baptist's "fruits of repentance" were spelled out (Luke 3:11–14; cf. Matt 3:7–12). In the story of Zacchaeus, salvation came to the "wee little man" only after he committed to share his wealth with the poor and restore those he had defrauded (Luke 19:8–9). And all throughout Luke-Acts, repentance and forgiveness are presented as the two basic elements of salvation. They are dependent upon one another.[52]

In conclusion, Luke's understanding of forgiveness places a strong

---

51. Heschel, *Prophets*, 288–89.
52. Luke 3:3; 17:3–4; 24:47; Acts 2:38; 5:31; 8:22.

emphasis on relational restoration. He highlighted the emotional aspects of reconciliation in order to remind his readers that forgiveness was something more than a cold transaction or settling of accounts. He set a "gold standard" for what interpersonal forgiveness had to look like. And he placed significant emphasis on the need for repentance in order that relationships would not continue experiencing the ravages of sin.

Temptation

Luke's short version of the Lord's Prayer concludes with the petition, "and lead us not into temptation" (Luke 11:2). Testing (or temptation) was another big theme for Luke, as he wrote more about this topic than any other Gospel author.[53] For him, falling into temptation meant giving up, falling away, or denying Christ. The secret to overcoming temptation was simple. It was "always to pray and not lose heart" (Luke 18:1). Many of Luke's readers were facing personal adversity. Some were discouraged that Jesus had not yet returned. Being committed to prayer and always "on the watch" was Luke's remedy for discouragement.[54]

To get his message across, Luke used the ideas of *sleep* and *alertness* as metaphors. Sleep represented spiritual dullness or faintness of heart. Alertness symbolized perseverance and attentiveness. On one occasion, Jesus invites three disciples to accompany him to a mountain. As he prays, "the appearance of his face was altered, and his clothing became dazzling white" (Luke 9:29). At first, the disciples missed what was happening because they were "heavy with sleep," but "when they became fully awake they saw his glory" (Luke 9:32). Shortly afterward in the narrative, Jesus tells a parable about a master who rejoices to

---

53. Overall, Luke displays a special concern for the theme of temptation, as he uses *peirasmos* with much greater frequency than the other Gospel authors. All three Synoptics include the term in their Gethsemane accounts "pray that you may not enter into temptation" (Matt 26:41; Mark 14:38; Luke 22:40). However, it does not appear elsewhere in Mark, and in Matthew the only other occurrence is in the Lord's Prayer (Matt 6:13). It appears a total of six times in Luke (Luke 4:13; 8:13; 11:4; 22:28, 40, 46), and once in Acts 20:19.
54. The initial champion of this view was Wilhelm Ott, who suggested that the *Sitz im Leben* of Luke's Gospel was the delay of the parousia (cited by Holmas, *Prayer and Vindication*, 40). Amid discouragement, ongoing trials, and anxieties, prayer was required for perseverance.

find his servants awake as he returns home in the middle of the night: "Blessed are those servants whom the master finds awake when he comes. . . . If he comes in the second watch, or in the third, and finds them awake, blessed are those servants!" (Luke 12:37–38).

The importance of alertness would take on a heavier tone as Jesus neared the end of his life. When speaking to his disciples of the coming tribulation, he warns them, "But stay awake at all times, praying that you may have strength to escape all these things that are going to take place" (Luke 21:36). In the garden, he tells them a second time, "Pray that you may not enter into temptation" (Luke 22:40). He himself then spends the night awake and in prayer. But "when he rose from prayer, he came to the disciples and found them sleeping for sorrow" (Luke 22:40). He says to them a third time, "Why are you sleeping? Rise and pray that you may not enter into temptation" (Luke 22:46). But it was too late. At that moment Jesus is arrested, and the disciples flee.

The petition "lead us not into temptation" was all about alertness and perseverance in prayer. Luke wanted his audience to put themselves in the shoes of the disciples. He didn't want them to miss the revelation of Jesus's glory like the disciples almost did. He didn't want them to fall asleep because of sorrow. If the disciples had only listened to Jesus—if they had only stayed awake and prayed this exact prayer—perhaps things would have turned out differently for them. Luke didn't want his audience to have those same regrets.

As the message of salvation continued its advance across the Roman Empire and beyond, Luke was deeply concerned that his readers should not fall into lethargy or discouragement. In his view, there was urgent need to stay awake, stay in prayer, and press on with the work of the kingdom. Luke wanted his readers to know that trials would be inevitable. But he wanted them to know that the simple request "lead us not into temptation," or "*give us strength in trial*," was a powerful prayer.[55] God was ready and willing to come to their aid, but they had to call on him for help.

A Shorter Form of the Lord's Prayer

We conclude this chapter with a discussion of why Luke's rendition of the Lord's Prayer was different from other ancient versions. Some differences were simply stylistic. For example, Luke gave preference to the present tense over the aorist, and used the Greek term for sin (*hamartia*) rather than the more Aramaic idea of debt (*opheilēma*). But a more strking distinctive of Luke's version is that he omits several elements of the prayer. Luke's prayer is addressed simply to "Father" and not "our Father in heaven." He excluded the petition "let your will be done" and the phrase "on earth as it is in heaven." And Luke's version does not include the petition "deliver us from evil." There are no simple answers as to why these different versions of the Lord's Prayer exist. I will present my theory on this subject, but first I will "put on the table" some of my thoughts about the origins of the Lord's Prayer.

First, no one can be certain about exactly what words Jesus chose when he taught his disciples this prayer. He would have spoken to them in Aramaic, and during the early years, the disciples would have prayed this prayer in that language. During the stage of passing along this prayer by "word of mouth," it is likely that its wording changed slightly. Ancient Jews were a bit averse to the stiff repetition of prayers, and their tendency toward spontaneity may have had some lasting effects. When this prayer finally did take written form, it was recorded in Greek. All this is to say that there was room for the text to change, and there is no way to know exactly what words Jesus originally used.

Second, there has long been a discussion about which version of the Lord's Prayer is *closest* to the original words of Jesus. The majority

---

55. Kistemaker points to the parallels between this petition and the words of Sirach: "'My son, if you come forward to serve the Lord, prepare yourself for temptation' (Sir. 2:1). 'No evil will befall the man who fears the Lord, but in trial (*peirasmos*) he will deliver him again and again' (33:1)" (Simon Kistemaker, "The Lord's Prayer in the First Century," *JETS* 21, no. 4 [1978]: 326).

of modern scholars have been inclined to argue that the Lukan five-petition form wins this prize. The rationale behind this view is summarized by Jeremias, who notes:

> The shorter form of Luke is completely contained in the longer form of Matthew. This makes it very probable that the Matthean form is an expanded one, for according to all that we know about the tendency of liturgical texts to conform to certain laws in their transmission, in a case where the shorter version is contained in the longer one, the shorter text is to be regarded as original. No one would have dared to shorten a sacred text like the Lord's Prayer and to leave out two petitions if they had formed part of the original tradition. On the contrary, the reverse is amply attested, that in the early period, before wordings were fixed, liturgical texts were elaborated, expanded, and enriched.[56]

I disagree with this assessment. Although there is a high degree of rationality to Jeremias's argument, there are in fact no "laws" governing the transmission of liturgical texts. My position is that the seven-petition forms found in Matthew and the *Didache* are more ancient and that Luke did in fact reduce the longer form that was more common at the time of his writing.[57] I believe that Luke shortened the Lord's Prayer out of a concern that certain ideas in the longer version would be misinterpreted by his Greco-Roman readers.

At this point, some readers may be asking (along with Jeremias), Would Luke ever do such a thing? Would he deliberately shorten the text of something so important as the Lord's Prayer? The answer is yes. Students of Luke-Acts have long been aware that Luke generally did not record the full text of prayers. As Holmas has commented, "Only sporadically does he record a prayer's content. Luke's penchant for very brief notes clearly lends emphasis 'upon the settings for prayer rather than the substance of prayers, contexts more than contents.'"[58] When Luke does offer the text of various prayers, they are often limited

---

56. Cited by Carruth and Garsky, *Documenta Q*, 76.
57. First, given the rapid and broad dissemination of the gospel tradition and the centrality of the Lord's Prayer within that tradition, it is highly unlikely that Luke would have been unfamiliar with the seven-petition form. Second, now that the literary independence of the *Didache* has clearly been proven, we accept that there were two independent traditions of the seven-petition form. This lends weight to the argument that the longer form is more ancient.
58. Holmas, *Prayer*, 59.

to the "gist" of their content.[59] He includes only that material he considers important for accomplishing his goals.

So we now turn to the more difficult question: *Why* would Luke shorten the prayer? Whereas there are no clear explanations for every edit, there is strong evidence that one petition in particular, "let your will be done," was worrisome for Luke. This is not to say that he disagreed with the idea of asking God to do his will. Quite the contrary, Luke had a very detailed theology concerning the purposes of God and their fulfillment in history. Rather, Luke was concerned that the phrase "let your will be done" might be misinterpreted by his gentile audience. Rather than focusing on an abstract notion that could potentially be misunderstood, Luke's strategy was simply to demonstrate how his gentile readers could put into practice the ways of the Father as revealed through the teachings of Jesus. He wanted to leave no room for confusion.

We will approach this matter in three stages. First, we will look at various characteristics of the Greco-Roman worldview that would have been a concern for Luke. Second, we will consider Luke's theology of prayer as a rationale for making these changes. And third, we will consider several examples in his Gospel where he removed reference to the "will of God" and replaced it with other words.

Greco-Roman Beliefs about the Will of God

In our discussion of the petition for daily bread, we alluded to the fact that the first-century Greco-Roman worldview was rather complex. On the one hand, there were the philosophical schools of thought, such as Platonism and Stoicism, that were influential particularly among the educated classes. On the other hand, there were the popular, or "folk," traditions that were followed by the population in general. In each of these streams, the "will of God" would have evoked different ideas. We will start with the philosophical worldview, and then look more closely at the "folk" belief in astrology.

---

59. E.g., Luke 22:41–42; Acts 1:24–25; Acts 4:24–30.

The Philosophical Schools

A point the major Greek philosophers tended to agree on was that the Supreme Being is absolutely transcendent and immutable. As we have mentioned above, this means that the Supreme Being is in no way affected or changed by human activities. He exists completely apart from the universe he has created and is entirely sufficient and satisfied in himself. For Plato, God is "that which always is and has no becoming."[60] He is unchangeable, impassible, and therefore perfect. If God could be changed, alter his course of action, or be swayed by any human activity (including prayer), then by implication God could not be perfect. Perfection requires absolute constancy.[61] For Aristotle, God is the unmoved mover, the power that acts upon all things, but is himself unaffected by anything. In this worldview, God's relationship to his creation is similar to that between a watch and its maker. God is the one who has set all the parts in motion. At the creation, he established the rules by which the universe operates. But he himself plays no ongoing role in the affairs of humanity.

A person coming from this worldview would not have thought of "God's will" as consisting of his desire or hopes for individuals. Rather, the will of God referred to the natural laws that he had set in place. So, for instance, if God designed the world in such a way that lying had negative consequences in life, then one might say that to tell a lie was not "God's will." God would experience no personal engagement (in the form of anger or grief) with the person committing this offense. In his immutability and transcendence, he would be far removed from such small human affairs. Thus, violating God's will was more a matter of breaking a law of nature than it was a personal offense against him.

Edwin Hatch has synthesized how this worldview found expression in the Stoic philosophers:

---

60. Plato, *Timaeus,* trans. Benjamin Jowett (Kindle ed.), loc. 1733.
61. The conceptualization of God presented in *The Republic* emphasizes the notion of his absolute immutability. Plato argues that "it is impossible that God should ever be willing to change; being, as it is supposed, the fairest and the best that is conceivable, every God remains absolutely and for ever in his own form." See Plato, *The Republic*, trans. Benjamin Jowett (Norwalk, CT: Easton, 1980), 117.

The world marches on to its end, realizing its own perfection, with absolute certainty. The majority of its parts move in that march unconsciously, with no sense of pleasure or pain, no idea of good or evil. To man is given the consciousness of action, the sense of pleasure and pain, the idea of good and evil, and freedom of choice between them. If he chooses that which is against the movement of nature, he chooses for himself misery; if he chooses that which is in accordance with that movement, he finds happiness. In either case the movement of nature goes on, and the man fulfils his destiny.[62]

But Heschel once again reminds us of how different this image of God is from that presented in the Bible: "The God of Israel, in contrast, is not a Law, but the Lawgiver. The order He established is not a rigid unchangeable structure, but a historic-dynamic reality, a drama. What the prophets proclaim is not His silence, but His pathos. To understand His ways, one must obey His will."[63] In the Jewish worldview, the will of God was not a natural law. It was an expression of his desires for each person and the world. To obey his will was a means of entering into relationship with him.

Astrology

Whereas the philosophical schools allowed for the idea of free will and held that a person's choices would have an effect on the outcome of his or her life, there was in "popular" Greco-Roman culture a strong pull toward fatalism. The idea behind fatalism is that the destiny of each person in the world is predetermined. Consequently, many of Luke's readers would have been inclined to think of the "will of God" as fate. In other words, everything that happened in life was already predestined, and the "will of God" was simply the unfolding that predetermined plan.

This expression of fatalism and predeterminism was strongly evident in the practice of astrology. In the first-century poem entitled *Astronomica*, the astrologer Manilius asserted that the stars are the medium through which the divinity controls all that happens on

---

62. Edwin Hatch, *The Influence of Greek Ideas on Christianity* (New York: Harper & Row, 1957), 222.
63. Heschel, *Prophets*, 304.

earth.[64] Referring to "God," "reason," and "the heavens" interchangeably, he wrote, "This god and all-controlling reason, then, derives earthly beings from the heavenly signs; though the stars are remote at a far distance, he compels recognition of their influences, in that they give to the peoples of the world their lives and destinies and to each man his own character."[65] The extent to which the stars determine the course of events of life is absolute: "Every sort of fact, every effort, every achievement, every skill and every vicissitude that through all the phases of human life may concern human fate; and it has disposed these in as many varied ways as there are positions of the stars; has attributed to each object definite functions and appropriate names, and through the stars, by a fixed system, has ordained a complete census of the human race."[66]

The enormous influence of astrology in Greco-Roman culture is well documented.[67] Astrological fatalism was the fundamental tenet of Roman creed in the first century CE, as the observations of Tacitus testify: "Most men, however, find it natural to believe that their lives are predestined from birth, that the science of prophecy is verified by remarkable testimonials, ancient and modern; and that unfulfilled predictions are due merely to ignorant impostors who discredit it."[68]

We can safely assume that Luke's readers would have been exposed to the influences of both astrology and Greek philosophy. In both cases, we see how their understanding of the "will of God" would have been very different than what the Bible presented. We now look at how Luke understood the idea of "God's will."

64. Pliny named Manilius as "the founder of astrology at Rome" (Tamsyn Barton, *Ancient Astrology* [London: Routledge, 1994], 34).

65. *Astronomica* 2.82–86. Cited by Katharina Volk, "'Heavenly Steps': Manilius 4.119–121 and Its Background," in *Heavenly Realms and Earthly Realities in Late Antique Religions*, ed. Ra'anan S. Boustan and Annettte Yoshiko Reed (Cambridge: Cambridge University Press, 2004), 35.

66. *Astronomica* 3.67–73. Cited by Barton, *Ancient Astrology*, 162.

67. Seutonius records astrologically based prophesies for all of the emperors, and notes that Augustus put Capricorn on his coins. Barton notes that images of Capricorn have also been found from the era of Augustus on sculptural reliefs, terracottas, paintings, and jewelry (*Ancient Astrology*, 40). Noting the broad influence of astrologers within Roman society, Barton also notes, "Between the death of Julius Caesar and that of Marcus Aurelius in 180 CE, no fewer than eight, and possibly as many as thirteen, decrees expelling astrologers and other groups from Rome and Italy are recorded" (ibid., 50).

68. *Annals* 6.22. Cited by Barton, *Ancient Astrology*, 53.

Fatalism and Prayer in Luke-Acts

Luke was a firm believer in the freedom of the human will. He believed that human choices could affect the outcome of history and that prayer could move God into action. His theology of prayer was straightforward: the initiative of salvation belongs to God, but human collaboration through prayer is necessary in order for God's purposes to be accomplished on earth. Luke believed that in many ways, history was hanging in the balance. Prayer was necessary if God's plan of salvation was going to stay on track.[69]

We also remember that Luke greatly emphasized the idea of persistence in prayer. For those who believe (including some Christians today) that all of human history is predetermined, the need for persistence is difficult to explain. If God has already determined what's going to happen, then why would he make his followers grovel in petition for what he has already ordained? This picture of God is at odds with the image that Luke presents: a loving Father who longs to be generous to his children, wants to respond, and yet insists that persistence is necessary because his good purposes are at times resisted. It is because people choose to oppose his ways, and because there is opposition in the spiritual realm, that Christians must continually ask God to intervene in the course of human affairs.

Finally, we recall Luke's emphasis on the emotional engagement of the Father with his children. As we have seen in his stories on forgiveness, Luke emphasized the emotional character of God. In a Greek philosophical worldview emphasizing God's transcendent remoteness, or in a fatalistic system in which everything is determined by the stars, there can be no true divine emotion. Sadness, joy, surprise, tenderness, and anger are all characteristics of dynamic and free relationships. If all things are predetermined by God, then any hint of God's emotional life is not authentic and can only be labeled as a mere anthropomorphism.

---

69. *Pace* my readers from Reformed schools of thought, who will disagree with my assessment of Luke's theology. Acts 13:48 will no doubt feature prominently in the counterargument. See Clark (2016), 150–74 for a more thorough treatment of Luke's theology.

It is for these reasons that we understand why Luke bristled at the thought of a remote, impassible God. With so much at stake, we see why he would loathe a view of history in which all things were preestablished and human choices weren't real. Luke's passion for free will and his vision to see the church take action drove his narrative. And this explains his reluctance to use the phrase "the will of God" with an audience that was so prone to misunderstand what this meant.

Your Will Be Done

The "rub" for Luke with regard to the petition "your will be done" was that within a fatalistic worldview, the accomplishment of God's will is a foregone conclusion. There is no basis for asking God to do his will if everything he wants is already predestined to happen. All there can be is the simple recognition that his will is going to be done. And all that prayer can ever be, in this light, is an act of human assent to the activity of God, a mere "Amen" to the monologue of human history.

This was a misinterpretation that Luke sought to avoid. Acutely aware of the potential for confusion, Luke chose to edit this expression out of the Lord's Prayer. Several passages in Luke's narrative reveal his inclination to reconfigure the idea of God's will for his gentile audience. We note the differences in the following texts (emphases mine):[70]

- Matthew had written, "Not everyone who says to me, 'Lord, Lord,' will enter the kingdom of heaven, *but the one who does the will of my Father who is in heaven.* . . . Everyone then who hears these words of mine and does them will be like a wise man who built his house on the rock" (Matt 7:21, 24). Working from the same source, Luke changed this teaching to say, "Why do you call me 'Lord, Lord,' *and not do what I tell you?* Everyone who comes to me and hears my words and does them . . . is like a man building a house, who dug deep and laid the foundation on the rock" (Luke 6:46–48).

---

70. These textual comparisons are from Carruth and Garsky, *Documenta Q*, 109.

- Mark recorded a story in which Jesus said, "Here are my mother and my brothers! For *whoever does the will of God*, he is my brother and sister and mother" (Mark 3:34–35). Matthew referred to the same incident: "Here are my mother and my brothers! For *whoever does the will of my Father* in heaven is my brother and sister and mother" (Matt 12:49–50). Luke recounted the same saying but changed the wording slightly: "My mother and my brothers are those *who hear the word of God and do it*" (Luke 8:21).

- In Matthew's version of the parable of the lost sheep, Jesus explains, "And if he finds it, truly, I say to you, he rejoices over it more than over the ninety-nine that never went astray. *So it is not the will of my Father who is in heaven* that one of these little ones should perish" (Matt 18:13–14). But in Luke, Jesus' choice of words is (again) slightly different: "And when he has found it, he lays it on his shoulders, rejoicing. . . . Just so, I tell you, there will be more joy in heaven over *one sinner who repents* than over ninety-nine righteous persons who need no repentance" (Luke 15:5–7).

It is clear in these passages that Luke deliberately modified his sources to replace terminology concerning the will of God with language emphasizing obedience and repentance.[71] *Doing the will of God* became *hearing my words and doing them*. The Father rejoiced not because *his will is done*, but because a *sinner has come to repentance*. Luke substituted the abstract notion of *God's will* with concrete notions that could in no way be subject to misunderstanding or misinterpretation by his gentile readers.[72]

---

71. One may attempt to make the opposite argument, i.e., that it was Matthew who modified Luke. This, however, does not explain Luke 8:21 vis-à-vis Mark 3:34–35, nor does it account for Luke's form of the Lord's Prayer vis-à-vis the *Didache*'s "let your will be done." The evidence weighs in favor a Lukan modification.

72. This is not to say, however, that Luke altogether avoids reference to the divine will (*thelēma*). Explicit reference to the will of God appears once in Luke's Gospel as Jesus prays, "not my will, but yours, be done" (Luke 22:42). It appears in Acts three times: (1) Paul cites God's characterization of David as a man "who will do all my will" (Acts 13:22); (2) when Paul's party could not persuade him against going to Jerusalem, they declared, "Let the will of the Lord be done" (Acts 21:14); and (3) Ananias prophesied to Paul that "the God of our fathers appointed you to know his will" (Acts 22:14).

Luke was willing to use this term under controlled circumstances. We find reference to the will (*thelēma*) of God when it can be explicitly linked to the predetermined purpose (*boulē*)

Conclusion

We conclude this chapter on Luke's presentation of the Lord's Prayer by reflecting on his genius as a missionary, historian, and theologian.

Luke the Missionary

Luke skillfully "translated" the meaning of the Lord's Prayer for his Greco-Roman audience. He took a Jewish prayer taught by a Jewish man embedded in Jewish culture, and made it comprehensible for the rest of the world. Luke understood people like Paquius Proculus: how he spoke, saw the world, and lived his daily life. Luke also understood the power of the Lord's Prayer as a symbol of the Christian faith. Something about it obviously resonated with the Christians in Pompeii.

By recounting a shorter version of this prayer, Luke demonstrated that sometimes practicality is more important than purity. This is a dilemma that missionaries frequently face. When I was living in southeastern Mexico, someone once gave me a copy of the Bible translated into classic Mayan. A group of translators had dedicated many years to studying the language and producing this work, and

---

of God for individual characters within the story. We note the following examples: it was the foreordained *boulē* of God for Jesus to die (Acts 2:23) and thus it was the specific *thelēma* of the Father for him to submit himself to arrest and crucifixion (Luke 22:42); God raised up David to serve his *boulē* (Acts 13:36) and therefore it was his explicit *thelēma* that he become king (Acts 13:22); God declared his overarching purpose for Paul's life (Acts 9:15–16), and subsequently the specific path to the fulfillment of this purpose was revealed as God's *thelēma* for him (Acts 21:14; 22:14). These were situations in which God had already declared what he intended to do, and consequently there were specific events in the lives of Luke's characters that must take place in order for the *boulē* of God to be accomplished.

The idea that certain things *must* happen is prevalent in Luke-Acts, as evident in his frequent use of *dei* ("to be necessary"). Many events in the life of Jesus occur by necessity. For example, "he must suffer many things" (Luke 9:22; 17:25; 24:26); he must go to Jerusalem (Luke 13:33); what was written about him must be fulfilled (Luke 22:37; 24:44); he must be crucified (Luke 24:7). This same sense of necessity continued to some extent in the lives of the apostles. For example: Paul must suffer (Acts 9:16), and Paul must testify in Rome (Acts 23:11; 27:24). In all of these instances, the basic notion was that certain things must occur in order for God's foreordained plan of salvation to be successful. That plan was summarized in Luke 24:46–47: Jesus must die, he must rise again, and the gospel must be preached. Luke presented God as intervening among human affairs in order to make salvation possible. However, he did not present God as controlling or predetermining all human activity.

Luke would not allow for the overarching predetermination of all human events and activities (see Marshall, *Luke*, 104–7). Luke sought to carefully guard the freedom of the human will and was unwilling to make reference to the divine *thelēma* in any way that his gentile readers might associate with the fatalistic worldview from which they were emerging.

from a philological standpoint, it was enormously valuable. What I discovered, however, was that many of my Mayan-speaking friends didn't understand it. What they actually spoke was a hybridized Mayan, and the language of their ancestors was largely unfamiliar to them. Sadly, the endeavor of these missionaries to give the people of the Yucatan a Bible written in their "heart language" was of little benefit to the average "yucateco" of the late twentieth century. Luke as a missionary was aware of this type of pitfall. He realized that a "purist" approach might render his labors ineffective. Knowing the life situations of his audience, he chose to be practical.

His missionary translation of the Lord's Prayer is a "dynamic equivalent" and not a literal, word-for-word transmission of the original. His rendition of this text was faithful to the teachings of Jesus, robust in its message, and concise in its wording. As a pragmatist, Luke emphasized *function* above *form*.

Luke the Theologian

Luke was a man deeply committed to the ideas of prayer, free will, and relationship. These are the recurring thematic backdrops to his stage drama. The themes of prayer and free will recur again and again because Luke believed people actually have a role in the unfolding of God's plan of salvation. God had moved powerfully in the lives of Jesus, the apostles, and the early church because they prayed. Free will was important to Luke because he feared that a collapse into the fatalism of Greco-Roman thought might lead to a slackening in prayer. There was a risk that his readers might conclude, "God will do what God will do, and my prayers won't change anything." Luke wanted them to know that history was hanging in the balance. Their *choice* to persevere in prayer had consequences.

Relationship with God was another important idea for Luke. For him the Lord's Prayer affirmed the relationship with God as Father. Luke presumed his audience generally had good impressions of their fathers. Fathers were generally viewed as being tender, loving, caring, attentive to their children's needs, and emotionally engaged. His readers, however, had not been in the habit of seeing God in this light. For some, God had been remote and distant. Others had once viewed relationship with God as more of a transaction. Luke wanted his audience to connect their positive image of fathers with their understanding of God. He was the Father who wanted to provide for their needs, waited to hear from them every day, and was emotionally invested in their lives.

Relationship in the church was also a priority for Luke. With regard to material provision, he understood that this was not just a "vertical" activity. The giving of "daily bread" happened through the people of the church. And regarding forgiveness, this was also "horizontal" as well as "vertical." And actions had to come as "fruits of repentance," not just words. Luke envisioned a church where no one would have need, and where forgiveness was requested daily and freely given.

Luke the Historian

Luke, as a historian, understood the times. He clearly saw how the plan of salvation was unfolding. God had worked through Israel and then through the man Jesus, and he was now at work in the world through his church. He didn't want his readers to think that the "glory days" had ended with Paul and Peter. Christianity was experiencing spectacular growth, and Luke saw the potential for this growth to continue.

Luke had a passion for shaping history. This was the age in which God was answering prayer powerfully. The Lord's Prayer called upon him to unveil his power and pour out his Spirit. As God sanctified his name by showing his mighty deeds, moved the kingdom forward through the work of the Spirit, and stirred the church from its slumber, the course of human history would be changed.

Luke's is the most vision-driven interpretation that we have yet encountered. Jesus, Matthew, and the *Didache* showed us a prayer that stood in continuity with the narrative history and theology of Israel. Luke's interpretation of this prayer, however, did not endeavor to build bridges to the past. He was a historian, but he utilized history primarily as a motivational tool. In his eyes the Lord's Prayer was, above all else, the prayer of a forward-looking, mission-driven church.

Luke's Lasting Impact

Luke's success as missionary, theologian, and historian are proven in history. It is estimated that in the early centuries of the church, the faith was growing at a rate of 40 percent per decade.[73] Thus, if there were 7,500 Christians at the time Luke wrote, there were about 215,000 one hundred years later and over six million after another hundred years had passed. This type of exponential growth can only be explained by mass conversions such as that encountered on the day of Pentecost (Acts 2). In other words, the growth of Christianity continued to be spectacular.

After many years had passed and the church continued to grow, another commentator on the Lord's Prayer would declare, "Prayer alone conquers God." It would seem that Luke's message got through. The church continued to see the absolute necessity of prayer. And as the decades went by, the Lord's Prayer remained *the* prayer of the Christian church. To the story of its conquering power in third-century North Africa we now turn.

73. Stark estimates that at this time, the faith was growing at a rate of 40 percent per decade. See Rodney Stark, *The Rise of Christianity* (San Francisco: HarperCollins, 1997), 6.

6

Tertullian: "Prayer Alone Conquers God"

As the sun rose upon the white beaches near the North African city of Carthage, Perpetua and her friends walked along the palm-lined streets toward the tombs. It seemed an odd place to hold their first day of class, but that's where the instructor had told them to meet. She had many questions. At the age of twenty-one, it seemed like everything in her world was changing: first marriage, then pregnancy, and now a new religion. Her husband wasn't happy about this, nor was her father. But her brother was rather passionate he when told her about Jesus. He made the message so clear. Her neighbors Saturninus and Secundulus, and even two of her slaves, Revocatus and Felicitas, had also believed. With these friends by her side, she was growing in confidence that this was the life she wanted to live.

The group exited the north gate of the city, walking through the ancient gardens of Megara, toward the burial grounds of the Christians. There they saw a gray-haired man standing in front of a tomb, with a handful of people sitting on the ground in front of him. Saturninus had told her a bit about the instructor. It was a bit unusual that this training was being conducted by a church administrator (called a "senior") rather than a priest or a deacon. But this man had earned a reputation for his sharp mind and his brilliant oratory. His name was Tertullian.

As Perpetua and her friends sat down to join the group, Tertullian began to speak.

You all know that according to Trajan's mandate eighty years ago, it is still technically legal for the authorities to punish any Christian brought before them. Whereas we have enjoyed seasons of peace, it would seem that our rulers (for whom we daily pray) wish to harass us once again. The Emperor Septimus Severus has decreed that no Christian may speak or write in such a way designed to bring about conversion to the Christian faith. Our governor Hilarianus has been particularly zealous to put this order into effect. Each and every day, someone in our midst is being arrested. Our brothers and sisters have been tortured before trial, exiled to remote islands, decapitated, thrown to wild beasts in the amphitheater, torn to shreds by iron hooks, burnt alive, and crucified. We are gathered today at the resting place of our brother Speratus who, when pressed to make an offering to the emperor, declared: "The empire of this world I know not; but rather I serve that God whom no man has seen."

Over the next several months, your commitment to the Christian faith will be tested. I will be teaching you on the prayer which the Lord has taught us, on repentance, and on baptism. If you persevere to the end, you will be received into the Christian church through the washing in water. Should it so happen that you are arrested before your training is completed, that washing may be in your own blood.

Perpetua could sense the other students shudder as Tertullian spoke. Their nervousness was palpable. And yet something about this new faith excited her. It gave her life a sense of purpose. "Those who have nothing to die for," she thought, "probably don't have much to live for."

The months passed and Perpetua attended her classes without fail. In the fall of the year 202, she gave birth to a son, and even though her husband and her father still refused to become Christians, they listened politely as she explained all the things that she was learning. Her father, however, was particularly worried for his daughter. He warned her that she was taking a risk. No one could predict when or who among the Christians would be arrested. As the word was getting out that the prominent young Perpetua was now a follower of Jesus, he feared that the authorities would choose to make an example out of her.

Then it happened. One morning she was on her way to class with the same group of friends that had accompanied her on that first day. A soldier detained them in the street, informing them that they had been accused of evangelizing and that Hilarianus had given an order for their arrest.

Early the next morning, Perpetua's father came to see her in prison, pleading with her to renounce the name "Christian." She picked up a pot that was in her cell. "Do you see this?" she asked. "Yes I do," he replied. "Could it be called by any other name than what it is?" she inquired. "No," he said, and then she replied, "Well, so too I cannot be called anything other than what I am, a Christian."

The next several weeks were nearly unbearable. She was shut up in a dark, crowded cell with nothing other than water. The heat was stifling, beatings were frequent, but most of all she worried about her baby boy. On the day she was arrested, she had left her son at home with her servant. She had not seen him since. But at last there came some reprieve. Deacons from the church had persuaded the guards to move the Christians to a different part of the prison. The conditions were a bit better, and most important, Perpetua was allowed to keep her son with her in the cell.

Word eventually came that there would be a trial. Her father came to see her once again. He kissed her hands and threw himself at her feet.

> "Daughter," he said, "have pity on my grey head—have pity on me your father, if I deserve to be called your father, if I have favored you above all your brothers, if I have raised you to reach this prime of your life. Do not abandon me to be the reproach of men. Think of your brothers, think of your mother and your aunt, think of your child, who will not be able to live once you are gone. Give up your pride! You will destroy all of us! None of us will ever be able to speak freely again if anything happens to you."[1]

---

1. "The Martyrdom of Saints Perpetua and Felicitas," in *The Acts of the Christian Martyrs*, trans. Herbert Musurillo (Oxford: Oxford University Press, 1972), 113.

Perpetua felt compassion for the old man, knowing that he spoke out of love. But the Lord had revealed to her in a vision that she would die for her faith, and she had already accepted this fate.

The trial came, and the Christians were sentenced to death. A cloud of uncertainty hovered over the sentence of her slave Felicitas, however, as she was eight months pregnant, and Roman law did not allow for her to be executed in that state. Felicitas was relieved, however, when the baby was born early. A member of the church adopted her new daughter, and her martyrdom would not be delayed.

Secundulus died in prison, leaving four young Christians to face their deaths in the arena. On that day they entered the crowded amphitheater with joy on their faces. The contest began as the attendants released upon Saturninus and Revocatus a leopard, and then a bear. Perpetua and Felicitas were stripped naked and bound in nets. The crowd shuddered, however, to see these nursing young mothers treated so dishonorably, and the women were thus given tunics to cover themselves.

A wild cow was released upon them, and Perpetua was knocked onto her back. Sitting up, she pulled the tunic over her naked thigh, and fixed her hair. Standing to her feet, she noticed that Felicitas had also been knocked to the ground. Perpetua extended her hand and helped her former slave to stand. She then called out to her fellow Christians in the stands, "You must all stand fast in the faith and love one another, and do not be weakened by what we have gone through."[2]

The young Christians were badly injured, but not dead. The crowd clamored for them to be finished with the sword. Gathering together in a circle, they comforted one another with a kiss of peace. Then, one by one, the gladiators did the deed. The young man assigned to dispatch Perpetua, shaken by what he had seen, missed the mark and struck her on the collarbone. Crying in pain, she took his trembling hand and guided the blade to her neck.

Tertullian wept as he watched his young student fall to the ground.

As he walked home that afternoon, his sadness was unabated, and

2. "Martyrdom of Saints Perpetua and Felicitas," 129.

yet he also felt an enormous sense of pride. His instruction had born fruit. His young disciples had passed the test. *Prayer*, he thought, *was the key*. He remembered the words that he once spoken to his students: "With our hands stretched out and up to God, let them rend us with their iron claws, hang us up on crosses, wrap us in flames, take our heads from us with the sword, let loose the wild beasts on us—the very posture of a Christian praying is one of preparation for all punishment."[3]

He thought about the prayer to which he had dedicated so many class sessions. Perhaps they were praying the Lord's Prayer as they died. He couldn't be sure, but he knew that as the perfect prayer—the prayer that summarized all that Jesus had taught—*this* was the prayer that had given them the strength to endure.[4]

Tertullian and the Lord's Prayer

What was it about Tertullian's teaching that produced such a radical transformation in the lives of his students? Why did he think of the Lord's Prayer as such an incredible source of strength? In this present chapter, we will have the opportunity to join Perpetua, Felicitas, Revocatus, Secundulus, and Saturninus as they sit at the teacher's feet.

Tertullian believed that unexamined beliefs made for weak Christians. He was frustrated by "simple" Christians who didn't know what they believed, didn't realize that there were contradictions in their beliefs, and (worst of all) didn't understand the *implications* of what they believed.[5] For Tertullian, right thinking led to right living.

---

3. See *Apologeticus* 30, ANF 3. I have slightly modified Thelwall's translation, rendering *habitus* as "posture" rather than "attitude."

4. Although this account has the appearance of fiction, most of the information here is based on historical records. "The Martyrdom of Saints Perpetua and Felicitas" includes the prison diaries of Perpetua and an eyewitness account of the events in the amphitheater, possibly written by Tertullian. All named characters are historical. The details concerning the catechesis and the interactions with Tertullian are my own reconstruction. See also "The Passion of the Scillitan Martyrs," in *The Ante-Nicene Fathers*, vol. 9, ed. Allan Menzies, trans. A. Rutherford (New York: Christian Literature Company, 1897), 285.

5. In *De baptismo*, Tertullian states that his teaching "will not be without purpose if it provides equipment for those who are at present under instruction, as well as those others who, content to have believed in simplicity, have not examined the reasons for what has been conferred upon them, and because of inexperience are burdened with a faith which is open to temptation" (*De baptismo* 1 [*ANF* 3]).

He lived in a day when many people were confused about the goodness of God. Some of this was due to poor biblical interpretation. The followers of a teacher named Marcion, for example, had difficulty seeing any goodness in the God of the Old Testament. They saw YHWH as cruel, vindictive, and unloving. They couldn't reconcile the Hebrew God with the loving Father revealed through Jesus Christ. Consequently, they concluded that the God of the Old Testament was evil and that the Father of Jesus was a different God. Tertullian's written response to Marcion (*Adversus Marcionem*) argued that there is in fact only one God revealed in both the Old and New Testaments. And in this work he beautifully presented the controlling idea in all of his theology: God is good and righteous in all of his ways.

In the Lord's Prayer, Tertullian saw a beautiful prayer that reflects the beauty of the creator: "For the prayer which He has taught us suits . . . none but the Creator . . . because He is the supremely and spontaneously good God!"[6] Each petition of the prayer tells of his goodness, and each petition is an invitation extended to God asking him to make his righteous character known on earth.

As Tertullian taught his students about the Lord's Prayer, he called upon them to pray, think, and live in a way that was worthy of this God. As part of his teaching methodology, he made a strong appeal to the philosophical ideas in which many of his students had been educated. The Greeks had explained the existence of the *Logos* as an operative force that held all things together and gave them shape, order, beauty, and continuity. For Tertullian and other early Christian teachers, everything that the philosophers had tried to explain in this teaching was now fulfilled in the person of Jesus. He was the true Logos: the *reason* or *organizing principle* of the created world.

Tertullian saw the Lord's Prayer as the means by which the Logos went into action. This prayer turned confusion into understanding; chaos into order; hatred into love; rebellion into obedience. If Christians could understand the meaning of this prayer, they would be persuaded of God's absolute goodness. If they would commit

---

6. *Adversus Marcionem* 4.36 (ANF 3).

themselves to praying this prayer, then that goodness and beauty would be seen by all of the world.

Tertullian and North African Christianity

The church father Jerome (c. 345–c. 419) wrote a brief account of Tertullian's life containing some information that is considered to be accurate.[7] He recounts Tertullian's fame as an author and his influence on later church leaders. Yet there is also information recorded by Jerome that has been called into question, such as his claim that Tertullian was a presbyter (a pastor) or that he later became a heretic. In actuality, Tertullian was most likely not a member of the clergy but rather a *senior*. This was a leadership position unique to North Africa, and the responsibilities of *seniores* included administration of church affairs, presiding over meetings, and (in the case of Tertullian) the training of those preparing themselves for baptism (catechumens). Most modern scholars doubt that he ever fell into heresy. He had strong "Pentecostal" tendencies, believing wholeheartedly in visions, prophecies, and new revelations. But he never joined any of the breakaway sects such as the Montanists, and he always maintained his formal ties to the catholic church.[8]

Tertullian's teachings and writings had an enormous impact on his own generation and many generations that followed. He is known as the "father of Western theology," and he introduced into our theological lexicon terms such as *Trinity, substance, person,* and *sacrament.* He was the first person to write a formal commentary on the Lord's Prayer, and his interpretation of this prayer laid a foundation that would be built upon by such men as Cyprian (200–258), Augustine (354–430), and Theodore of Mopsuestia (350–427).

Tertullian was a scholar, and his writings prove him to be a man with a high level of education. He was most likely trained in rhetoric, theoretical law (*juris consultus*), as well as poetry, philosophy, and history. It also is apparent that he came from a wealthy and respected

---

7. See the introduction to *ANF* 3:5.
8. See David Rankin, *Tertullian and the Church* (Cambridge: Cambridge University Press, 2005), 3–5.

family. Tertullian's close friendships with the powerful of his day, probably established in school, may explain why he himself was never arrested. It's possible that his pagan friends gave him protection he didn't want or even know about. But he used this apparent immunity to his own advantage. He launched vitriolic counterattacks against all those who criticized or persecuted Christians, and he showed little concern or fear regarding the possible repercussions in his own life.

He had the uncanny ability to irritate pretty much everyone. Among his friends and allies, he was never one to conform, and he was no diplomat toward his enemies. Tertullian was a typical North African Christian, and this meant that he was rigidly moralistic, harsh, passionate, and uncompromising in his convictions. He recognized long before many others that there could be no reconciliation between the pagan Roman culture and the Christian faith. One worldview would win, and the other would lose.

Tertullian and his fellow Christians were in many ways out of place in the cosmopolitan and tolerant city of Carthage. This was a culturally and religiously diverse metropolis in a flourishing region of the Empire.[9] The inhabitants of this city had always extended a warm welcome toward the various religions represented by the numerous ethnic groups living within their walls. Amid all of this "tolerance," however, there was one group that the people of Carthage could not accept, and that was the Christians. This group simply did not know how to get along with others. They claimed that theirs was the only true religion and that all others were false. For this reason, the citizens of Carthage thought that Christianity was tearing apart the very fabric of their society. Consequently, in a city that prided itself on tolerance toward all, Christianity was seen as intolerable.[10]

9. Decret notes that at its height (150–250 CE), Roman Africa had between four and seven million inhabitants and nearly five hundred cities. Carthage, which competed with Alexandria for the title of the "second" Roman city, had around 150,000 inhabitants. François Decret, *Early Christianity in North Africa,* trans. Edward L. Smither (Eugene, OR: Cascade, 2009), 5.

10. Decret notes that "Christianity had not come simply to revive the ancient cults; rather. It wanted to destroy all other worship forms and become the only religion. . . . This claim to one unique religion and a resulting uniformity in belief from East to West was not only insulting to pagans whose gods and long-standing worship would be reduced to the level of superstition, it also touched upon an inherent African aversion to particularism and to becoming aligned to any

In this hostile environment, Christians naturally felt threatened. Michael Brown notes, "The average African saw the world as a battlefield upon which she must be prepared to fight for survival."[11] Tertullian's training course (catechesis) was an intense and vigorous process. Even before students were admitted to the group, they had to pass through an intense period of screening. If they passed, they could attend the classes, which in some cases might last for as long as three years. At the end of their instruction, they were subject to a final examination, testing whether "they have lived soberly, whether they have honoured the widows, whether they have visited the sick, whether they have been active in well-doing."[12] Once baptized, they were then allowed, for the first time, to recite the Lord's Prayer in the company of the congregation.[13]

The Lord's Prayer was considered to be one of the secrets and mysteries of the church, and a great amount of caution was exercised with regard to who could say it. Tertullian had criticized "breakaway" groups because they let the unbaptized participate in all the prayers and customs of the church.[14] For Tertullian and others, this prayer was a pearl that should not be offered to the swine. The privilege of praying the prayer taught by Jesus required years of preparation. And that was the purpose of his classes.

Tertullian's classroom notes have come down to us in three documents known as *De oratione* ("On Prayer"), *De baptismo* ("On

ideological system."Worse still, by planting itself in the midst of the masses, the new religion began to tear at the tightly woven African social fabric. As paganism penetrated every aspect of daily life, it was necessary for Christians, desiring to remain faithful to their convictions, to cut themselves off from their fellow citizens. They were essentially removed from family life and its traditional veneration of ancestors. Unable to participate in weddings and funerals with pagan rituals, African family life was becoming threatened. Christian convictions also proved to be a serious attack against social life in Roman Africa. Town council sessions typically opened with some act of pagan homage. Public festivals and ceremonies—gladiator games in the arena, chariot races around the circus, and plays that depicted mythological characters—were all inaugurated with sacrifices to the chief gods" (*Early Christianity*, 19).

11. Michael Brown, *The Lord's Prayer through North African Eyes* (New York: T&T Clark, 2004), 192.

12. *Traditio apostolica* 20.1 (Hippolytus, *Traditio apostolica*, trans. Burton Easton [Cambridge: Cambridge University Press, 1934]).

13. *Traditio apostolica* 21.25.

14. "It is doubtful who is a catechumen, and who is a believer; they have all access alike, they hear alike, they pray alike—even heathens, if any such happen to come among them. 'That which is holy they will cast to the dogs, and their pearls,' although (to be sure) they are not real ones, 'they will fling to the swine.'" *De praescriptione haereticorum* 41 (*ANF* 3).

Baptism"), and *De paenitentia* ("On Penance"). Our main source will be *De oratione*, which is a detailed, expository teaching on the meaning of the Lord's Prayer. We will make reference, however, to these other two documents and additional writings of Tertullian that help illuminate his thought.

Tertullian's Understanding of the Prayer

De oratione is not an easy read. It is heavily steeped in the thought and vocabulary of the Stoic philosophy that Tertullian used as a framework to explain the Christian faith. It is a deeply theological treatise. And yet there was something about Tertullian's explanation of this prayer that produced a radical transformation in the lives of his students. We now take a seat alongside the young Christians, soon to be martyred, and listen to some of the highlights from Tertullian's teaching on the prayer.

Tertullian's Introductory Remarks (*De oratione* 1)

Our teacher begins his lecture on the Lord's Prayer by explaining that through Jesus, God can be known to us. He is the Word, or the Logos, of God. The students are familiar with this idea from their studies in Greek philosophy. In school they had been taught that the thoughts of a person are unknowable until he or she speaks. When a word (*logos*) is uttered, then the inner world of that person is revealed. In this same way, God would be unknowable if he didn't speak to us, if he didn't make himself known by his Logos.

Tertullian explains that Jesus is the true Logos that the philosophers had been seeking. He is the "the Spirit of God and the Word of God and the reason of God."[15] As the Spirit of God, he is the one through whom God's power is revealed; as the Word of God, he is the one by whom all things were spoken into being; and as the Reason of God, he gives us understanding.[16]

15. Unless otherwise noted, all quotations from *De oratione* are from Stewart-Sykes, *Tertullian.*
16. Bear in mind that Tertullian is writing about 125 years before the Nicene Council. The language

Our teacher goes on to explain that this Logos, by whom God can be known and understood, has "marked out for his new disciples of the new covenant a new form of prayer." Just as a new bottle is required for new wine, and a new patch for a new garment, so it is necessary that a new prayer be given for the new revelation of God that is found in Jesus Christ. Tertullian says (in terms that would now be regarded as supersessionist) that in the Old Testament, people said prayers, but all of the ideas expressed in those prayers are now out of date. All of the hopes and longings addressed in them have been fulfilled. The "fleshly" covenant that God had made with the Jewish people has now been replaced by the gospel of Jesus Christ, which is "spiritual." Therefore, a new prayer is necessary. Even though John had taught his disciples to pray, all he did was lay the foundation for Jesus. No one even remembers the prayer that John taught, Tertullian argues; it was still part of the old system. "Earthly things must yield to heavenly," he explains. "Whoever is of the earth . . . speaks earthly things. . . . And whatever is heavenly is of the Lord Christ, as is this rule of prayer likewise."[17]

Tertullian tells his students that just as Jesus is three things: the Word of God, the Spirit of God, and the Reason of God—so the prayer that he has taught us "is made up of three parts: out of word, by which it is spoken, out of spirit, by which it is powerful, out of reason, in that it reconciles." What he means is that there are three ingredients to this prayer that make it effective. First, it is the mind of God put into words. Second, it is a spiritual (not a fleshly) prayer, and therefore it is powerful. And third, it is rational prayer, and therefore it will win over people's minds and reconcile them to God.

By tying this prayer to the very identity of Jesus the Logos, Tertullian

that he uses to describe the relationship between Jesus and the Spirit represents a more primitive form of Trinitarian theology.

17. I include this quotation from his teaching not because I agree with him but rather because he stands as a representative of the de-Judaization of the Christian faith. He shows little interest in exploring any notion of continuity between the Old Testament concept of prayer and that taught by Jesus. In his eyes the Jews, because of their infidelity, have been replaced by the Christians. The previous covenant has been supplanted by the new covenant in Christ. Whereas his teaching here may reflect the attitudes of his day and therefore merit mention, we must recognize that such a position today would be very unhelpful in any context of Jewish-Christian dialogue.

is communicating the idea that prayer transforms chaos into order and moves all of creation toward the fulfillment of its purpose. Jesus the Logos is the power that brings order and beauty to all the universe. The prayer he gave to his church is the means by which this power operates. What Tertullian wants his students to know is that they are part of God's plan to redeem the world. They are not just bystanders, watching God do his thing. Prayer is collaboration between God and humanity. Jesus took the initiative by teaching this prayer. It expresses the fullness of God's plan for the world. But this plan is only fulfilled when people actually pray the prayer.

Our teacher wraps up his introduction with a few comments on the attitude that we should have as we pray the Lord's Prayer. First, when we're not in church, this prayer should be said in secret. God will hear us even if we pray it silently. Second, we shouldn't be worried about the fact that this is such a short prayer. God provides even without our asking, and he doesn't require long prayers. Finally, we must bear in mind that "as much as it is restricted in words, it is comprehensive in meaning." The Lord's Prayer is the summary of the entire gospel. It embraces every function of prayer, whether worship or petition. It covers the entire "discourse of the Lord" and "the whole record of his instruction." There is nothing that can ever be said in prayer that is not somehow not expressed in the words of the Lord's Prayer. It is the perfect prayer.

God as Father (*De oratione* 2)

The teacher explains that the opening address of the Lord's Prayer is an affirmation of the identity of God as Father. "It begins with bearing witness to God and with the reward of faith when we say, 'Father, you who are in the heavens.'" To call God Father is a "form of address which demonstrates both *pietas* and *potestas*." Both of these words are laden in meaning for the students. *Pietas* describes the "rules" that govern their relationships in family and society. And *potestas* means the ability to actually get things done.

All of their lives they have been taught about the idea of *pietas*. They always have to be aware of the person with whom they are dealing. They might talk to a slave or a friend in a casual, careless way. But in the presence of people who held positions of honor, they have to be very conscientious about how they act and what they say. This is especially true in their relationships with their fathers. In school they had read the writings of Epictetus, who had explained what *pietas* meant in the father-son relationship: "Next, remember that you are a son. What is the commitment made by this role? That he considers all that is his own as being under his father's sway, that he obeys him in all matters, never criticizes him to someone else, and neither says nor does anything to harm him, defers to him, and concedes to him on all occasions, cooperating with him as much as he can."[18] Tertullian wants his students to view the relationship with God the Father in this same way. *Pietas* implies both honor and intimacy.

By tying together this idea of *pietas* with *potestas*, the teacher is explaining that a right understanding of God as Father is what makes prayer effective. When we render to God what is rightfully his, namely faith, his power is at work on our behalf. This is seen in John 1:12, which states, "To those who believe in him, he gave the power to be called children of God."

Tertullian then explains that addressing God as Father is a way of recognizing "those who are his." Our duty is not fulfilled by honoring the Father alone. We must also show honor to all that all are connected to him. This includes the Son, "for now we know that the Son is the new name of the Father." But it also means that we give honor to the church: "Nor is the mother, the church neglected, since the mother is found within the Father and the Son, for the name of Father and Son find their meaning in her."

In summary, the teacher wants his students to understand that it is a tremendous privilege to call God Father. There is great authority in the prayers we lift up as sons and daughters of God. But he wants us to

---

18. *Diatribai* 2.10.7 (Epictetus, "*Diatribi*," in *The Stoics Reader: Selected Writings and Testimonia*, trans. Brad Inwood and Lloyd Gerson [Indianapolis: Hackett, 2008]).

know that with this privilege come the responsibilities to show honor to God as Father, his Son, and his people on the earth, the church.

Hallowing the Name of God (*De oratione* 3)

"The name of God the Father has been revealed to nobody," the teacher goes on to say, "but to us it is revealed in the Son. For now we know that Son is the new name of the Father." To honor the name of Jesus, therefore, is to honor the Father.

We seek to honor God's name, Tertullian explains, but we should not think of God as somehow *needing* this from us.

> It's not appropriate for us to give God our "good wishes" as if it were even possible for people to do that, or as if he might experience some kind of hardship if we didn't wish him well. . . . Is there any time when God's name is not holy or being hallowed? . . . Don't the angels surround him declaring, "Holy, Holy, Holy"? . . . Thus, when we say "hallowed be your name" our petition is for his name to be honored in those of us who belong to him, as well as for those who are yet to come to grace.[19]

Tertullian is affirming here certain aspects of what his students have always believed about the Supreme Being. They have studied Plato, who said that God "always everywhere and in all things has the most perfect sufficiency, and is never in need of anything else."[20] Thus, they don't have any difficulty understanding the idea that God doesn't have needs. He doesn't ask us to honor his name as if there were some deficiency in his nature or character that requires this from us.

But even as honoring God's name is not necessary for God's personal well-being, *it is necessary* in order for people to be saved. What Tertullian touches upon here ties into a broader theme of his teachings. God does not command us to pray because of some personal need within his being. But prayer is necessary for people to come to salvation and for God's desires to be accomplished on earth. There is a difference between the *ontology* of God and the *economy of salvation*.

---

19. This is my own "dynamic equivalent" of Stewart-Sykes' translation. Unfortunately, many translations of Tertullian's works, especially those from the nineteenth century, are rendered in difficult English. Where appropriate, I will update certain passages.
20. Plato, *Philebus*, trans. Benjamin Jowett (Kindle Edition, 2012), 84.

The ontology of God describes who he is apart from anyone or anything else. In this sense, Plato was right—God is perfectly sufficient in himself. There is no deficiency in his nature that somehow needs to be filled. But the *economy of salvation* describes the "house rules" that God set in place when he created the world. For example, he could have made salvation possible by any number of means, but he made it possible through Jesus. This means that honoring the name of Jesus is now *necessary* in order for salvation to occur. Or put another way, God *needs* people to believe in Jesus and find forgiveness in him. There is no other way that his desire for all to be saved can be fulfilled. Thus, in the *ontology* of God, he has no needs. But in the *economy of salvation* that God has set in place, he does have needs.

Tertullian is introducing this idea slowly to his students because he is aware that it requires a "leap" in their thinking. He will be coming back to this idea again. He knows that they will struggle reconciling the sovereignty of God with the need for prayer. He is affirming here what they may see as a paradox: God is the perfectly sufficient, all-powerful ruler of the universe who needs nothing and no one. And yet God is the loving, caring Father who has chosen to entwine his life and his desires with the human race. He desires all people to honor his name, and prayer is necessary to bring that about.[21]

The Will of God (*De oratione* 4)

Tertullian continues his teaching with an explanation of the petition, "Let your will be done in the heavens and the earth."[22] There are two aspects of the will of God that Tertullian wants to emphasize. One is the human choice to actively do God's will by obeying his commands. The other is the passive acceptance of the things that God brings to pass in our lives, that is to say, the act of surrendering to God's will.

---

21. For a more thorough discussion of Tertullian's "harmony of opposites" and how it relates to Stoic thought, see Clark, *Lord's*, 190–92.
22. Note that Tertullian places the petition for the *will* before the *kingdom*. The exact wording and order of the Lord's Prayer in *De oratione* is unique to Tertullian. We remember that his aim with his students was to explain the meaning of the prayer and not necessarily to train them in how the prayer was to be recited. They weren't yet allowed to say the prayer, thus Tertullian may have been deliberately casual about the wording.

Regarding the second point, Tertullian reminds his students that "there is nothing evil" in the will of God. The teacher seems to foresee that some of his students will be put to the test and explains that "let your will be done" is a prayer for endurance. Jesus prayed, "Father, take away this cup" because he was in great suffering. Yet he also prayed, "Let not my will but yours be done." In the same way, our request here is for the strength to accept whatever cup God asks us to drink.

The teacher also explains that there is an active dimension to this petition. God's will is accomplished when people choose to obey his commands. "For what would God wish other than that we should act in accordance with his direction?" Tertullian reminds his students that this petition does not suggest that God needs our help to accomplish his will. We pray "let your will be done . . . not because someone is opposing that God's will be done and he needs our prayers in order to be successful in implementing it."[23] Rather, we pray for his will to be done in all people. "We ask then for him to supply us with the substance and effect of his will, that we may be saved both in heaven and in earth: because the sum-total of his will is the salvation of those he has made his children."[24]

At this juncture, we may be a bit confused. On the one hand, Tertullian has said that the doing of God's will is brought about by human obedience. On the other hand, he has said that no one can resist the will of God and that human prayer can have no bearing on God's success in carrying it out. This seems like a contradiction. He commands us to pray for his will to be done, and yet no one can resist God, and he doesn't need anyone's help to carry out his desires. This may not make sense to us. But Tertullian's students, particularly those who have studied Stoic philosophy, are comfortable with this paradox. To get to the bottom of what he is saying, we must "dig in" to the Stoic ideas that here served as a framework for Tertullian's thought.

Stoics believed in the unalterable path of providence (*fatum*), and yet

---

23. My translation, based on Stewart-Sykes'.
24. From *Tertullian's Tract of the Prayer*, trans. Ernest Evans (London: SPCK, 1953), 9.

at the same time, they maintained that the human will is free.[25] They saw the "final destination" of human history as being determined by God, and yet they believed that people have the ability to make choices along the way. Think of a group people on a boat traveling along the Nile to Alexandria. They can move about freely, sit or stand, talk or keep silent, or even jump off—but nothing that they do can change the fact that the boat will end up in Alexandria. Stoics believed that people have the ability to choose between good and evil, but nothing that people do can have any final bearing on the outcome of human history. The goal of the Stoics was to not rock the boat. *You may not be able to change the final destination, but you can at least make the choices that will lead to a pleasant journey for yourself and others.* They called this "living according to nature."[26]

Tertullian's concept of God's will in many ways parallels Stoic thought, with some modifications. He believes that the final destination of history has been determined by God's will. No human activity or choices can alter that. At the same time, Tertullian believes that people have a free will. They can choose between obedience and disobedience, faith and disbelief. All people have the ability to choose whether they will align themselves with God's will or reject it.

His thoughts on these matters have been more fully explained in his other writings. In his text *Against Marcion*, for example, he writes regarding humanity, "Entire freedom of will, therefore, was conferred upon them . . . so that, as master of himself, he might constantly encounter good by freewill observance of it, and evil by its freewill

---

25. Stoics argued that the existence of evil serves as evidence that providence does not control human behavior. Greene notes, "Cleanthes, perceiving the fact of evil, sought to relieve Providence, though not Fate, from responsibility for it, arguing (unlike Chrysippus) that though all that comes through Providence is also fated, not all that is fated is providential. He goes further, and places the moral responsibility for evil squarely on the shoulders of man, holding that God nevertheless knows how to make evil contribute to good" (William Greene, *Moira: Fate, Good, and Evil in Greek Thought* [Gloucester: Peter Smith, 1968], 344–45).

26. Greene describes this aspect of Stoic thought in the following way: "What must be, must be; but man, by his insight, may will to do what must be done, and so may act in harmony with nature; or, again, he may resist. The result, considered externally, will be the same in either case, for man cannot overrule Nature, or Fate; but by willing cooperation, by making its law his law, he can find happiness, or by resignation he can at least find peace" (ibid., 340).

avoidance."[27] In another work, Tertullian explores the relationship between the free human will and the divine will:

> The person with a good and sold faith should never refer to "all that happens" as God's will, and no one should flatter himself by saying that "nothing happens apart from what He allows," as if to say that there is nothing that we, in our own power, cannot do. If this were the case—if everything that happens were God's will—then sin would be excused. That way of thinking would lead to the destruction of our way of life (nay) and even of God Himself—if it can be said that He makes happen by His own will things that He does not will, or if there is, in fact, nothing that He doesn't will. . . . Accordingly, we should not blame "God's will" for those things that we ourselves choose.[28]

Tertullian is saying in this passage that we should never think of God's will as *everything that actually happens*. If this were the case, then people might argue that sinful, evil choices were somehow part of "God's will." This mindset, Tertullian says, threatens to destroy the Christian faith, and even God himself! There are many things in this world that God does not *will* to happen, but they do happen because people make choices that are contrary to what he wants.

Thus we ask: What was Tertullian talking about when he said that no one can resist the will of God? The answer is this: no one can change the final destination of the creation. Individuals can resist the will of God in their own lives, but in the end God's will for the world prevails. In other words, this boat is heading to the New Jerusalem. All of creation is going to be renewed and restored. Nothing that any person does can alter the fact that this renewal is coming. Yet to each person is given the freedom to choose whether he or she will ride this boat by obeying God's commands or jump off by disobeying. God's providence is guiding the creation toward its final destination. At the end of human history God's righteous character—his absolute goodness and justice—will be seen by all. In his justice he will save those who have believed and condemn those who have not. All things

---

27. *Adversus Marcionem* 2.6 (ANF 3). I have translated *sponte* as "freewill" instead of Thelwell's "spontaneous." See also 2.5, 9.
28. *De exortatione castitatis* 2.2, 4 (ANF 4). My own rendering of Thelwell's translation.

are working toward this end, and no human activity can alter this course upon which creation has been set.[29]

To say that God's will cannot be resisted means that the goodness of God will always prevail. Individuals will exercise their free wills, sometimes choosing to obey God's commands and sometimes choosing evil. But God in his resourcefulness will always do what is necessary to bring about the good. This doesn't mean that everyone will be saved in the end. But it does mean that all of creation will recognize God's justice and righteous character. Everything in human history is moving toward this goal. People and evil powers may oppose the doing of God's will, but in the end his goodness will be seen by all. Tertullian wrote to Marcion, giving this explanation for God's actions in history:

> He will be moved, but not subverted. He will respond accordingly in each circumstance. Every action provokes a feeling in him: anger in response to the wicked, and indignation in response to the ungrateful, and jealousy in response to the proud. . . . But he shows mercy when people lose their way, and he is patient even with the unrepentant . . . he does whatsoever is necessary to bring about the good.[30]

God will be "moved but not subverted." God is affected by the activities of human beings. He acts and reacts as they exercise their free will. But ultimately, God will triumph in his purpose for humanity.

In conclusion, the teacher has explained that there is, on one hand, a fixed, unalterable element of God's will. On the other hand, there is also a conditional element to it as well. We have the freedom to obey or disobey God's commands, and we have the freedom to accept or reject the things that he brings to pass in our lives. Consequently, we must

---

29. In *Adversus Marcionem* Tertullian has made this clear. He argues there that God created the world in goodness and justice and that it was out of God's goodness that he gave humans free will. In the beginning, the goodness of God was manifest without opposition. "But yet, when evil afterwards broke out, and the goodness of God began now to have an adversary to contend against, God's justice also acquired another function, even that of directing His goodness according to men's application for it" (*Adversus Marcionem* 2.13 [*ANF* 3]). God offers his goodness to the worthy and denies it to the unthankful. "The entire office of justice in this respect becomes an agency for goodness: whatever it condemns by its judgment, whatever it chastises by its condemnation, whatever . . . it ruthlessly pursues, it, in fact, benefits with good instead of injuring. . . . Thus God is wholly good, because in all things He is on the side of good" (*Adversus Marcionem* 2.13 [*ANF* 3]).
30. This is my paraphrase of *Adversus Marcionem* 2.16 (*ANF* 3).

seek God for both obedience and endurance. This is what we do when we pray, "let your will be done."[31]

Let Your Kingdom Come (*De oratione* 5)

Tertullian goes on to explain that our understanding of the petition "let your kingdom come" is similar to "let your will be done." We don't ask for the kingdom because we imagine that God is not already king: "For when is God, in whose hand is the heart of all kings not the king?" He is the sovereign ruler. This prayer is for ourselves, that every choice we make would be submitted to his choices, and every hope that we have would be aligned to his hopes.

He then says that God desires to openly reveal his kingdom to the world and that he has put this desire and expectation in his people. Consequently, the church should not ask for a prolongation of this earth because the coming of the kingdom means "the consummation of the world."[32] Even if Christians were not instructed to pray this way, we should still desire the speedy coming of the kingdom, for this is what even the martyrs in heaven pray.

What we see here is consistent with what Tertullian has said in his other works. The kingdom of God is not, in his view, a present reality. The kingdom only comes to the earth when Jesus returns. Consequently, neither here nor anywhere in his writings does Tertullian express the hope that this world can somehow be transformed: "One thing in this life greatly concerns us," he wrote,

31. Thus we see that in Tertullian's view, God's will is not always done in individual lives, but it ultimately will be accomplished for the whole of creation. This tension is similar to that found in Stoic thought, which maintained that the choices of individuals would have no bearing on the final outcome of human history. The difficulty of maintaining this separation between the *summands* and the *summation* of human activity was not lost upon the critics of Stoicism, namely Plutarch, who argued that Stoicism ultimately collapsed into determinism (cf. Greene, *Moira*, 337–70). What appears to be Tertullian's resolution of this problem is the notion that the exercise of human freedom does *in fact* contribute to the fulfillment of God's ultimate purpose. Because humanity has been endowed with divine reason, many will in fact choose to believe. God's goodness and justice will be manifest as he rewards each person according to his or her deeds, and the power of Christ will result in the salvation of those who have believed.
32. Tertullian here contradicts what he has said elsewhere: "Without ceasing, for all our emperors we offer prayer. We pray for life prolonged; for security to the empire; for protection to the imperial house; for brave armies, a faithful senate, a virtuous people, the world at rest, whatever, as man or Cæsar, an emperor would wish" (*Apologeticus* 30 [*ANF* 3]).

"and that is, to get quickly out of it."[33] The citizenship of the Christian was in heaven, not on earth: "But as for you, you are a foreigner in this world, a citizen of Jerusalem, the city above. Our citizenship, the apostle says, is in heaven. You have your own registers, your own calendar; you have nothing to do with the joys of the world; nay, you are called to the very opposite, for 'the world shall rejoice, but ye shall mourn.'"[34]

In this respect, Tertullian represented the mindset of his times. François Decret points out, "In Tertullian's day, the Christian movement did not integrate into the life of the African city or pursue social justice. The church perfectly tolerated the Roman Empire and the African society to which it belonged and managed to focus effectively on its interests, which did not include challenging the political order."[35] Tertullian believed that the day of the Lord was near. The prayer "let your kingdom come" was simply a request for its hastening.

Daily Bread (*De oratione* 6)

As Tertullian begins his remarks on the fourth petition, he acknowledges that the nature of this request is for "earthly needs." He goes on to say, however, that "Give us this day our daily bread" is better understood in a spiritual sense. For Jesus had said, "'I am the bread of life,'" and the "bread is the word of the living God." And his body is the bread of the Lord's Supper. He concludes that "when we ask for our daily bread, we are asking that we should perpetually be in Christ and that we should not be separated from his body."

The teacher's main point is that even though a material understanding of bread is acceptable, the deeper understanding of this petition is the request for spiritual bread. When Jesus spoke of bread in his parables, it was always a metaphor for spiritual provision. The gentiles preoccupy themselves with material gain. The children of God

---

33. *Apologeticus* 41 (*ANF* 3).
34. *De corona* 13 (*ANF* 3).
35. Decret, *Early Christianity*, 44.

are not to share in their anxiety. Thus, even though there is a material aspect to the request for bread, it is limited. He emphasizes that we only request one day's provision, and thus follow Christ's command, "Take no thought for what you should eat tomorrow."

We see this same line of interpretation elsewhere in Tertullian's writings: "(He) who was wont to profess 'food' to be, not that which His disciples had supposed, but 'the thorough doing of the Father's work'; teaching 'to labour for the meat which is permanent unto life eternal'; in our ordinary prayer likewise commanding us to request 'bread,' not the wealth of Attalus therewithal."[36] We may ask why Tertullian had such a discomfort with a material application for this petition. Michael Brown suggests:

> Being somewhat insulated from the vagaries of the production and distribution of food, it is understandable that high-status Christians would be somewhat disinclined to further the idea that a thoroughly benevolent God should be asked for something as necessary to survival as food.... And yet at the same time, Tertullian would have sought to avoid the implication that "God was not fundamentally concerned with material matters."[37]

Our teacher is trying to strike a balance. He acknowledges that God is concerned with our physical well-being and that there is a place for material requests. But he argues that the better understanding of the request for bread is the spiritual. Thus, what we really ask for is to remain in Christ.

The Forgiveness of Sins (De oratione 7)

As Tertullian continues his teaching with an explanation on "forgive us our debts," we are shocked to learn about the practice of penance in the church of Carthage. "A confession is a request for pardon, because whoever asks pardon confesses a wrongdoing. So it is shown that penance (exomologesis) is acceptable to God, because he desires this, rather than the death of a sinner."[38]

36. De ieiunio 15 (ANF 4).
37. Brown, Lord's Prayer, 20.

Exomologesis is a word that strikes fear into the hearts of the students. They have heard rumors about this practice, and the time is approaching for them to participate. In his other lectures he has explained more fully what is involved. In his class on penance, he says:

> And thus exomologesis is a discipline for man's prostration and humiliation, enjoining a demeanor calculated to move mercy. With regard also to the very dress and food, it commands (the penitent) to lie in sackcloth and ashes, to cover his body in mourning, to lay his spirit low in sorrows, to exchange for severe treatment the sins which he has committed; moreover, to know no food and drink but such as is plain—not for the stomach's sake, to wit, but the soul's; for the most part, however, to feed prayers on fastings, to groan, to weep and make outcries unto the Lord your God; to bow before the feet of the presbyters, and kneel to God's dear ones; to enjoin on all the brethren to be ambassadors to bear his deprecatory supplication (before God). All this exomologesis (does), that it may enhance repentance; may honour God by its fear of the (incurred) danger; may, by itself pronouncing against the sinner, stand in the stead of God's indignation, and by temporal mortification (I will not say frustrate, but) expunge eternal punishments.[39]

And during his class on baptism he also explains:

> They who are about to enter baptism ought to pray with repeated prayers, fasts, and bendings of the knee, and vigils all the night through, and with the confession of all bygone sins. . . . To us it is matter for thankfulness if we do now publicly confess our iniquities or our wickedness: for we do at the same time both make satisfaction for our former sins, by mortification of our flesh and spirit, and lay beforehand the foundation of defences against the temptations which will closely follow.[40]

Perhaps no other practice in the North African church better illuminates their attitude toward sin. In language that rings familiar to us today, Tertullian refers to this practice as *enhanced repentance*. The idea is to create (for the students) an association between suffering and sin. In the time leading up to their baptism, they will confess their sins and punish their bodies. They will starve, weep, spend sleepless nights,

38. It is notable that Tertullian here uses the transliterated Greek term, indicating that it is a formal practice of the church known by this name.
39. *De paenitentia* 9 (*ANF* 3).
40. *De baptismo* 20 (*ANF* 3).

and lay prostrate before the church leaders as they publically confess their sins. This practice will no doubt "weed out" those who are not serious about becoming Christians. This is their "boot camp." If they can make it through this difficult time of training, the foundation will be in place for them to resist temptation throughout their lives.

The teacher's hope is that every time they say "forgive us our debts," they will remember their *exomologesis* and shudder. The purpose of confessing sins within the Lord's Prayer is not simply to engage in a transaction to cancel debt. Every sin must be dealt with in sincere repentance, and the purpose of that painful initiation is to encourage repentance as a way of life.

Temptation and the Evil One (*De oratione* 8)

Tertullian goes on to say that God's intention is not only for Christians to receive forgiveness from sin but to avoid it altogether. He explains that there is a petition in the Lord's Prayer that says, "Do not lead us into temptation." He acknowledges the fact that there has been some confusion among Christians with regard to the meaning of these words. God doesn't tempt his children, and therefore it seems strange that we should ask him not to tempt us. He says that we should never think of God as trying to get us to stumble. "For God is not ignorant of the condition of our faith, nor does he seek to dethrone it." Therefore, the petition "do not lead us into temptation" means this: "do not allow us so to be led by the one that tempts," that is, the Devil. He is "the leader and worker of temptation." Thus, the last two phrases of the Lord's Prayer, "do not lead us into temptation" and "remove us from the evil one," are really one and the same request.

Reflecting on Tertullian's words, we see that he takes on one of the most difficult challenges in the interpretation of the Lord's Prayer. The simplest and most logical interpretation of the petition is that we are asking God not to tempt us. But Tertullian recognizes that this suggestion reflects poorly on the character of God: *Why would he want to tempt us? Does he want to see us fall?* So he resolves this problem in a very cavalier way. He first cites the proper Latin rendition of the phrase "do not lead us into temptation" (*ne nos inducas in tentationem*). But then he rephrases it (without any exegetical or grammatical justification) as, "do not allow us to be led by the person who tempts" (*ne nos patiaris induci, ab eo utique qui temptat*). In other words, he doesn't like the way this petition sounds, so he changes it. Tertullian's "correction" to the text of the Lord's Prayer will become so influential that the churches of North Africa will actually pray the prayer his way instead of Matthew's![41]

Tertullian bases his interpretation on theological reasoning rather than grammar. In another one of his writings (*De fuga in persecutione*) he explains his rationale. The topic is persecution, and he wants to make it clear that this type of trial comes from the Devil and not from God. God allows persecution to happen because it creates the opportunity for Christians to demonstrate the strength of their faith. God permits it to happen, but the actual deed is inflicted by Satan. God's purpose in allowing persecution is that "righteousness may be perfected in injustice, as strength is perfected in weakness."[42]

But even if the testing of persecution is something that God periodically allows, Tertullian argues that we can still ask God to preserve us from it. So it is "that both things belong to God, the shaking of faith as well as the shielding of it, when both are sought from Him—the shaking by the devil, the shielding by the Son."[43] He then ties these arguments into the final petitions of the Lord's Prayer:

> But in the prayer prescribed to us, when we say to our Father, "Lead us not into temptation" (now what greater temptation is there than persecution?), we acknowledge that that comes to pass by His will whom we beseech to exempt us from it. For this is what follows, "But deliver us from the wicked one," that is, do not lead us into temptation by giving us up to the wicked one, for then are we delivered from the power of the devil, when we are not handed over to him to be tempted.[44]

---

41. Cf. Robert Simpson, *The Interpretation of Prayer in the Early Church* (Philadelphia: Westminster, 1965), 63–64; and Stewart-Sykes, *Tertullian*, 39. Cyprian incorporated Tertullian's explanatory gloss (*De oratione* 8.4) into the actual text of the prayer.
42. *De fuga in persecutione* 2 (ANF 4).
43. Ibid.
44. Ibid.

What we see in Tertullian's teaching is a somewhat nuanced argument on temptation. First, he says that persecution and injustice come from the Devil. But God may sometimes let the Devil have his way with us if God deems that such a test may strengthen our faith. We can ask God to exempt us from these testings, but the teacher acknowledges that this may not always be a successful prayer. In spite of our plea not to be tested, God may still allow persecution to come. In *De oratione*, he notes that both Abraham and Jesus were subject to trial. Thus it is natural that the believers should expect the same.

We find Tertullian's thoughts on these matters intriguing. What he envisions is a dynamic relationship between God and the believer. We think about what the teacher had said before: "God will be moved, but not subverted." He will always "get his way," but there are many paths to the fulfillment of his will. Tertullian invites us to engage God in relationship. God will act and react in response to what we do, how we think, and how we pray.[45] He invites us to plead with him and persuade him, to show him what is in our hearts. Maybe God, in the end, will determine that the testing of our faith is not necessary. Maybe he will determine that it is necessary. Or perhaps God will decide that even as our faith is strong, he wants to give us the opportunity to show the world how strong it is.

Perhaps it was this understanding that helped the Christians of Carthage sort out all that was happening in their world. When Perpetua, Felicitas, and their friends did eventually die in the amphitheater, Tertullian and the other Christians in the stands may have asked themselves, "Why them and not us?" These events would make no sense apart from the fact that God knows each person's heart and has a different plan for each one. It was Perpetua who had cried out to her brothers and sisters, "You must all stand fast in the faith and love one another, and do not be weakened by what we have gone through." Her suffering became a source of strength for the church.

---

45. It is within this same framework that Tertullian defends the notion of God's repentance. In *Adversus Marcionem* 2.24 (*ANF* 3) he argues that sometimes God alters a previously declared course of action as a consequence of human activity. This repentance is simply a change of mind, "which in God we have shown to be regulated by the occurrence of varying circumstances."

She had prayed that this trial would never come, but when it did, she was able to take a great evil and turn it to good.

Tertullian's Concluding Remarks (*De oratione* 9, 29)

As he wraps up his thoughts on the Lord's Prayer,[46] the teacher reminds his students that this brief prayer is not only a summary of the gospel but of the entire Bible: "How many are the statements of the prophets, gospels, and apostles, the words of the Lord, parables, illustrations, instructions, touched performed on one occasion!" So much is accomplished in this prayer: the giving of honor, the witness to faith, the offering of obedience, the remembrance of hope, the quest for life, the confession of sin, and the awareness of temptation. Only God himself could have created such an effective form of prayer.

He goes on to say that because the Lord's Prayer proceeds from the Spirit and the Truth, and because it is God who commanded them to pray as such, God cannot deny these requests. "Prayer alone conquers God," he says. The purpose of prayer is only for the good, and all that it accomplishes is for the good of the church and the entire world. Prayer is an invitation to God, asking him to make his goodness seen on earth. God is infinitely good. But in order for that goodness to be fully revealed on earth, the people of God on earth must pray.

Conclusion

To conclude, we consider once again the question presented at the beginning of this chapter: What was it about Tertullian's teaching on the Lord's Prayer that produced such a radical transformation in the lives of his students? Reflecting on his teaching, three overarching themes are of note: (1) his insistence on the absolute goodness of God; (2) the freedom and responsibility he attributed to women and men; and (3) his emphasis on *relationship* with God. We shall look at each of these in turn.

---

46. In what would have been Tertullian's oral delivery of this teaching, my position is that *De oratione* 9 and 29 represent his conclusion, while chapters 10–28 were added to the "print" version.

First, Tertullian deeply believed in the fundamental *goodness* of the Christian God. Tertullian's God was righteous in all of his ways and fully trustworthy in his character. We are challenged to seek his honor because *he is good.* With joy we look to the time when he will be king over all of the earth because *he is good.* We obey his commands and we surrender to his ways because his will for us *is good.* We look to him for provision, we ask him for protection, and we trust in his mercy because he is good.

For Tertullian, the Lord's Prayer was proof of God's character. Against Marcion's claim that this prayer was addressed to a different god than YHWH, Tertullian appealed to the goodness of God revealed in the Old Testament and celebrated in the Lord's Prayer:

> Who can I call Father? Him who had nothing at all to do with making me, from whom I do not come—or him who by making me became my Creator? Whom will I ask for the Holy Spirit? A god who cannot even instill an earthly spirit, or the one who created the angels, and whose Spirit hovered over the waters in the beginning? Shall I ask the one who is not the king of glory to send the kingdom, or should I ask the one who holds the heart of kings in his hands? Who will give me daily bread? Will it be the god who has never even created a grain of wheat, or him who provided his people the daily bread of angels? Who will forgive my sins? The god who does not judge them and does because he forgets about them? Or him who if he does not forgive, will remember and will judge? Who is it that will not allow us to be led into temptation? He whom the tempter does not fear, or he who since the beginning of the world has condemned the angel who became the tempter?[47]

Tertullian believed that the Lord's Prayer was an effective prayer because it appealed to the goodness of the one true God.

Tertullian's God could accomplish his purposes among the human race without the need for coercion or control. With the Stoics, he shared the conviction that in the end, God will win. But unlike those who assert that God must predetermine all things in order for his purposes to prevail, Tertullian saw no conflict between the freedom of the human will and the sovereignty of God. God is the all-powerful

---

47. *Adversus Marcionem* 4.26 (Tertullian, *Adversus Marcionem*, trans. Ernest Evans [London: Oxford University Press, 1972]). This is my "updated" rendition of Evans.

king of the universe who will use all means necessary to display his righteousness to all of humanity. Tertullian's God is confident that this manifestation of goodness will win over the human heart. Not all will be saved, but all will recognize his justice.

Second, and in correlation with the first point, we note that Tertullian's God has given humanity both freedom and responsibility. Prayer is not a process of personal alignment to fate; it is truly an invitation to participate with God in shaping the course of human history. In the economy of this creation, prayer is necessary for the fulfillment of God's purposes. Jesus is the Logos, the power that brings order and beauty to the universe. Jesus is the Word of God, the Spirit of God, and the Reason of God. The Lord's Prayer also consists of word, spirit, and reason. What this means is that the Lord's Prayer (and all prayer) is the instrument by which the Logos fulfills his purpose in the world. Prayer transforms chaos into order and moves all of creation toward the full display of God's goodness.

Women and men are part of God's plan to redeem the world. But in order to fulfill this calling, we must exercise our free will. We must choose to pray. An enormous responsibility has been given to us, and we must act.

Third, we note in Tertullian's teachings an emphasis on relationship. His God is not an impersonal force at work in the world to carry out his foreordained decrees. He is a living God who invites women and men into dynamic relationship. He listens to them, wrestles with them, and takes their pleas into account. He is not predictable, and he is not easy to serve. Those who wish to be called by his name must be willing to pay the price. Admittance into the church is not an easy path. The Christian life may quickly turn into a Christian death. But Tertullian invites his students to count the cost and consider the reward. In his view, relationship with the creator of the universe is the highest good that anyone could ever hope for.

It is my conviction that this presentation of God's goodness, humanity's freedom, and relationship resulted in a compelling call to the Christian faith. Tertullian understood that right thinking about

God led to a right way of living for God. A woman will not die for a God that she does not believe is good. She will not pay the ultimate price if she does not believe that her choice will shape history. And she will not suffer for one whom she does not intimately know. Somehow, Tertullian instilled these convictions in his students, and consequently Perpetua could see no alternative in life: "I cannot be called anything other than what I am, a Christian."

7

Conclusion

The Story of the Lord's Prayer

The Lord's Prayer was born out of the Jewish experience of first-century Palestine, during a time of religious upheaval. Many people were frustrated with "the system." Most still participated in the sacrifices and festivals, even as they were searching for a deeper level of encounter with their God. The perceived weakness of the priestly system was that it created a barrier between the people and YHWH. The experience of the divine glory was limited to the confines of the temple, where the priests owned the ritual. They said the prayers and offered the sacrifices while the common people were relegated to the role of bystanders.

In this setting, a movement was taking shape to extend the holiness of YHWH into the home, village, and synagogue. The men saw themselves as priests, the community was the temple, and the synagogue was their inner sanctuary. The offering being lifted up to God was the sacrifice of prayer. In this way they entered into his presence, reaffirmed their faith, and made their needs known. First-century Palestine was experiencing a revival of prayer. People were taking ownership of their worship. It was in this setting that Jesus taught his followers to pray the Lord's Prayer.

This prayer was not radically different from other Jewish prayers. The people had long thought of YHWH as their father. The honoring of his name, his rule over all things, and the accomplishment of his will were common themes in their prayers. Material dependence, the need to confess and forgive sin, and victory over temptation and evil were also well-worn motifs. What made the prayer of Jesus unique—even revolutionary—was the idea that all of these requests and longings had now found their fulfillment in him.

In the framework of the Deuteronomic Covenant, Israel had been chosen by YHWH as the one people to whom he would reveal himself and through whom he would make himself known to the nations. God had made a contract with Israel, but the people had struggled to honor the terms of the agreement. Consequently the nations had not come to worship Israel's God. Jesus called Israel to renew the covenant with YHWH. In the temptation, he figuratively went back to the wilderness, where he modeled his vision of covenant faithfulness. The Lord's Prayer was his invitation to join him in the community of covenant renewal. Israel could restore its relationship with YHWH and draw all nations to worship him by saying and living out this prayer.

Those who responded to his invitation came to see themselves as the new Israel. Just as the *Shema* and the *Amidah* had been the signature prayers of the synagogue communities, so the Lord's Prayer became the identity marker of Jesus's disciples. This was the prayer they said together every day. And everywhere that the gospel was preached, the new followers of Christ were being taught to pray in this way.

For several decades, the teachings of Jesus and the story of his life were passed along orally. Then, in the latter half of the first century, a wave of texts was written to record what he had said and done. The Gospels of Matthew and Luke and the *Didache* each included the Lord's Prayer, and each text presented this prayer in a unique way. To a large extent, their interpretations were built on the foundation that Jesus had established. The notions of *prayer as sacrifice, community as temple,* and *covenant fulfillment* were now firmly established in Christian thought.[1] The basic vocabulary of the prayer remained intact, yet each author instilled new meaning within it.

Matthew

Matthew believed that through the Lord's Prayer, the church could transform the cosmological order. He saw an unnatural separation between the realms of heaven and earth that the church was called to bridge. The Lord's Prayer turns one's gaze toward the heavenly realm: the place where *things are right,* where God's name is honored and his will reigns supreme. It then invites the person praying to look at the situation of this world: our need for food, our tendency to sin, our struggles with temptation and evil. Through the words "on earth as it is in heaven," this prayer brings the two realms into union. It draws the cosmological order toward the *palingenesia* ("second Genesis"), where heaven and earth will once again experience the perfect unity that they had in the beginning.

The effectiveness of the Lord's Prayer lies in its power to move both God and people. Matthew envisioned the progress toward the *palingenesia* as an act of collaboration between God and his church. As we pray the Lord's Prayer, the Father wages war against Satan. He forgives our sins and helps us to forgive others. He gives us strength to resist Satan and drives away evil. But the prayer also changes us. It calls for a present, earthly way of living that stands in the light of a heavenly reality. Everything that the church envisions God doing in the heavenly realm must be implemented in our lives on earth. The church cannot ask for God to sanctify his name if we are not honoring him with our choices. Christians cannot ask for the kingdom to come if we do not seek righteousness. And we cannot ask for the Father's will to be done on earth if we do not practice it in our own lives. Matthew's point is that heaven must be manifest in the lives of people before it can take its hold on the earth.

---

1. See, for example, Rom 12:1; 1 Cor 3:16–17; 2 Cor 3:6; Eph 2:19–21; 1 Pet 2:5; Heb 7:22; 13:5.

Matthew had a highly refined theological agenda for the Lord's Prayer. Yet his genius is evident in his ability to preserve the *original sense* instilled by Jesus, even as he crafted his own unique interpretation. For Jesus, the meaning was innately tied to the history and theology of Israel. This prayer called up images of Israel in Sinai, its unique calling among the nations, and the supremacy of Israel's God. Matthew passed along this story and yet found a way to give new meaning to the Lord's Prayer. A text rooted in narrative theology became a treatise on the cosmological order.

The *Didache*

Matthew's lofty theology stands in sharp contrast to the practical concerns displayed in the *Didache*. For the Christians who followed this text, the value of the Lord's Prayer was found in its effectiveness for community discipleship. These were believers who aspired to follow the Torah and walk in the way of life. In their quest for holiness, however, they had to deal with the messiness of everyday life. By necessity, they had a high level of tolerance for disorder. The neat structure that many of the leaders had once enjoyed in the synagogues was now vanquished by hordes of converts from paganism. With the outpouring of the Holy Spirit there had come a new order of wandering apostles and prophets for whom the "rules of conduct" were just beginning to take shape.

As these communities navigated the tension between order and chaos, their commitment to pray the Lord's Prayer three times a day helped them stay on the path toward sanctification. Theirs was a "spirituality of the road," as they knew that perfection would not come all at once. They experienced moments of messiness and chaos. Yet they believed that the way of life had been clearly set before them. God was in their midst, and he was making them holy. When they said the Lord's Prayer, they were reminded of who they were and what they stood for. This prayer summarized the foundational elements of their worldview and values: the holiness of the community, the coming restoration, the moral commitment to be righteous, the responsibility to share, the need for ongoing confession and mercy, and the call to overcome evil and sin. The Lord's Prayer was a prayer that reaffirmed their identity as a community grounded in grace. It shifted their attention toward the final goal, even as it reiterated the everyday values that would enable them to stay on the way of life.

Luke

Whereas the Lord's Prayer began as the intellectual property of the Jewish people, Luke made it comprehensible to the masses. He recognized the power this prayer held to communicate and recapitulate the Christian message beyond the confines of the Jewish world. He was the first author to "translate" this message for gentile Christians living in cities throughout the Roman Empire. Luke spoke in words that they could understand and portrayed characters with whom they could relate. When the cultural experiences of his audience assisted in his presentation of the Lord's Prayer, he allowed those associations to remain. When he judged that their pagan background might make certain words and concepts in the prayer confusing, he simply trimmed them from the text. The result was a form of this prayer that was concise, robust, and immediately applicable.

Luke wrote with an agenda. His vision was that the spectacular expansion of the Christian faith would continue into the next generation. Having told the story of Jesus and the apostles, he intended for his readers to write the next chapter in the progress of salvation history. All the heroes in Luke's story had been women and men deeply committed to the practice of prayer. Luke believed that he and his readers were living in the era of "answered prayer." Just as prayer had been the driving force behind the successes of the past, so it would be in the future. He did not want his readers to fatalistically think that God's will would be accomplished with or without their prayers. Prayer was necessary because Luke believed that people actually have a role in God's unfolding plan of salvation.

In Luke's writings, the Lord's Prayer is a missionary prayer. It calls into being a Spirit-empowered church boldly advancing the Christian faith among the nations. Yet even with its visionary orientation, this is also a prayer about relationships. The church needs to maintain relationship with the Father and walk in daily dependence on him. We need to share what we have with one another, practice forgiveness, and encourage each other in our calling. As we pray the Lord's Prayer and put its words into practice, we can be assured that God will continue working in us to advance his kingdom on earth.

Tertullian

More than a century would pass before anyone (that we know of) would write about the Lord's Prayer again. It was the Carthaginian *senior* Tertullian who applied himself to this task. By the year 200, the world and the church had dramatically changed. Christian doctrine was becoming increasingly untethered from its Jewish roots, and it adopted more of a Greek flavor in its outlook and content. Many elements of the Judaic symbolic universe had now been "lost in translation." The Lord's Prayer was no longer the prayer of a rabbi and his disciples. It was now a Christian ritual, embedded in the liturgy and traditions of the church.

Tertullian's expository teaching on the Lord's Prayer is representative of the changes that had taken place in the Christian movement. As a new form of prayer taught by Jesus, the Lord's Prayer was new wine. The wineskin to hold it—that is to say, the framework by which it was to be understood—was no longer the Old Testament but rather a philosophical theology governed by reason and ordering principles.

To create this wineskin, Tertullian (at times unconsciously) drew upon the Stoicism of his earlier education. Jesus was the Logos, the organizing principle of the universe. The prayer that he taught his followers to pray was the instrument by which the Logos became operational in the world. And the purpose of this prayer was to display the goodness of the Christian God. Tertullian believed that in the economy of this present creation, God had established prayer as the means by which his purposes are accomplished. As the perfect prayer, and as the summary of the gospel, no prayer could accomplish this task more effectively than the Lord's Prayer.

Despite the intellectual character of his presentation, there was found within his teaching a radical and life-transforming message. Tertullian does not represent a shift away from the heart to the mind. Rather, he believed that the heart could only remain steadfast in Jesus when the mind was fully aligned to the truth. And even though Tertullian utilized a vocabulary that Jesus never employed, the voice of the Palestinian rabbi still resonates in his words. Tertullian's work bears witness to the enduring capacity of the Lord's Prayer to be reincarnated in new cultures, languages, and historical settings. He demonstrated that this prayer appeals to people everywhere and in all times. Goodness, evil, honor, forgiveness, and struggle are themes unconstrained by time and culture.

Reflections on Reception History: How Meaning Changes

To understand the Lord's Prayer is to take note of the experience in which it originated and the history in which it has been encountered.[2] The meaning of this prayer is not something that can be pinpointed to a fixed moment in the past. Even as the words may remain the same, the lived response to this prayer is an ever-unfolding story.

We began this book talking about the Mississippi River, taking note of the fact that the source is something different from the river itself. Surely, the discovery of Lake Itasca increased our understanding, as the river would not exist without it. Yet the only way to understand the Mississippi in its entirety would be to follow it from Itasca to New Orleans, from beginning to end.

In this same way, the meaning of the Lord's Prayer is to be

---

2. Luz notes:

> Understanding the texts means taking note of the experiences they originate in, comprehending the reality they reflect, and listening to the fundamental history to which they refer. One way or the other, understanding biblical texts means dealing with history. In contrast to the widespread current idea that the historical is, in the end, relative and therefore secondary, we must say that for biblical texts the history to which they refer and which they reflect is primary. (Ulrich Luz, *Studies*, 275)

discovered in the *history of its meaning*. Surely when we exegete this text in order to uncover its original sense, we gain essential knowledge. Apart from this original sense, we can never hope to understand what it has legitimately meant in later history. And yet we are cautious not to confuse that original sense with the entirety of its meaning.

The transmission of the Lord's Prayer over the past two thousand years has not merely been a process of oral repetition or a simple rerecording of words. As it has been passed down from person to person and generation to generation, new interpretations have also been transmitted. These have each been shaped by language, culture, theology, personal experience, and historical setting. The prayer taught by Jesus over two thousand years ago has traveled a long road to reach the modern ear. Those who seek to fully understand *what it means* must endeavor to understand *what it has meant* along the way.

This is not to say that we can or should try to study what the Lord's Prayer (or any biblical text) has meant to every person in every place since the time it was written. Such a task is impossible. Rather, the aim is to hear this prayer (and all of the Bible) with a historical consciousness. In this, we accept that our understanding of the text is in many ways the result of history. Scripture comes to us in a mediated form. The voice by which the Bible speaks to us is in fact a symphony of voices. Many people over many generations have contributed to what the Word of God means to us today. We cannot separate out each one of these, but we can focus on some of those voices that are more prominent.

A geologist can explain the course of the Mississippi. Every change it experiences along the way has a cause. Confluence with other rivers, soil types, climate, and human factors all affect what the river looks like and how it behaves. Explaining how and why the meaning of the Lord's Prayer has changed over the past two thousand years is a more complicated task. Unlike a material phenomenon such as a river, the history of ideas cannot be explained in concrete terms. Historians of theology must resort to theories in order to explain the progression of thought over time.

The study of how meaning is communicated through a text is known as *hermeneutics*. One hermeneutical theory suggests that there is a limited number of meanings that a word can have based on what it has meant in the past. For example, if I hear someone say, "I need some bread," there is a set number of meanings this sentence can have. It might be referring to the grain-based food people eat. It might be referring to money. Or, if the speaker is a child of the seventies, it might be referring to a music group known for its sentimental, depressing songs. I would have to learn more about the context of the statement before I could figure out what it means. But the possibilities are somewhat limited. "Bread" can only mean so many things at this present moment in history, and that range of meaning is determined by how this word has been used in the past. This is known as a synchronic understanding of communication, and again, the theory is that there is a pre-set range of meaning imposed upon any word that a person speaks or writes.

Alternatively, another hermeneutical theory looks for the ways that words can be given new meaning. For example, consider what terms such as *mouse*, *tag*, and *text* meant fifty years ago: a small annoying rodent, a small piece of fabric to identify a garment, and a series of words written on paper. Whereas these terms still have those same meanings today, we realize that they have also taken on new meanings. How did this happen? The answer is that somebody took the inherited meaning of these words and gave them new associations. Obviously, the new meanings were tied to the old. A computer mouse may be small and black. A tag on Facebook is a discreet tool of identification, and a text is still a written message, just on a screen instead of paper. In each case, creators of new meaning had to build on what a word meant in the past. But they also had to find a way to convey to their audiences that they were talking about something different. In sum, new meaning is possible, but new meaning must always be tied, in some way, to the old meaning. This is known as a diachronic approach to communication.

Most biblical interpreters today agree that the scriptural authors communicated both diachronically and synchronically. In other words, sometimes they wanted their audience to understand their words in a conventional sense, and at other times they wanted to give new meaning to old ideas. For example, someone once asked Jesus which commandment was the most important of all. Quoting from Deuteronomy 6, he replied, "The most important is, 'Hear, O Israel: The Lord our God, the Lord is one. And you shall love the Lord your God with all your heart and with all your soul and with all your mind and with all your strength'" (Mark 12:29–30). Then followed a happy moment in which everyone agreed on this answer. On this occasion, Jesus had no intention of putting a new twist on a familiar verse. He wanted the text to mean exactly what everyone had always understood it to mean. This is an example of synchronic communication.

On other occasions, however, Jesus wanted to give familiar passages new meaning. One of the most famous examples is found in the Sermon on the Mount. Five times he introduced a teaching with the words, "You have heard that it was said," rejoined by the declaration, "but I say . . ." (see Matt 5:21–43). In each case, he had to affirm some aspect of what was meant in the past. For example, adultery in the past meant having sex with another person's spouse. For Jesus, it *still* meant that, but he wanted to expand the meaning into new territory. In order to do this, he had to explain to his listeners *why* it meant something more than what they had always thought. He wanted to communicate in a diachronic way.

One of the most important tasks in the interpretation of a biblical text is to determine whether the author was speaking synchronically (wanting continuity) or diachronically (wanting discontinuity). In other words, did he want to continue with the old, conventional meaning of his words? Or was he trying to discontinue the old understanding and thus create new meaning for old words? In each case, the interpreter must find clues in the context of the passage in order to uncover the author's intention in this regard.

In our study of the Lord's Prayer, we have seen how various interpreters approached this prayer in a diachronic fashion, attaching new meaning to old words and ideas. Jesus took imagery and symbols that were familiar to the Jews of first-century Palestine and tied their meaning to his own life and proclamation. Embedded in his personal narrative, these historical symbols took on new significance. Matthew created new meaning for the prayer's symbols primarily by means of the literary and theological context with which he surrounded the prayer. The *Didache*'s presentation of the Lord's Prayer was shaped by the discipleship ethos of the community. Luke created meaning for the prayer by means of association with the characters and events in his narrative. Tertullian conveyed new significations for this prayer by means of its integration into the thought world of Greco-Roman culture. Each interpreter of this prayer found a way to give new meaning to old words.

In the course of this study, however, we have also seen a significant amount of continuity. Our survey has shown that this prayer could signify many things but that each interpreter sought to honor how it had been understood in the past. Each wanted to give new meaning to this prayer for new situations even as they kept this prayer tethered to the historical Jesus and his teachings. In the midst of new understandings and applications, it never ceased to be the prayer that Jesus had spoken. As long as its words were acknowledged as *his* words and as long as it remained the prayer of *his* church, it could mean *many things*, but it could not mean *anything.*

We conclude then, that the meaning of the Lord's Prayer changed over two centuries because the various communities that prayed this prayer *needed* it to change. The Galilean Jewish fishermen who followed Jesus lived in a different world than Perpetua and Felicitas. In order for the Lord's Prayer to be meaningful in their lives, it had to speak uniquely to their different life situations. And yet Perpetua, Felicitas, Peter, and James all followed the same Jesus. Regardless of who they were, where they lived, or what was going on their lives, this prayer was powerful for them because it was *his* prayer. It was tied to his life, mission, and teaching. In that sense, some elements of this prayer could never change.

At any point along the path of the Mississippi, we can find water from Lake Itasca. The source will always shape its makeup. With respect to the path it takes, there are geographical and human factors that limit where it can go. There are numerous possibilities as to how this river can change, but there are also set factors that create boundaries around what will happen. In the same way, to understand the reception history of the Lord's Prayer is to understand both the potentialities and the boundaries that shape its interpretation. Any legitimate understanding of this prayer must demonstrate how it stands in continuity with the source: Jesus. We also accept that theological orthodoxy places boundaries on what this prayer can mean for us. But within these parameters, there are and have always been numerous possibilities for this prayer's meaning and application in our lives.

Where Do We Go from Here?

For those who feel bored or isolated in their relationship with the Word of God, my hope is that this study will reawaken your imagination. Our task has not been to uncover *the* meaning of the Lord's Prayer, as if this were a single, finite set of ideas. Rather, we have explored a brief season in the history of its meaning. Many other opportunities for research still lie before us, as Hans-Georg Gadamer reminds us: "The discovery of the true meaning of a text or a work of art is never finished."[3]

Each interpretation of the Lord's Prayer can be compared to the artistic framing of a painting: a wooden border crops the image, highlighting certain features while muting others. It creates either a synthesis or contrast of colors. The frame may not necessarily alter the painting itself, but it does determine how the image is perceived. Each interpreter of the Lord's Prayer took the bare image of its words and placed a frame around them. This frame was created by their life experiences, belief systems, and desires to meet the needs of others

3. Gadamer, *Truth*, 298.

around them. Each interpreter's unique experience in life led to the crafting of a unique and beautiful frame, which in turn led to unique and beautiful understanding of this prayer.

Jesus was a narrative theologian, while Matthew was a systematic theologian. Luke was a missionary. The authors of the *Didache* were discipleship leaders, and Tertullian was a philosopher. What the Lord's Prayer means to us today is, in part, the consequence of their experience. We are the heirs of their legacy. Yet the question that now lies before each one of us is: Who am I, and what will be my role in shaping what the Lord's Prayer will mean to future generations?

A seed has an objective character when it stands alone, but its full potential is only realized when it begins to interact with soil, light, and water. In the same way, the Lord's Prayer comes alive when it is sowed in our life experience. This prayer—and the entire Word of God—is a garden yet to come fully alive in each of us. Thomas Merton has said that

> every moment and every event of every man's life on earth plants something in his soul. For just as the wind carries thousands of winged seeds, so each moment brings with it germs of spiritual vitality that come to rest imperceptibly in the minds and wills of men. Most of these unnumbered seeds perish and are lost, because we not prepared to receive them: for such seeds as these cannot spring up anywhere except in the good soil of freedom, spontaneity and love.[4]

May the seed of the Lord's Prayer find good soil in your life. May it produce much fruit and new seeds for generations to come!

4. Thomas Merton, *New Seeds of Contemplation* (New York: New Directions, 1962), 14.

Appendix: Praying the Lord's Prayer

Early Christians often used the Lord's Prayer as template for prayer. This is a modernized adaptation that can be used in groups or individually.

Our Father in heaven

- *Thank God that we have been made his sons and daughters through Jesus.*

- *Declare the fatherhood of God over our lives.*

- *Praise him as the one and only true God.*

Let your name be honored as holy

- *Pray that our own lives may be honoring to God.*

- *Pray that God would show his power, so that the nations may honor him.*

Let your kingdom come

- *Pray for everything that a righteous king establishes: peace between peoples and nations, justice, provision and care for the poor, freedom for the captives, physical healing and restoration, the end of corruption, exploitation, trafficking, and the like.*

- *Pray that by the manifestation of the Holy Spirit, God's kingship may be revealed on earth.*

Let your will be done

- *Release to God your plans and desires, committing yourself to his will above your own.*
- *Pray for God to move in such a way that his desires and dreams may be fulfilled in our lives.*
- *Pray for the transformation of hearts, so that the peoples of the earth would choose to do his will.*

On earth as it is in heaven

- *Pray that heaven would come to earth.*

Give us today the portion of bread we need for this day

- *Pray for our material needs.*
- *Ask God to show us what we can share with others.*

Forgive us our sins

- *Confess to God any sins that need to be brought before him.*

As we forgive those who have sinned against us

- *By name, release before the Lord everyone who has sinned against you.*

Do not lead us into testing

- *Pray that what is in our hearts would be made open before God.*
- *Pray that God would preserve us from falling during times of testing.*

Deliver us from evil

- *Pray that God would give us victory over the power of sin and Satan.*

The kingdom and the power and the glory are yours forever and ever

- *Close your prayer in a time of worship.*

Index of Ancient Sources

OLD TESTAMENT

Genesis
12:2–3 29
3:6 38
3:15 56
3:18 56
22:1 55
22:17–18 29

Exodus
12 9
16 38
16:4 54
32 38

Leviticus
2 9
11:44–45 44
19:18 53

Numbers
14, 20 38

Deuteronomy
4:34 54
4:39 43
6:5 . . . . . . 50, 202
6:4 43
6: 4, 7 30
6:13 39
6:16 . . . . . . 39, 54
8:2 . . . . . . 39, 54, 55
8:3 . . . . . . 39, 52
8:16 54
13:3 54
28:1, 1, 10 30
28:10 44
28:36, 63–64 46
30:1–8 . . . . . . 46, 47
33:8 54

Joshua
2:11 43

1 Samuel
2:2 44
6:20 44

15:22 13
17:39 55

2 Samuel
15:24–26 49

1 Kings
10:9 55

1 Chronicles
16:26 43
16:29 44
17:5–6 17
29:11 112

2 Chronicles
6:19–21 17
20:6 43

Ezra
1:2 43
5:11–12 43
6:10 43
7:12, 21,23 43
9:6 43

Psalms
2:4 43
26:2 55
40:9 49
51:16 14
72 47
78:18,41, 56 54
95:8–10 54

95:9 54
96:4–5 43
99:5 44
103:19 46
103:19–21 77
113:11 (LXX) 49
115:6 43
115:3 49
115:13 49
115:16 50
106:14 54
132:14 3
134:6 (LXX) 49
135:5–6 49
136:26 43
145:11–13 46

Ecclesiastes
8:1–3 49

Isaiah
1:11–13 14
1:15 131
5:16 44
6:3 ...... 44, 77
7:12 54
11:12 99
14:12–13 43
29:23 ...... 44, 136
43:3 44
43:5–6 32
45:23–25 32
49:5 40
49:6–7 32

49:8 40
49:26 32
52:8–9 32
55:11 49
56:6–7 . . . . . . 20, 131
58:9 131
59:2 131
60:1,3 52
61 40
63:15 43
65:17,24 131
66:1 43

Jeremiah
7:9–15 20
10:11 43
31:33 50

Ezekiel
16:1–52 37
16:60–62 37
36:20 44
36:23 . . . . . . 44, 136

Daniel
2:18–19,28,37,44 43
3:33 46
4:34 46
6:26 46
4:37 43
5:23 43
6:10 11
9:3–19 30

Hosea
1:2–2:13 37
2:14–16 37
6:6 14

Joel
2:28–32 128

Obadiah
2:1 46

Jonah
1:9 14
1:14 49

Habakuk
1:12 44

Zechariah
8:20 44

Malachi
1:11 . . . . . . 109, 131

DEUTEROCANONICAL BOOKS
Tobit
13:1–6 . . . . . . 26, 46
13:11–16 . . . . . . 25, 26
14:5–7 27

Wisdom
6:4 46
10:10 46

Sirach
2:1 149
42:24–45 101

OLD TESTAMENT
    PSEUDEPIGRAPHA
2 Baruch 71

1 Enoch
1–36 71
89:73–74 17

4 Ezra 71

Jubilees
10:1,9,11 101
8:19 3

Psalms of Solomon 71
1,2,4,8 17

Sibylline Oracles
5:248–250 3

DEAD SEA SCROLLS
1QHa
14:8–13 34

1QM
1:14–16 13
2:5–6 13
13 33

1QS 5
3:13–4:26 101
3:20–21 101
8:4–10 14
9:3–5 13
11:11 104

1Qsa 5

4Q174 5

4Q177 5

4Q252 5

4Q265 5

4Q266 13

4Q504 34

CD 5

JOSEPHUS
Antiquitates Judaicae
18:15 10

Bellum Judaicum
2.427 18
6.259 . . . . . . 2, 8

NEW TESTAMENT

Matthew

3:2 66

3:7–12 146

3:13–17 131

4:1–11 38

4:3 39

4:7 39

4:8–9 72

4:10 39

4:17 . . . . . . 63, 66

4:21–22 69

5:3 . . . . . . 48, 63

5:6 . . . . . . 72, 73

5:6–9 . . . . . . 67, 73

5:10 . . . . . . 66, 72

5:12 64

5:16 . . . . . . 65, 82

5:19–20 . . . . . . 48, 64

5:21–22; 27–28; 31–32; 33–34; 38–39;
    43–44 . . . . . . 68, 124, 202

5:22 124

5:34 77

5:48 16

6:1–2 69

6:2–3; 5–6; 16–17 68

6:5 10

6:9–10 79

6:9–11 122

6:10 78

6:11 78

6:13 147

6:12 78

6:14–15 83

6:19–20 69

6:25–34 77

6:33 . . . . . . 48, 72, 82

7:7 82

7:11 . . . . . . 65, 77, 139

7:20–21 . . . . . . 48, 65, 72, 82

7:21,24 156

7:28–29 8

8:11 64

8:21 69

9:2–3 8

9:4 77

9:14 8

10:21 69

10:23 127

12:1–8 19

12:26 72

12:34, 39 77

12:45 72

12:49–50 157

12:50 . . . . . . 64, 82

12:28 48

13:11 . . . . . . 48, 66

13:18–23 48

13:24–30, 37–43 . . . . . . 69, 72

13:31–33 66

13:41 . . . . . . 69, 72

13:41,43 69

13:44 66

13:44–47 48

15:1–9 8

15:13 65

15:19 77

16:4 77

16:13–20 . . . . . . 74, 75

16:19 . . . . . . 75, 80

16:24 140

17:1–2 131

17:24–27 18

18:3–4 48

18:7 77

18:13–14 . . . . . . 65, 157

18:15–20 75

18:18–20 . . . . . . 74, 75, 80

18:22–35 77

19:14 66

19:23 64

19:28 70

19:29 69

20:14 78

21:13 19

22:23–34 8

22:34–40 8

23:9 69

23:2 8

23:13 66

23:15 90

23:23 10

23:22 77

23:35 83

24:38–39 78

24:29–51 62

25:1–30 67

25:31–36 . . . . . . 48, 62

26:41 147

26:61 21

27:40 21

27:46 124

Mark

1:9–11 131

1:12–13 38

1:15 63

2:1–12 19

2:18 8

3:1–6 8

3:13–14 131

3:35 63

3:34–35 157

4:11,47 48

4:15 40

4:30–32 69

5:41 124

7:1–3 9

7:1–8; 9–13 8

7:1–23 124

8:34 140

9:1 127

9:2–4 131

10:14–15 48

12:18–27; 28–33; 35–37 8

12:29–30 202

13 128

13:2 19

13:28–30 127

14:38 147

14:49 18

14:58 21

15:29 21

15:34 124

Luke

1:1–3 123

1:10 . . . . . . 11, 130, 131

1:46 . . . . . . 130, 131

1:68 . . . . . . 130, 131

1:46–48 137

1:46–55 . . . . . . 136, 137

1:49 137

1:52–53 144

1:67 134

2:4 124

2:29–32 131

2:33 134

2:38 130–31

2:41–51 18

3:3 146

3:11–14 146

3:21 130

3:21–23 . . . . . . 131, 132

4:1–13 . . . . . . 38, 132

4:13 147

4:18 144

4:21 40

5:16 130

5:19 125

5:20–21 . . . . . .8, 135

5:33 8

6:12 . . . . . . 130, 132

6:12–13 131

6:20 . . . . . . 48, 63

6:24–26 137

6:36 135

6:46–48 156

7:22 144

7:47 135

8:10 . . . . . . 48, 135

8:13 147

8:21 157

8:24 125

8:26 124

9:2, 11–20 48

9:12–17 137

9:18 130

9:22 158

9:23 140

9:27 128

9:28–29 131

9:28–36 132

9:29, 32 147

9:38 134

9:48, 49 137

10:17 137

10:21–22 . . . . . . 130, 132, 135

11:1 130

11:1–2 . . . . . . 112, 132, 147

11:1–4 . . . . . . 122, 145

11:2 . . . . . . 134, 136, 138, 140

11:9–10, 11–12 143

11:4 147

11:5–13 132

11:11–13 134–35

11:13 . . . . . . 135, 139

11:20 138

12:30, 32 135

12:37–38 148

12:38, 45 128

12:54–56 128

13:33 158

13:34–35 2

15:5–7 157

15:11–32 ...... 134, 145

17:3–4 146

17:11–14 137

17:25 158

18:1 147

18:1–8 133

18:7–8, ... 128

18:9–14 10

18:18–25 137

18:21–28 128

18:32–33 128

19:1–10 145

19:8–9 146

19:11–27 128

20:27–40, 41–44 8

21 128

21:1–4, 8, 17 137

21:20–21 22

21:36 148

22:37 158

22:18 138

22:28 147

22:39–46 132

22:40 ...... 147, 148

22:41,42 ...... 130, 151, 157, 158

22:46 ...... 147, 148

23:34 146

24:3 18

24:7 158

24:26 158

24:44 158

24:46–47 158

24:47 ...... 138, 146

John

1:12 175

2:19–21 ...... 16, 21

5:1 18

7:10 18

Acts

1:3 138

1:3–8 139

1:6–8 128

1:14 ...... 130, 132

1:24 ...... 130, 151

2 161

2:1–4 132

2:4 135

2:14–21 128

2:21 138

2:23 158

2:28 138

2:38 146

2:42 130

2:43–47 144

2:46 18

3:1 ...... 11, 18, 130

3:6 138

3:16 138

4:10,12,18, 30 138

4:24–30 ...... 132, 151

4:29–30 138

4:31 130

4:34 ...... 135, 144

5:31 146

5:42 18

6:4,6 130

7:59–60 . . . . . . 132, 146

8:12 138

8:16 138

8:22 146

9:10–19 132

9:11 130

9:15–16 158

9:40 130

10:2 130

10:4 132

10:9 130

10:9–16 132

10:48 138

11:17 78

12:12 130

13:2–3 132

13:3 130

13:22 . . . . . . 157, 158

13:33 78

13:36 158

13:48 155

14:23 130

15 91

15:26 138

16:18 138

16:25 130

17:25 144

17:28 78

19:5, 8, 13 138

20:19 147

20:35 138

20:36 130

21:5 130

21:13 138

21:14 . . . . . . 157, 158

22:14 . . . . . . 157, 158

22:17 130

23:11 158

26:9 138

27:24 158

28 129

28:8 130

28:23 138

28:28 129

28:31 138

Romans

12:1 195

1 Corinthians

3:16–17 195

7:7 78

7:29–31 127

9:5 78

10:11 127

2 Corinthians

3:6 195

5:17 80

Ephesians

2:19–21 195

5:23 78

1 Thessalonians

1:10 127

4:13–18 127

2 Timothy

3:9 78

Hebrews

3:2 78

7:22 195

13:5 195

1 Peter

2:5 . . . . . . 22, 195

2 Peter

2:1 78

3:10–13 61

Revelation

3:21 78

4:2–11 77

18:6 78

21:1–5 80

MISHNAH AND RABBINIC
    LITERATURE

m. Berakot

1–4 35

4:1 11

m. Kelim

1:6–9 3

m. Taanith

4:2–3 6

Tanhuma, Way-yislah

9 23

APOSTOLIC FATHERS

The Didache

1.1

1.3 108

1.3–4 103

1.4 109

1:6 112

3.1 110

3.8 109

3:10 104

4.3 109

5.1 110

6.2–3 92

7.1 97

7.1–4 93

7.4 112

8.1 97

9.1 99

9.2–3 113

9.4 112

9.5 . . . . . . 97, 112

10.2 113

10.3 107

10.4–5 113

10.5 . . . . . . 100, 110

10.6 . . . . . . 105, 112

10.7 93

11.3–12 94

11.4 112

12.1 . . . . . . 97, 112

12.3 112
12.5 94
13.1–2 94
14:1–3 109
14.2 112
16 103
16.2 106
16:5 111

GRECO-ROMAN LITERATURE
Aristotle
Eudemian Ethics 142

Cato the Elder 141

Cleanthes
Hymn to Zeus 104, 141–42

Epictetus
Diatribi
2.10.7 175

Manilius
Astronomica
2:82–86 154
3:67–73 154

Plato
Philebus 176
Phaedo 61–62
Timaeus 152

The Republic 152

Tacitus
Annals
6.22 154

PATRISTIC LITERATURE
Eusebius
Historia ecclesiastica 22

Hippolytus
Traditio apostolica
22.5 171

Irenaeus
Adversus haereses 61

Minucius Felix
Octavius 61

Origen
Contra Celsum 61

Tertullian
Adversus Marcionem
2.6 180
2.13 181
2.16 181
2.24 188
4.26 190
4.36 168

Apologeticus
30 . . . . . . 167, 182
41 183

De baptismo
1 167
20 185

De corona
13 183

De exhortatione castitatis
2:2, 4–5 180
8 180

De fuga in persecutione
2 187

De ieiunio
15 184

De oratione
1 172–74
2 174–76

3 176–77
4 177–82
5 182–83
6 183–84
7 184–86
8 186–87
8.4 187
9 189
29 189

De praescriptione haereticorum
41 171

Unknown
The Passion of the Scillitan Martyrs
. 167
Martyrdom of Saints Perpetua and
Felicitas 165, 166

Index of Modern Authors

Ayo, N., 83

Barton, T., 154
Berger, P., 95
Binder, D. D., 7
Bockmuehl, M., xi
Boyd, G., 60
Brown, M. J., 144, 171, 184

Carruth, S. & A. Garsky, 140, 150,
  156
Clark, D., xvi, 133, 155, 177
Conn, H. M., 122
Conzelmann, H., 128, 131,
Crossan, J. D., 4, 78, 83
Crump, D., 146, 169

D'Orta, E., 117
De Boer, M. C., 70 – 71
Decret, F., 170, 183
Deissler, A., 42
Draper, J. A., 90
Dunn, J. D., 19, 47, 128, 129, 139

Esler, P. F., 129

Flint, P. W. & J. C. VanderKam, 12
Flusser, D., 90, 91, 101, 102

Gadamer, H. G., xii, 204
Gartner, B., 13, 14, 15,
Geertz, C., 95
Giordano, C & Kahn, I., 119
Gladwell, M., 5
Greene, W. C., 179, 182

Haran, M., 7
Hatch, E., 152 – 153
Heinemann, J., 11
Heschel, A., 142, 143, 145, 146, 153
Hoffman, 35,
Holmas, G. O., 128, 147, 150
Hurvitz, A., 49

Jefford, C. N., 102
Jeremias, J., 42, 150

Kistemaker, S. J., 149

Kloppenburg, J. S., 102

Levine, L. I., 7
Lewis, C. S., 60 – 61
Longenecker, B., 117, 120
Luz, U., xi, xiii, 83, 199

Marshall, H., 137
Matyszak, P., 117
Meeks, W., 125, 126
Merton, T., 205
Metzger, B., 112
Milavec, A., 90, 111

Neusner, J., 3, 10, 11
Nickelsburg, G., 18, 46

O'Loughlin, T., 91, 102

Patte, D., 11, 68
Pennington, J., 63, 69, 70, 79
Petuchowski, J. J., 6, 11, 35, 42
Plymale, S., 132

Rankin, D., 169
Riches, J., 71, 72,
Rivkin, E., 8, 9, 10

Sanders, E. P., 31
Sandt & Flusser, 91, 101, 102
Schiffman, L., 7
Schoolcraft, H. R., vii
Scott, E. F., 111
Simpson, R. L., 187
Smalley, S. S., 130, 132, 139
Stagg, F., 111
Stark, R., 161

Thompson, G., 78

Van der Horst, P., 61
Volk, K., 154
Voobus, A., 90

Wright, N. T., 4, 18, 19, 31, 37, 41, 47, 48, 57

Yeivin, Z., 8